Management for Professionals

More information about this series at
http://www.springer.com/series/10101

Gerrit Heinemann • Christian Gaiser

Social – Local – Mobile

The Future of Location-based Services

Gerrit Heinemann
eWeb Research Center
Niederrhein University
Mönchengladbach
Germany

Christian Gaiser
Chief Executive Officer (CEO)
Bonial International GmbH
Berlin
Germany

Translation from German language edition:
SoLoMo – Always-on im Handel
by Gerrit Heinemann
Copyright © Springer Fachmedien Wiesbaden 2014
Springer Fachmedien Wiesbaden is a part of Springer Science+Business Media
All Rights Reserved

ISSN 2192-8096 ISSN 2192-810X (electronic)
ISBN 978-3-662-43963-0 ISBN 978-3-662-43964-7 (eBook)
DOI 10.1007/978-3-662-43964-7
Springer Heidelberg New York Dordrecht London

Library of Congress Control Number: 2014953248

© Springer-Verlag Berlin Heidelberg 2015
This work is subject to copyright. All rights are reserved by the Publisher, whether the whole or part of the material is concerned, specifically the rights of translation, reprinting, reuse of illustrations, recitation, broadcasting, reproduction on microfilms or in any other physical way, and transmission or information storage and retrieval, electronic adaptation, computer software, or by similar or dissimilar methodology now known or hereafter developed. Exempted from this legal reservation are brief excerpts in connection with reviews or scholarly analysis or material supplied specifically for the purpose of being entered and executed on a computer system, for exclusive use by the purchaser of the work. Duplication of this publication or parts thereof is permitted only under the provisions of the Copyright Law of the Publisher's location, in its current version, and permission for use must always be obtained from Springer. Permissions for use may be obtained through RightsLink at the Copyright Clearance Center. Violations are liable to prosecution under the respective Copyright Law.
The use of general descriptive names, registered names, trademarks, service marks, etc. in this publication does not imply, even in the absence of a specific statement, that such names are exempt from the relevant protective laws and regulations and therefore free for general use.
While the advice and information in this book are believed to be true and accurate at the date of publication, neither the authors nor the editors nor the publisher can accept any legal responsibility for any errors or omissions that may be made. The publisher makes no warranty, express or implied, with respect to the material contained herein.

Printed on acid-free paper

Springer is part of Springer Science+Business Media (www.springer.com)

Preface

Mobile Internet and smartphones enable communication anywhere and anytime. Furthermore, in combination with social media, they create a new kind of interaction and revolutionize buying behavior, as users increasingly share information about their whereabouts and local offers. This exchange is no longer time-delayed, but shared in real time via the network. The social network, in conjunction with mobile devices, is a companion for all life situations and all topics, which changes the definition of privacy by making part of our lives public. Virtual identities serve as a means of self-expression and are becoming essential, particularly for younger Internet users – termed "digital natives." "People are happy to share information about themselves with others," says Mark Zuckerberg. In this respect, the use of social media can no longer be viewed in isolation. Social media are increasingly used in combination with localization and location-based services (LBS) as well as mobile Internet usage. Such interaction forms the basis for "SoLoMo synergies," which result from social, local, and mobile (SoLoMo) networking and give rise to new opportunities for marketing efficiency. Given that the number of intensive users of smartphones and mobile Internet is set to grow dynamically in the next few years, SoLoMo networking might well increase to the same extent. As of the end of July 2013, 46% of the residential population in Germany already uses a smartphone – according to a recent survey by kaufDA, which will be discussed in detail in this book. The number of smartphone users in Germany exceeded the threshold of 40 million at the start of 2014.

The SoLoMo phenomenon is also fueled by the fact that users want to stay constantly informed online. The same applies today to "smart natives," for whom permanent access to the digital data stream is normal. They demand mobile offers, which they can continuously keep up to date and share with their network. In this regard, local real-time offers with geotargeting, increasing response speeds, real-time information, and augmented reality create interesting mobile added value for SoLoMo users. Added value is undoubtedly provided by online buying and mobile shopping, which is convenient and varied, and can be carried out 24 h, regardless of location. Most customers can no longer imagine a world without online shopping. This is exactly why brick-and-mortar retailing should not get left behind, especially since the Internet has become a central part of many people's lives. Consumers do not want to buy everything online, nor do they want to forego the advantages of the online channel just because they also visit shops. Some companies therefore let their customers shop in parallel and tie them to the brick-and-mortar store through location-based services. Location-based services (LBS) are mobile services which access localized and situation-based data. These services are becoming largely important, particularly in terms of the situational adequacy of mobile commerce offers. They also have a huge impact on existing commercial and retail structures, since the mobile Internet – in combination with LBS – has become a disruptive technology, which is redefining commerce as a whole.

The "Potential for Location-based services" study, conducted by the eWeb Research Center at Niederrhein University of Applied Sciences (Germany) in collaboration with kaufDA/Bonial International Group, the global provider of location-based advertising services, and in cooperation with the Edelman agency until September 2013, provided the impetus for this book. Our primary aim was to build a bridge between theory and practice and create a user-friendly design. LBS specialists in the Bonial International Group – at international locations in the USA, Germany, France, Russia, and Spain – observed that retailers have identified the explosive nature of increasing mobile Internet usage for their own store and want to develop a better understanding in order to respond with appropriate measures. This book is intended to help close the information gap. The ongoing Delphi study on the subject of the "Future of Commerce," which is being conducted under the auspices of eBay GmbH Deutschland and APCO Worldwide, was also a source of encouragement and support.

We would like to express our thanks to Ms. Sarah Stevens for actively supporting us in the conceptual design, evaluation, and documentation of the study. We are also grateful to the Edelman agency, and in particular to Ms. Susanne Richardsen, for their constructive and uncomplicated cooperation.

Mönchengladbach, Germany	Gerrit Heinemann
Chicago, USA/Berlin, Germany	Christian Gaiser

List of Abbreviations

2G	2nd Generation
2.5G	2.5th Generation
3D	Three-Dimensional
3G	3rd Generation
3.5G	3.5th Generation
Fig.	Figure
Admin	Administration
AGB ("GTC")	General Terms and Conditions
AGOF	German Online Research Consortium
API	Application Programming Interface
App	Application
ARM	Advanced RISC Machine
Asw	Absatzwirtschaft (marketing journal)
BITKOM	German Federal Association for Information Technology, Telecommunications and New Media
Bn.	Billion
B2C	Business-to-Consumer
B2B	Business-to-Business
BVH	German E-Commerce and Distance Selling Trade Association
CAGR	Cumulated Average Growth Rate
CATI	Computer-Assisted Telephone Interviewing
CBC	Customer Buying Cycle
CCRP	Customer-to-Customer Reference Points
CEO	Chief Executive Officer
CGA	Consumer-Generated Advertising
CGC	Consumer-Generated Content
CIC	Customer Interaction Center
CM	Category Management
CNC	Costs New Customer
Comp	Company
CPI	Cost per Interest
CPC	Cost per Click
CRM	Customer Relationship Management

Disc	Discount
DMB	Digital Multimedia Broadcasting
DIY	Do-It-Yourself
DSL	Digital Subscriber Line
DVB	Digital Video Broadcasting
e	expected
E-/e-	electronic
EAN	European Article Number
EAV	Electronic Added Values
EBIT	Earnings Before Interest and Taxes
EBITDA	Earning Before Interest, Taxes, Depreciation and Amortization
EC	Electronic Cash
ECC	E-Commerce Center
ECR	Efficient Consumer Response
EDGE	Enhanced Data Rates for GSM Evolution
EHI	EHI Retail Institute
et al.	et alii
etc.	et cetera
e.V.	Incorporated Association
FAZ	Frankfurter Allgemeine Zeitung (newspaper)
F	Following (et seq.)
Ff	Following Pages (et seqq.)
GfK.	Gesellschaft für Konsumforschung (consumer research company)
GmbH	Limited Liability Company
GPRS	General Packet Radio Service
GPS	Global Positioning System
GSM	Global System for Mobile Communications
P/L	Profit and Loss Statement
HMWVL	Hessian Ministry of Economic Affairs, Transport and Regional Development
ed.	Editor
HSDPA	High-Speed Downlink Packet Access
HSPA+	High-Speed Packet Access+
HSUPA	High-Speed Uplink Packet Access
HTML	Hyper Text Markup Language
http	Hypertext Transfer Protocol
ifH	Institute for Commercial Research
IEEE	Institute of Electrical and Electronics Engineers
IMS	IP Multimedia Subsystem
incl.	Inclusive/Including
IPS	In-Plan Switching
IPTV	Internet Protocol Television
ISDN	Integrated Services Digital Network
IT	Information Technology

List of Abbreviations

IVR	Interactive Voice Response
KB	Kilobyte
kBit/s	Kilobit per Second
LBS	Location-Based Services
Log	Logistics
LTE	Long-Term Evolution
m	Mobile
m	Million
M ("m-")	Mobile
MAV	Mobile Added Values
MAC	Media Access Control
Max	Maximum
MB	Megabyte
Mln.	Millions
MMS	Multimedia Messaging Service
MP3	Moving Picture 3
NGMN	Next Generation Mobile Networks
NFC	Near Field Communication
N	Number/Number of Cases
No.	Number
OHA	Open Handset Alliance
OS	Operating System
PAN	Personal Area Network
PC	Personal Computer
PDA	Personal Digital Assistant
PDF	Portable Document Format
PIN	Personal Identification Number
POI	Point of Interest
P&L	Profit & Loss
POS	Point of Sale
QR	Quick Response
RFID	Radio Frequency Identification System
ROI	Return on Investment
ROPO	Research Online–Purchase Offline
RP	Rheinische Post (newspaper)
Pg	Page
Sec	Seconds
SKU	Stock Keeping Unit
SMS	Short Message Service
Hr	Hour
SSID	Service Set Identifier
SU	Service Units
TIFF	Tagged Image File Format
TV	Television
UMTS	Universal Mobile Telecommunications System

URI	Uniform Resource Identifier
URL	Uniform Resource Locator
US	United States
USP	Unique Selling Proposition
Cf	Compare/See
Vs	Versus
VDA	German Association of the Automotive Industry
VoIP	Voice over Internet Protocol
WAMS	Welt am Sonntag (newspaper)
WAP	Wireless Application Protocol
WEP	Wired Equivalent Privacy encryption
WiMAX	Worldwide Interoperability for Microwave Access
WLAN	Wireless Local Area Network
WWW	World Wide Web
ZAW	Central Association of the German Advertising Industry

Contents

1 **"Always on and Always in Touch": The New Buying Behaviour** ... 1
  1.1 What Customers Want: The Mobile Universe 1
  1.2 Social: Internet and Social Networks as a Central Part of Life 3
  1.3 Local and Mobile: Smartphones as Accessories for Shopping 5
  1.4 SoLoMo: Key Issue for Future Commerce 6
  1.5 Future of Commerce: Challenge for Brick-and-Mortar Formats ... 9

2 **Social Commerce as Base Factor No. 1 for SoLoMo** 13
  2.1 Importance and Significance of Social Media 13
    2.1.1 Current Trend in Social Media 13
    2.1.2 History and Phases of Social Media 15
    2.1.3 Significance and Relevance of Social Media 16
    2.1.4 Future Prospects for Social Media 16
  2.2 Social Commerce as a New Form of Commerce 17
    2.2.1 Special Characteristics and Relevance of Social Commerce 18
    2.2.2 Stages of Development in Social Commerce 23
    2.2.3 Categorization of Social Commerce 25
    2.2.4 Future Prospects for Social Commerce 26
  2.3 Manifestations of Social Commerce 27
    2.3.1 Socialization of E-Commerce 27
    2.3.2 Commercialization of Social Media 30
    2.3.3 Facebook Commerce as a Hybrid Form of Social Commerce 33
    2.3.4 Business Models for Social Commerce 35
  2.4 Changes in the Buying Process Due to Internet and Social Media 37
    2.4.1 The New Buying Process 37
    2.4.2 Customer Involvement in the Buying Process 41
    2.4.3 "Always-on" in Omni-Channel Use 43
    2.4.4 Smartphone Usage and Smart Natives 46
  2.5 "Always-in-Touch": The SoLoMo Mindset 49
    2.5.1 SoLoMo Usability 50
    2.5.2 SoLoMo Efficiency 50

xi

		2.5.3	SoLoMo Communication...........................	51
		2.5.4	SoLoMo Convergence.............................	51
	2.6	The Role of SoLoMo in Brick-and-Mortar Retailing...........		52
3	**Location-based services as Base Factor No. 2 for SoLoMo**........			55
	3.1	Mobile Applications with Local Relevance.................		55
		3.1.1	Local Search Optimization......................	55
		3.1.2	Bundling and Aggregation Platforms................	58
		3.1.3	Local and Social Referral Marketing................	60
		3.1.4	Local Real-time Offers........................	62
	3.2	Digital In-store Applications........................		63
		3.2.1	Reinforcing Brick-and-Mortar Benefits as a Basic Approach..................................	63
		3.2.2	Gamification for Enhancing Experience...............	65
		3.2.3	QR Scan Retail and Showrooming..................	67
		3.2.4	AR App Retail and In-store Navigation...............	69
	3.3	New Formats with Digital In-store Applications..............		71
		3.3.1	Pop-up Stores by Online Retailers..................	71
		3.3.2	Flagship Brick-and-Mortar Stores with Digital In-store Fittings....................................	73
		3.3.3	Showrooming with Mobile Shopping Option...........	74
		3.3.4	Renovation of Existing Formats with In-store Apps......	76
	3.4	Relevance to Situational and Real Environment as a Success Factor..		77
		3.4.1	Situational Adequacy and Potential in Mobile Marketing...................................	77
		3.4.2	Situation-Oriented CRM.........................	81
		3.4.3	Context-Sensitive Services and Localization Functions...	84
		3.4.4	Bargaining and Couponing.......................	86
	3.5	Dynamic Pricing and E-Payment with Local Relevance.........		88
		3.5.1	Special Characteristics of Dynamic Pricing with Local Relevance..................................	88
		3.5.2	Virtual Coupons and Bonus Cards..................	90
		3.5.3	Mobile E-Payment in Brick-and-Mortar Retailing........	91
		3.5.4	Integration of Mobile Pricing in the Multi-channel Environment.................................	93
	3.6	Prospects for Brick-and-Mortar Stores and Potential of Location-Based Services...................................		95
4	**Mobile Commerce as Base Factor No. 3 for SoLoMo**..............			101
	4.1	Development and Future Prospects for Mobile Commerce.......		101
		4.1.1	Development and Status of Mobile Commerce..........	101
		4.1.2	Popular Applications in Mobile Commerce............	106

		4.1.3	Tablet Shopping and Future Prospects for Mobile Commerce	107
		4.1.4	Mobile Commerce Added Value	111
	4.2	Technological Principles of Mobile Commerce		112
		4.2.1	Mobile Transmission Technologies	112
		4.2.2	Mobile Devices	114
		4.2.3	Mobile Operating Systems	117
		4.2.4	Mobile-Relevant Trends	120
	4.3	Business Models in Mobile Commerce		123
		4.3.1	Prospects and Value Chains in Mobile Commerce	124
		4.3.2	Business Concepts in Mobile Business	127
		4.3.3	Telematics and Cross-technology Platforms in Mobile Commerce	129
		4.3.4	Websites Versus Applications/Apps	130
	4.4	Special Characteristics of Mobile Marketing		131
		4.4.1	Specific Applications in the Mobile Marketing Mix	131
		4.4.2	mCRM: Customer Relationship Management in Mobile Commerce	138
		4.4.3	NFC: Near Field Communication in Mobile Commerce	141
		4.4.4	Mobile Viral Marketing	144
	4.5	Forms of Mobile Commerce		148
		4.5.1	Pure Mobile Commerce	149
		4.5.2	Cooperative Mobile Commerce	149
		4.5.3	Multi-channel Mobile Commerce	150
		4.5.4	Hybrid Mobile Commerce	151
		4.5.5	Vertical Mobile Commerce	151
	4.6	Relevant Success Factors for Mobile Commerce		153
5	**Study: Status and Potential of Location-based services**			155
	5.1	Concept and Objectives of the Study		155
		5.1.1	Initial Situation and Reason for Study	155
		5.1.2	kaufDA as an LBS Provider	155
		5.1.3	Initial Position and Core Issues	156
		5.1.4	Study Design and Socio-Demographics	156
	5.2	Smartphone Ownership and Usage in Relation to LBS		157
		5.2.1	Ownership and Usage of Smartphones	157
		5.2.2	Planned Purchase of New Devices	159
		5.2.3	Functions Used on Smartphones and Tablets	159
		5.2.4	Channels Used for Product Information Searches	161
	5.3	"So": Social and LBS-Relevant Buying Aspects		161
		5.3.1	Current and Future Information-Seeking Behavior	162
		5.3.2	Impact of Attractive Offers on Buying Behavior	163
		5.3.3	Usage Locations for Information Searches	164
		5.3.4	Use of Social Media Channels for Local Offers	165
		5.3.5	Awareness and Expectations of LBS from a Social Perspective	165

5.4	"Lo": Attraction and Usage of LBS at POS		169
	5.4.1	Attraction of Location-based services	169
	5.4.2	Previous Usage of LBS and Frequency of Use	170
	5.4.3	Reasons for Using and Not Using LBS	171
	5.4.4	Relevant LBS Contents	172
	5.4.5	Interest and Buying Based on LBS Usage	173
5.5	"Mo": Mobile Usage of LBS		175
	5.5.1	Product Information Searches via Smartphones	175
	5.5.2	Prerequisites for Greater Use of Mobile Devices	177
	5.5.3	Requirements for Information Searches on Mobile Devices	180
	5.5.4	Use of Smartphones/Digital Displays When Shopping	180
	5.5.5	Preferences for Private or Provided Devices	181
5.6	Relevance of Results to Brick-and-Mortar Retailing		182
	5.6.1	Differentiation of Customers and Users	182
	5.6.2	Conclusions and Twenty Tips on Use of LBS	183
5.7	Comprehensive Recommendations for Brick-and-Mortar Retailing		184

Bibliography ... 187

Index ... 203

About the Authors ... 205

"Always on and Always in Touch": The New Buying Behaviour

1.1 What Customers Want: The Mobile Universe

Mobility and mobile Internet will definitely play a prominent role in commerce in future: the number of smartphone users is climbing sharply and expected to double again in the next few years (cf. AGOF 2013). More than 40 % of the German-speaking population already regularly uses web-enabled mobile devices to access the World Wide Web (cf. Fig. 1.1). People are no longer only using their devices for telephone calls, email correspondence or chatting, but increasingly also to search for product information or directly shop online (cf. AGOF 2013). Buyers at brick-and-mortar stores are now starting their buying process with research in the mobile network and are increasingly using local services to do so. Although smartphone owners also use other types of devices for this purpose, i.e. desktop, mobile or tablet, information searches are predominantly started using smartphones. Such searches are frequently conducted during idle periods, e.g. when stuck in traffic, standing in line, or in the waiting room. Customers continue the information process on their desktop at home, where more and more shopping is being done. Google refers to this phenomenon as "multi-screening" (cf. Google 2012). However, people are increasingly surfing the mobile Internet not only in idle periods, but also while watching TV, either on the mobile phone or a tablet (cf. Google 2012). Customers often make decisions about purchases, which are sometimes realized on the online shop or at a brick-and-mortar store the next day (cf. Google and Ipsos OTX MediaCT 2012). But where are the limits to smartphone usage? That question can only be answered from the perspective of users, since they are the ones driving this trend: This is what customers want (cf. PBS-Business 2013). Based on the latest studies, use of the Internet and mobile technology is still in its infancy, especially in Germany (cf. kaufDA 2013). Several firm growth factors are only just taking effect, such as a gradual improvement in the low-level and slowly progressing connectivity and network infrastructure in Germany. Additional factors include the growing range of offers from brick-and-mortar retailers on the net, as well as international online competition, which is gradually appearing on the German market and is set

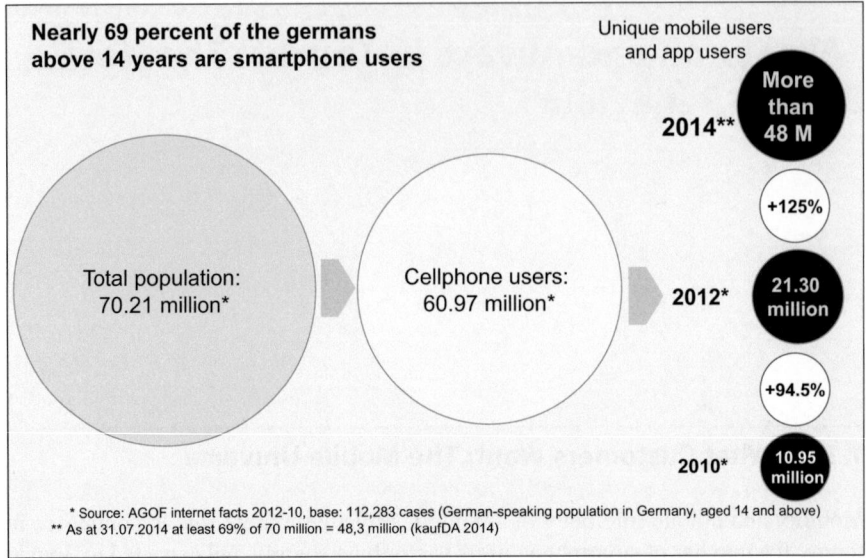

Fig. 1.1 The mobile universe (Source: Based on AGOF (2013))

to come increasingly from Asian countries in the future. The next Amazons and Googles will probably come from China, which is undergoing an enormous digital upgrade.

These new digital giants will be able to exploit a strategic window, because most German online and mobile shops are lagging behind international providers and will have to become more professional in the next few years. Above all the "digital natives" or rather "smart natives" entering the markets will demand such professionalism, in particular the "smart natives". Such "heavy smartphone users" are still young and in most cases not yet legally competent. As they enter the commercial landscape as customers, online and mobile growth will accelerate further in the next few years and the disruptive trend of recent years will therefore continue. In the course of this development, mobile commerce sales made directly on smartphones are currently growing progressively, and at least twice as strongly as for "normal online commerce" (cf. Schürmann 2012). Figure 1.2 shows that the mobile share of online commerce had already reached approximately 10 % in Europe in 2012, but only 7 % in Germany. In comparison with the previous year however, this was equivalent to a growth of 141 % (cf. BVH 2013). Mobile commerce sales volume is expected to increase more than tenfold by 2020, and could then make up around 35 % of total online retail sales. Mobile commerce turnover would then be equivalent to more than 200 billion euros in Europe and over 27 billion euros in Germany, i.e. the total of all online retail sales revenues in 2012. However, such a level of turnover in no way reflects the actual importance of mobile commerce. In the event of parallel usage of the different buying and information channels – also referred to as omni-channel use – a significant feeder role for brick-and-mortar stores is also

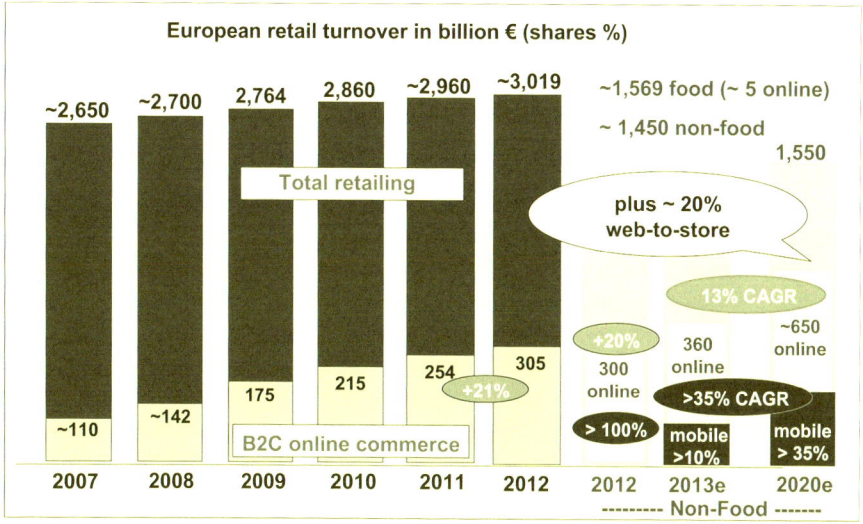

Fig. 1.2 Future share of mobile commerce in online commerce in Europe (Source: eWeb Research Center (2013) based on IMR (2011))

ascribed to mobile Internet. The role of the mobile net in making general preparations for shopping is therefore gaining importance and has a sustained effect on shopping in-store. Smartphones and tablet PCs are increasingly being used for this purpose and have already become the "main access device" for social networks.

1.2 Social: Internet and Social Networks as a Central Part of Life

Nearly two thirds of the more than 2.6 billion Internet users worldwide are active in social networks. Facebook alone has approximately 1.15 billion users, as of April 2013, and Google+ has just broken the 200 million barrier (cf. Statista 2013). The huge numbers of social network users are spending an ever greater share of their spare time on the Internet. Social networks are increasingly being accessed via mobile devices. By 2014 at the latest, the number of mobile Internet users – at around 1.6 billion – will exceed the number of desktop users (Grebarsch and Zalando 2012). Mobile Internet is upgrading the cellphone from a communications medium to an interaction medium, and turning it into a central part of the "digital lifestyle" (cf. Go-Smart study 2012, p. 18), where online offers are available at any time. The difference between mobile and stationary Internet is disappearing as far as "smart natives" are concerned. The new "digital reality" is experienced wherever its heavy users may be. Situational availability largely constitutes mobile added value for users, while changing their demands and usage habits at the same time. Diverse communications options are created based on new technologies and tools.

In this respect, people are doing what they have always done, but with different resources (cf. Mindwyse 2011, p. 6): Facebook "likes" are probably the most used tool in this regard. But ratings, bookmarking, commenting and discussing are also popular. Additional options include uploading the user's own contents, status updates and sharing or asking questions, to mention just a few of the popular social media activities. Sharing involves people telling stories about what they do and what they find interesting, whether about hobbies, vacation photos, funny and bizarre stories, or partnership experiences. Rating remains quite high up on the popularity scale. Decisions are increasingly being made based on other people's opinions. Everything and everyone is rated: doctors, playgrounds, employers, restaurants, and even restrooms. Questions are raised in the community and answered there (cf. ibid.). Bloggers and community members are even increasingly responding to service inquiries among themselves (cf. Ich-sag-mal 2011; Heinemann 2012a, p. 10). Only 19 % of the 1.15 billion Facebook users exclusively use a desktop to access Facebook. As Fig. 1.3 shows, 52 % use both mobile and stationary devices. Around 20 % use the network solely via a mobile device, meaning that the overall rate of mobile usage of Facebook could be around 60 %. Seven hundred and fifty one million users therefore utilize Facebook through mobile apps and the mobile website (cf. Statista 2013). Sixty-three percent of mobile users check their newsfeed several times a day. Facebook users always carry their smartphones with them and Facebook is by far the most commonly used app on Android and Apple iOS. Furthermore, many apps have a Facebook login. The mobile trend also continues in summertime, when there had previously been a summer break in Internet usage. Jan Firsching from Futurebiz states that mobile Facebook users even check their news feed while sitting in the beer garden. The

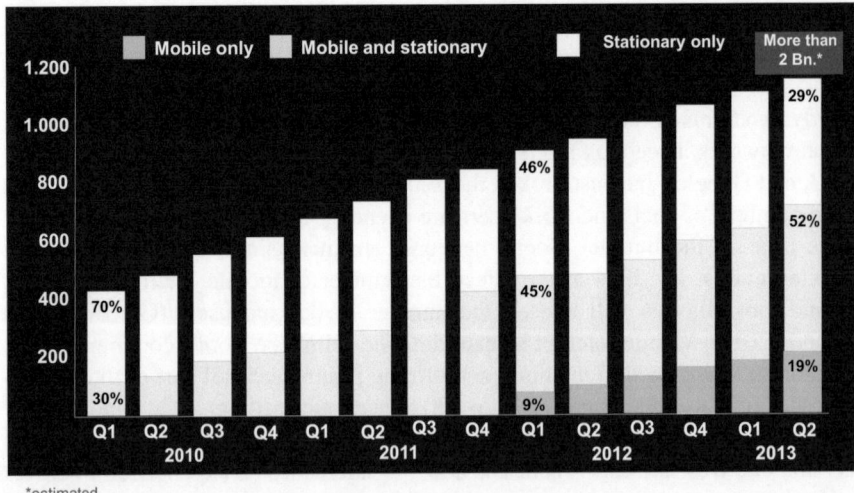

Fig. 1.3 Users of social networks worldwide (Source: Own illustration with data source from Statista (2013))

smartphone is taken to the beach, swimming pool and barbecues, and is always on hand. When it comes to vacations, consideration is now given to favorable data rates, because after all, vacation photos should immediately be published on Facebook and Instagram (cf. Firsching 2013b).

It is imperative in this respect that companies optimize their contents for mobile usage. Concise texts, attractive photos and mobile optimized websites should be considered essential. Online retailers need to realize that not only is the number of mobile users increasing, but also session time, which is 21 % longer on Facebook when accessed via mobile devices (cf. ibid.). Mobile usage of social networks is also pushed by the sharply rising number of users. Seventy-three percent of smartphone users already visit social networks on their mobile devices, with 38 % visiting every day. Mobile advertising is therefore also becoming an additional driver of growth. In 2012, relevant gross advertising volume grew around 70 % as compared to the previous year (cf. Hofmann 2012). Gross advertising expenditure in newspapers and magazines is falling accordingly, to the benefit of online advertising (cf. BVDW 2012, p. 13). This trend can also be observed for brick-and-mortar retailers (cf. Haug 2013; EHI/KPMG 2012, p. 37).

1.3 Local and Mobile: Smartphones as Accessories for Shopping

The extremely rapid growth rates for web-enabled mobile phones mean that by the end of 2014, the majority of mobile phone users will be on the move with a web-enabled device, which they are able to use when shopping at brick-and-mortar stores (cf. Haug 2013; Aquino and Radwanick 2012). The role of the mobile net in general preparations for shopping is therefore growing and has a sustainable impact on buying in-store. Around 70 % of smartphone users in the USA already use their device at the point of sale. Roughly half of them do so to find a store and compare prices. Almost a quarter of smartphone owners always carry their device, enabling them to compare prices and obtain information about products (cf. Fig. 1.4). Smartphones are also being used more often in German chain stores, according to expert opinion at least. In all probability, the importance of mobile devices will match the American trend by the end of 2014 (cf. Haug 2013). Surprisingly, a large number of major German online shops are not yet equipped for the increasing mobility of their users. One study conducted by the United Digital Group (UDG) revealed that many online retailers are losing out on sales because their range of offers is not yet really mobile-capable. As a result, it is not uncommon for users to abandon purchases. Very few online shops have a clear display adapted to the screen size. "Especially in this area, the mobile e-commerce landscape could still be upgraded in Germany", remarks Matthias Thürling, e-commerce specialist at UDG (cf. Springer-Professionals 2013). There is pressure to take action here, because the latest studies reveal that 33 % of Europeans are willing to complete purchases on a

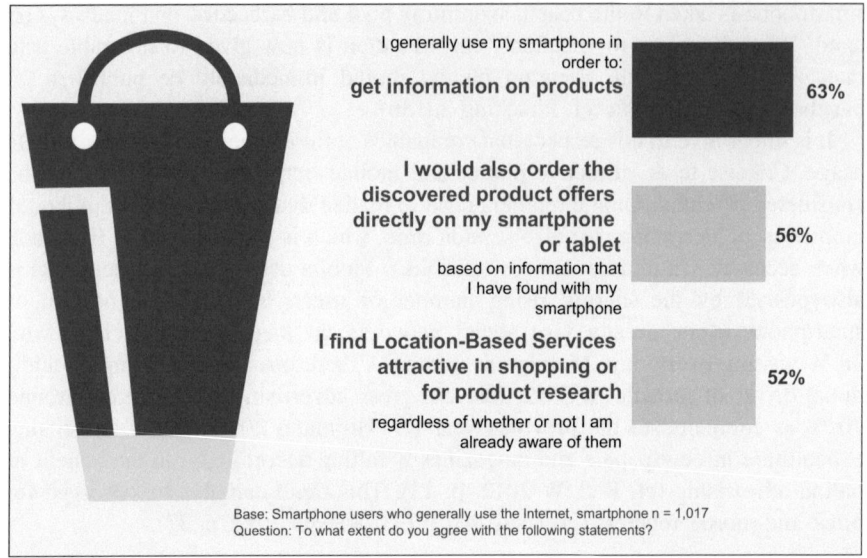

Fig. 1.4 Smartphones as accessories for shopping (Source: Own illustration with data source from kaufDA (2013); eWeb Research Center (2013))

smartphone or tablet PC. And 29 % of the smartphone owners surveyed have already used their mobile device for shopping (cf. ibid.). In turn, this could result in even greater participation of smartphone users in social networks (cf. Google and Ipsos OTX MediaCT 2012).

The same factor applies to multi-screening and mobile format diversity: Internet users can no longer be assigned to a specific type of device, but rather use different formats in different situations, or even in parallel. This trend has recently been termed "multi-screening" and indicates that flexible format solutions will increasingly be in demand. The quote "mobile commerce is couch commerce" (cf. Heinemann 2013b; DDV Dialogue 2013, p. 22) best describes the parallel use of media.

1.4 SoLoMo: Key Issue for Future Commerce

The mobile Internet and new smartphones make communication possible anywhere and anytime. Users increasingly share information about their whereabouts and local offers (cf. Mindwyse 2011). This exchange is no longer time-delayed, but shared in real time via the network. In this respect, the social network is a companion for all life situations and all topics, which changes the definition of privacy by making part of our lives public. Virtual identities serve as a means of self-expression and are becoming essential for digital natives (cf. Mindwyse 2011). "People are happy to share information about themselves with others", says Mark

Zuckerberg (cf. von Kuhnhardt 2012). Such use of social media can no longer be viewed in isolation, but is increasingly taking place in combination with localization and location-based services, as well as mobile Internet usage. Such interaction forms the basis for "SoLoMo synergies", which result from social, local and mobile networking (SoLoMo) and give rise to new opportunities for marketing efficiency (cf. von Kunhardt 2012). Given that the number of heavy users of smartphones and mobile Internet is set to grow dynamically in the next few years, SoLoMo networking could also increase to the same extent. Most heavy users surf the mobile Internet every day. This group of "smart natives" forms a significant basis for SoLoMo.

The SoLoMo networking associated with smartphone penetration is revealed by the combined response or solution to the following questions (cf. von Kunhardt 2013):

- **Social:** How do fans move on social media platforms and what do they expect from their retailers and favorite brands there?
- **Local:** What options does localization of customers provide for local offers and offers at brick-and-mortar stores?
- **Mobile:** What options do mobile marketing and mobile commerce offer, and how can companies pick up their "mobile" fans/consumers?

Social networking is certainly regarded as a key driver of this trend, in combination with advancing smartphone penetration. In just a few years from now, the majority of Germans will use a smartphone and view it as a natural part of their buying processes (cf. Go-Smart study 2012, p. 31). These future customers will expect a far greater range of services on their smartphone than those they are familiar with from stationary Internet usage. In particular, local functions and social networks will play an even greater role than today. The "SoLoMo phenomenon" is also fueled by the fact that users want to remain relevant online. The same applies today to smart natives, for whom permanent access to the digital data stream is normal. They demand mobile offers, which they can continuously keep up-to-date and share with their network. In this regard, local real-time offers with geo-location, increasing response speeds, real-time information and augmented reality create interesting mobile added value for SoLoMo users. Added value is undoubtedly provided by online buying (cf. Go-Smart study 2012, pp. 30–31; Mindwyse 2011; Heinemann 2012b), which is convenient and varied and can be done 24 h a day, regardless of location. Nevertheless, experts do not make the assumption that brick-and-mortar stores will completely disappear, quite the contrary (cf. eBay 2012a). Consumers do not want to buy everything online, "without touch & feel", but nor do they have to forego the advantages of one channel just because they happen to use another. Some companies therefore let their customers shop in parallel (cf. Heinemann 2012b). But an online shop is not enough on its own, since this matter concerns channel excellence, which so far has predominantly been offered by international online retailers. Brick-and mortar retailing should not get left behind, since this would inevitably result in an exodus of customers (cf. ibid.).

In the future, customers will probably no longer want to distinguish between the supplier's different channels – as shown by the outcome of a recent eBay study on the subject of "Future Commerce" (cf. eBay 2012a). Usage of the mobile Internet by many buyers in brick-and-mortar stores means that a separation cannot be made between shopping online or offline. A greater number of customers will also shop online in-store and even ask for goods to be delivered to the store, as is often the case in the UK. In this respect, brick-and-mortar shop space will increasingly be converted into showrooms, where the customer enjoys the touch & feel experience, but can't immediately take the merchandise with them. All of the products are displayed, but only one of each. Customers can test products at their convenience, and try them out or on. Customers who decide to buy a product can easily make the purchase using their smartphone, by means of a QR code, without having to wait directly in the showroom. A new version is then supplied directly – in the shop, to the customer's home or any other location of his or her choosing. The same situation can essentially still be found in a traditional furniture retail store, not with a QR code, but with home delivery and long delivery times. Examples from other countries show that shopping with QR codes is already possible from anywhere. For example, Tesco in South Korea has set up images of food shelves in subway stations, showing the supermarket's product range. All customers have to do to make a purchase is to scan the QR codes over the images. Magalogs, a combination of magazine and buying functions via augmented-reality functions on the smartphone, allow for a new kind of "QR purchase". However, it should not be assumed that shopping via images will be feasible for all products. As far as cars and clothing are concerned, for example, many consumers will not want to forego a test drive or trying on items before buying. The assumption can therefore be made that the use of new shopping options, depending on the type of product, will produce different forms of shopping. The "compulsory purchase" of consumer goods, such as food, will increasingly be done online, as is already possible in South Korea. The "shopping experience" however will continue to take place in showrooms or salesrooms in the future, equipped with more innovative fittings, in order to attract customers. However, it will still take some time for a virtual supermarket at a bus stop to become prevalent in Germany. German retailers are already lagging far behind English-speaking countries in such developments. Whereas customers are encouraged to use a smartphone to make a price comparison while shopping at a Best Buy store, it is not uncommon for this to be prohibited in Germany or for jammers to be installed in shops, so that customers are unable to access their cellphones. In this respect, Germany and USA, and especially Japan, are worlds apart. But experience suggests that such bans will not manage to keep the trend towards SoLoMo in check. Nor will they be able to prevent customers becoming better informed than ever before by using the mobile Internet. Sales personnel are finding it increasingly difficult to keep up with emancipated and well-informed consumers. The role of sales staff will be subject to major changes in this respect. Given that the distinction between different channels is becoming blurred, the pressure to close a deal is growing. Customers unable to make a decision to buy in-store do not have to return to the store if they change their mind at home. They

1.5 Future of Commerce: Challenge for Brick-and-Mortar Formats

can then buy the product easily from the living room sofa on the Internet, not necessarily from the same retailer, but rather from the best supplier.

Greater use of the Internet is generating "new" site visits on the net, which have an impact on previous brick-and-mortar retail locations and are increasingly replacing or at least complementing them. Parallel usage of different buying and information channels – also referred to as omni-channel usage or multi-screening – means that a significant feeder role for the brick-and-mortar store is assigned to the mobile Internet, as previously mentioned. As a result, it will be less and less possible to talk about purely online and offline worlds in the future, since both are amalgamated into "no-line" systems, in which operating forms merge into one another. This produces great opportunities for troubled brick-and-mortar retailers.

Technological innovations enable a completely new customer focus, which particularly takes account of the multi-options demanded by customers. The assumption can be made that at least 20 % of all purchases in brick-and-mortar stores will be affected by mobile ROPO (Research Online Purchase Offline) by 2020 (cf. Bruce 2011). Recommendations from friends on social networks already play a leading role in this. In combination with social interaction and localization, "SoLoMo" mobile commerce has excellent prospects for the future. Brick-and-mortal retailers in particular should therefore start to deal with "SoLoMo" mobile commerce. However, any retailers already steering clear of the online issue should really do the same when it comes to mobile commerce. Optimization is necessary for mobile-compatible contents and format-compliant websites. The range of offers for mobile services and applications, or killer applications, should also be expanded. Situational and lifestyle-related adaptation of offers to customers' individual shopping habits certainly represents a master class in mobile commerce. That is the only way to leverage the synergies that result from social, local and mobile networking. Such individualized features include customizable virtual shelves and the use of augmented reality in all conceivable facets. Mobile 2.0, i.e. mobile-oriented implementation of social media tools with networking to Facebook, Twitter and the like, is standard. Twitter accounts do not only function as a service tool used to reply to customer questions, as practiced at Best Buy with Twelpforce. They can also sustainably fuel other sales channels, as demonstrated by Whole Foods Market (WFM). Much greater attention should be paid to the highest level of mobile navigation and mobile usability in mobile commerce than the online shop. Flexible formatting also helps in this regard, which allows for the use of different types of devices, including tablet PCs. Page loading speed and accessibility should also be implemented as optimally as possible, particularly with regard to transmission problems. Content-heavy websites with loading times lasting minutes scare customers away and drive them to competitors, which are only a click away.

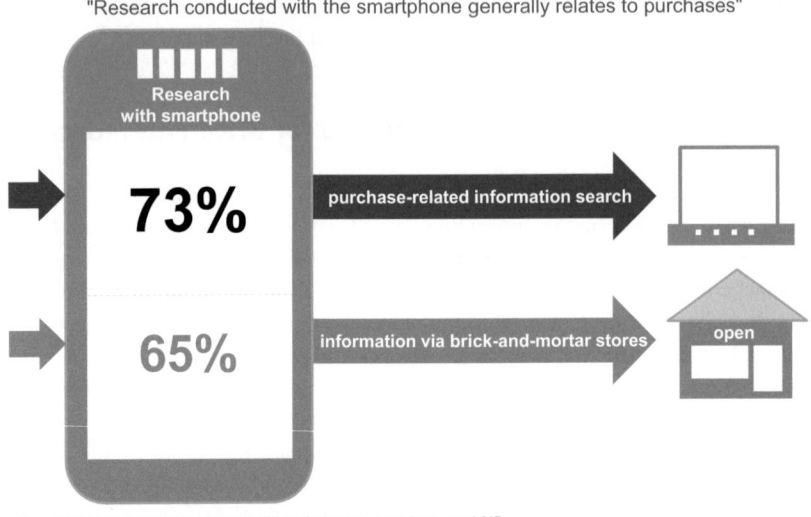

Fig. 1.5 "Feeder" function for mobile commerce (Source: Own illustration with data source from kaufDA (2013); eWeb Research Center (2013))

Fourth-generation smartphones in particular allow for a completely new shopping experience, which suppliers can take advantage of, for example by linking consumers to a professional and informative mobile website in their stores.

Studies conducted by Google on this topic show that 65 % of online purchases are already initiated through information searches via the smartphone and 61 % subsequently finalized on the desktop. In any case, 73 % of mobile Internet searches are purchase related and 65 % of them look for relevant informations about local stores (cf. kaufDa 2013). Mobile devices thus have a prominent role as a "feeder function" not only for online shops, but also for brick-and-mortar retail formats (cf. Fig. 1.5). Today, it is already possible to target customers on a shopping trip with adverts, as already practiced in the USA. Electronics retailer Best Buy, fashion chain American Eagle Outfitter and department store operator Macy's have already upgraded their stores to track exactly where a consumer is situated. They combine new geo-location technology with immediate cellphone advertising, which is tailored to location, time, person and before long, even to the shelf. Customers are then sent a coupon for a specific shop or notified about the availability of the desired product in surrounding stores. In combination with their intuitive navigation functions, smartphones literally bring customers into stores. This is the only way to interpret the comment from e-commerce experts that: "The future of online is offline". Such developments represent great opportunities for innovative suppliers, which are able to anticipate trends and implement them in new concepts, since technological innovations allow for a completely new form of customer orientation, which in particular takes account of the multi-options demanded by the customer. The winners will include genuine multi-channel retailers, which merge their online or mobile and offline channels into an enclosed overall system, a development that can already be found in English-speaking countries (cf. Heinemann 2013a).

Customers who are already "online in-store" with a smartphone will not accept any differentiation between a supplier's channels in the future, since in the majority of cases, they already use several channels for the buying process. In this respect, new forms of sales will emerge, which already exist in English-speaking countries abroad, and there will be "no-line systems", where, as described above, the boundaries between online and offline disappear. The trend towards no-line systems will define all retail sectors. Customers are driving this development. They expect a flagship store on the net, including the greatest variety of choice, enabling them to prepare for making a purchase in brick-and-mortar stores, or conversely to complete the purchase at home in the online shop after a visit to the store. Such "showrooming" – sometimes called "advice theft" by German retailers – does not involve a complete halt to visits to downtown locations. However, in order to avoid a drop in sales revenues, every retailer will need its own online shop sooner or later. But this requires a refocussing in terms of investment decisions – as Wilhelm Josten from Butlers rightly states (cf. Josten 2013). This means: an investment freeze in stores and in space expansion, and "full steam ahead" for online systems, because the Internet has changed our buying behavior, but is also subject to constant changes.

Brick-and-mortar retail formats will have to change their appearance in the future, in some cases in the form of a showroom or with showroom or pop-up areas, and in other cases through automation or downsizing (Heinemann 2013a). Otherwise, brick-and-mortar non-food retailers will not be able to escape from reducing fixed costs for the space as a result of dwindling sales. The first fully automated store with robots already exists. Clothing retailer Hointer in the USA, which will be mentioned again in the following chapters, is the pioneer in this area. There will no longer be many stores in large downtown areas, and in particular in small and medium-sized centers, and some of these towns and cities will become desolate. Brick-and-mortar B2C retailers with a "classic" small shop in a B or C location will especially be at risk within the emerging structural change because they have so far largely steered clear of the Internet, or joined an unpromising retail federation solution. Brick-and-mortar retailing is at risk of degenerating into a showroom in which products are only tried out and experienced in a tactile way, or specialist advice is given. In view of dwindling sales revenues, the provision of goods and expensive sales personnel might no longer be easily justifiable. Consequently, after visiting the showroom, it is often only possible to place orders via the Internet. But despite the availability factors, increasing numbers of customers are placing orders online when visiting a store or afterwards. Price advantages are not solely decisive in this respect – reasons could also include a lack of availability of sizes and colors, or a laborious and uninspiring buying process (cf. Haug 2013).

Nor will conventional small retailers be able to avoid being present on the net. There are already some prime examples, from many sectors, which show that the launch of an additional, complementary online shop is no longer a question of company size, but rather primarily a matter of the owner's commitment. Unfortunately, retail associations obscure the true force of the development and in particular lead small and medium retailers to believe everything will be fine and the Internet is only a transitory phenomenon. This often prevents the necessary clarity of vision – and action. But it is not only brick-and-mortar retailers that are affected. Mail order companies will substitute catalog sales almost completely with online sales revenues and will have to find replacement solutions for the "catalog cost driver", including in the B2B area, which in any case is several times larger in e-commerce than in the B2C area (cf. BITKOM 2007). Sooner or later, contracted suppliers will sell directly to customers themselves and transform into vertical providers. This model is already customary in the fashion industry and other sectors. Manufacturer-direct retailing is a big success story and a company like Boss already makes more than 50 % of sales revenues in direct sales to end customers (cf. Focus.de 2013a). The large B2B mail order companies also have good prospects, viewing the development as an opportunity and taking a "disintermediation" approach. Combined B2B and B2C models are also emerging in other sectors of online commerce. Amazon has managed to sell at least a quarter of its products to business customers. Boundaries are increasingly becoming blurred, but where is the limit to online commerce? Horst Norberg, CEO of the Media-Saturn Group, recently indicated a 25 % limit on the market share for online commerce. The question arises here of whether the strongest growth years in Internet technology are already over. That is definitely not the case. In 2012, the entertainment electronics and PC/telecommunications product groups already exceeded the 25 % online share threshold and are close to 30 % for 2013. The 25 % limit might be a pipe dream which no longer exists, especially as Media-Saturn-Holding, even in combination with Redcoon, does not even have a 5 % online share, or half of that without Redcoon. Mobile commerce will no doubt replace large parts of e-commerce and limit it to a certain extent. As the extended arm of online commerce, sales revenues via mobile commerce ultimately remain in the same channel. Pure brick-and-mortar retailers however, without any online or mobile activities, will fall by the wayside. Today, German retailers have by far the largest retail shop space per capita and simultaneously generate the lowest sales revenue per square meter in Europe (cf. Jahn and Müller 2011). The "Key European Retail Data 2011 Review and 2012 Forecast" study shows that Germany already has the most retail space, at 1.45 square meters per capita, following the Netherlands with 1.66 square meters per inhabitant (cf. ibid.). If brick-and-mortar retailers in Germany want to grow, they should start thinking about the subject of SoLoMo right away.

Social Commerce as Base Factor No. 1 for SoLoMo

2.1 Importance and Significance of Social Media

2.1.1 Current Trend in Social Media

The term social media or, more recently, social Internet can be used as a synonym for the term Web 2.0. Within the framework of social media, information can be used both in verbal and multimedia form. This includes, for example, photos, videos, music, voice recordings and games (cf. Heymann-Reder 2011, p. 20). Communication on social media is usually networked worldwide and creates new interaction opportunities for users and companies. Well-known social media platforms include Facebook, Twitter, Google+, YouTube, LinkedIn, Pinterest and Polyvore. MySpace is regarded as a "social media pioneer", but has more or less had its day. In contrast, YouTube now plays a prominent role as a video-sharing platform and is a global institution, without which we can no longer imagine our lives. By far the most popular form of social media today is connecting to a website with Facebook, but many German online retailers have not yet made use of this phenomenon. There is often uncertainty about which aims should be pursued through social media. As a result, the potential of a Facebook connection is not fully exploited and usually amounts to nothing more than a "Like" button. Often only the shop itself is rated, but not the individual product. An automated dissemination mechanism therefore remains unused (cf. Social Media 2011, p. 36). Groupon provides a good example of potential social networking. Four links to Facebook are offered per page, with two direct share buttons, a multifunctional recommendation box for friends, and a "Like" box, which shows numbers and pictures of fans. Groupon quantifies traffic generated from Facebook at 3–5 % of the total visitor rate (cf. ibid.). However, there is a lack of penetration in Germany for most plug-ins. Moreover, the button increases the page loading time and the advertiser has to explain the use of Facebook social plug-ins in its data privacy information. Of the eight standard plug-ins, only the "Like" button and single sign-on actually prove useful. However, many experts view social plug-ins as just the

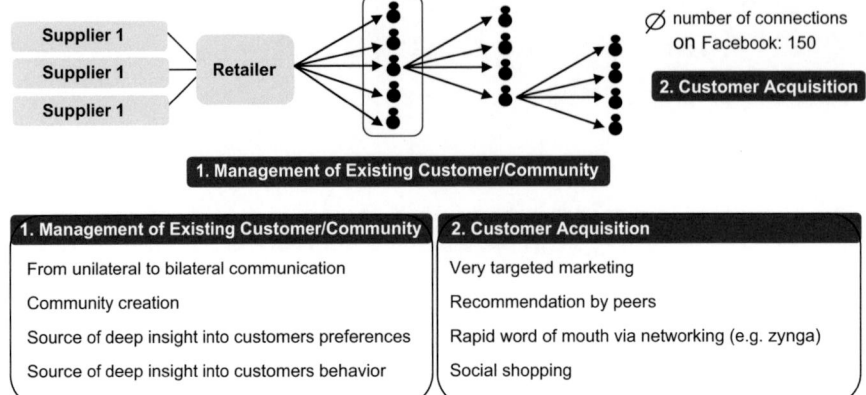

Fig. 2.1 Leverage of social graph (Source: Own illustration based on BV Capital 2011)

start. Implementing our own ideas based on the Open Graph model is regarded as the supreme test, in order to utilize data and images from the user's profile.

Etsy, for example, coordinates user and friend data with its own product features, in order to make birthday recommendations. Facebook's reach does not have to end with integration in the web shop. Integration is also suggested at the POS (point of sale). Leveraging the social graph offers considerable potential. As Fig. 2.1 shows, one Facebook member has an average of 150 contacts, meaning 150 times 150, i.e. 22,500 members can be reached in the second phase, and over 3.3 million members in the third stage. This can be used to manage existing communities as well as to acquire customers.

Google Incorporation, which according to its former CEO has for too long underestimated the importance of social networking, has now hit the ground running with Google+ and precisely targeted the weakness of Facebook: not every contact necessarily signifies friendship. Google+ enables online acquaintances to be combined into groups, to which targeted information is then assigned. As far as Google is concerned, this may well involve offering a Facebook-like platform, in order to close the social circle and no longer be forced to depend on Facebook (cf. Internet World Business 2011e, No. 12, p. 3; Die Welt dated June 30, 2011e, p. 12). Within a very short space of time, Google has clearly managed to put Facebook and Twitter on the defensive (cf. FAZ 2011e, No. 156, p. 11). In this respect, Google+ should register high growth in its numbers of members within a relatively short period of time. Experts expect that with this private/professional network, initially launched in 2011, this new giant will draw level with Facebook in the future (cf. Spiegel 2011).

2.1.2 History and Phases of Social Media

Social media are not as new as might be assumed in light of the current discussion. The beginnings of social media go back to community marketing in the music industry and thereby to pre-Internet times. This emerged from the Arpanet, predominantly used for military purposes, which started at the end of the 1960s and went public in 1993 (cf. Beckmann and Schulz 2008, pp. 138 et seqq.). The first online music communities, such as "MySpace", were formed back in the start phase of the Internet in the 1990s (cf. ibid.). After the Internet bubble burst in 2001, the net was reinvented as "Web 2.0" (cf. Weinberg 2010, pp. 4 et seqq.). Web 2.0 and later social media essentially represent users "recapturing" the web. The emancipation of users was also the original idea of the Internet, which had been pushed into the background somewhat by its later commercialization. Social media aims to involve users more intensively and form communities of all types, in order to create dialogues. Passive users should therefore turn into active "prosumers". Participants are described as prosumers if they are not only "active and mature partners to companies" in a dialogue, but also help to design the net overall. Forums and web blogs of all type were **initially** used for this purpose. Private social networks later emerged in conjunction with the further development of MySpace and then the founding of Facebook. With a huge number of members, they have become part of our everyday lives.

The development of virtual community forms, which include social media, is depicted in Fig. 2.2. Social media describe the opportunity to share experiences and information on community websites, such as blogs, Internet forums, networks, image and video portals, wikis, podcasts and user-generated websites, and to enter into relationships with other users (cf. Weinberg 2010, pp. 23 et seqq.). On the whole, however, social media no longer represent a pure communication platform. Social platforms are clearly used for communication purposes as well as for the direct sale of products and are therefore becoming more heavily

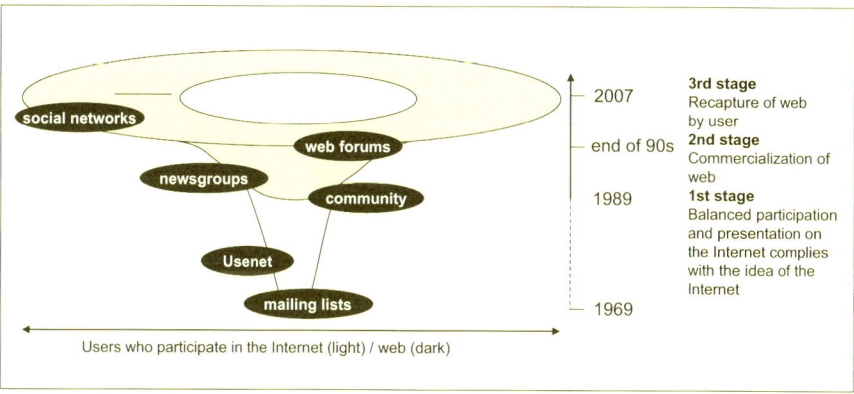

Fig. 2.2 Development of virtual community forms since the creation of Arpanet (Source: Beckmann and Schulz 2008, p. 139)

commercialized than previously, as expressed by the term "F-Commerce", which stands for "Facebook commerce" (cf. von Kuhnhardt 2012).

2.1.3 Significance and Relevance of Social Media

The significance of social media can be seen in the context of global Internet penetration, as documented impressively by the size of the Facebook community. Over one billion users are now said to be members, with around 26 million in Germany (cf. Fanpagelist 2012). Google+ could now have over 200 million monthly users worldwide (cf. Firsching 2013a) and is growing dynamically. Altogether, at least 1.5 billion people are active in social networks. The exchange of information between such users is developing a completely new dynamic in the course of "social networking". Users tend to be young and are slightly more likely to be male. However, more than one in two of over-50s already use this medium (cf. ARD/ZDF 2012). Social networks are increasingly accessed through mobile devices, with around 54 % of Facebook users already doing this (cf. Socialbakers 2012; von Kunhardt 2012).

As the LG Electronics case study shows, this factor is relevant to 70 % of service inquiries. With just a few posts on the net from the company itself, an unusually high reach can be achieved. Just 47 blog posts at LG Electronics were capable of answering more than 30,000 service inquiries in advance, without placing any strain on the hotline (Ich-sag-mal 2011; Heinemann 2012a, p. 10).

2.1.4 Future Prospects for Social Media

In 2014, almost one in two Germans use a smartphone and view it as a natural part of their buying processes (Go-Smart study 2012, p. 31). These future customers expect a much greater range of services on their smartphone than they are familiar with from stationary Internet usage. Due to smartphones, local functions and social networks in particular will play a greater role than today. The SoLoMo phenomenon is also fueled by the fact that users want to remain relevant online. The same applies to smart natives, for whom permanent access to the digital data stream is normal. They demand mobile offers, which they continuously keep up-to-date and share with their network. In this regard, local real-time offers with geo-location, increasing response speeds, real-time information and augmented reality create interesting mobile added value for SoLoMo users. Added value is undoubtedly provided by online shopping (Go-Smart study 2012, pp. 30–31; Mindwyse 2011; Heinemann 2012b), which is convenient and varied, and can be done 24 h a day, regardless of location. Nevertheless, experts do not make the assumption that brick-and-mortar stores will disappear completely (eBay 2012a). Consumers do not want to buy everything online, but nor do they have to forego the advantages of one channel just because they use another one. Some companies therefore let their customers shop in parallel. However, this approach should not lead to an exodus of

2.2 Social Commerce as a New Form of Commerce

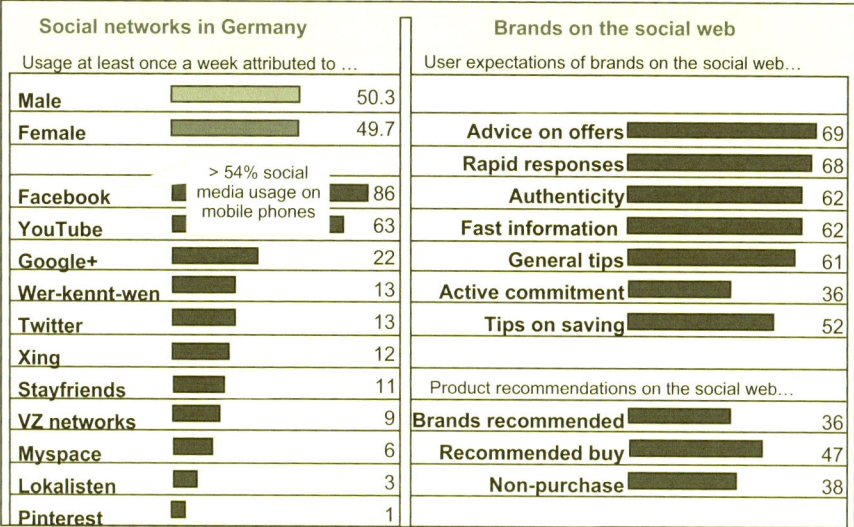

Fig. 2.3 Expectations of brands in social network (Source: Own illustrations based on Horizont 44/2012 with data source from Social Minds 2012, Press Release Media Agency Vivaki from 2.11.2012. Base: 2.000 online users aged 14 and above)

customers. As a result, various retailers are currently working on social media strategies (cf. Heinemann 2012b). The question of which role social media will play in the future is also increasingly being examined in the branded goods industry. In this respect, a study by Social Minds from 2012 provides interesting evidence of customer expectations of the brand in the social network (cf. Horizont 44/2012). As Fig. 2.3 shows, credibility and authenticity are the key factors here. In addition to prompt and honest information on the supplier side, users are primarily concerned with recommendations for specific brands (36 %) and concrete purchase recommendations (47 %). In 38 % of cases, users also expect specific recommendations not to buy in the event of bad experiences with the product.

2.2 Social Commerce as a New Form of Commerce

Social commerce may be regarded as the symbiosis of e-commerce and social media (cf. Haarhaus 2013). The online environment is already heavily influenced by social media today. Crossovers are more or less fluid in this respect. The development stages and different forms of social commerce are therefore discussed below. The comments also refer to a master's thesis by Heike Haarhaus on this subject, which was supervised by the author (cf. Haarhaus 2013).

2.2.1 Special Characteristics and Relevance of Social Commerce

Although social commerce is certainly one of the most widely discussed online issues of recent times, there is no precise definition of the term yet (cf. Haarhaus 2013). The current definitions are generally very broad. While almost everyone is talking about social commerce, it is clear that very few companies understand the underlying concept correctly. In most cases, the term includes social marketing (cf. Chaney 2012b). In order to bring more clarity to the discussion, reference is made to the two components e-commerce and social media. Heike Haarhaus has produced a checklist for social commerce based on these two components. The first component – "e-commerce" – clearly emphasizes transactional relevance, in which the sale and purchase of products or services on the Internet is a significant prerequisite (cf. Haarhaus 2013; Wikipedia 2012a). With reference to Kollmann, e-commerce essentially consists of four components: content, commerce, context and connection. In the initial years, the Internet was dominated by e-content and e-connection (cf. Kollmann 2009, pp. 12 et seq.). In recent years however, a wide variety of online services have become established, which combine more than one of these components, making it difficult to categorize them exactly. Wirtz defines e-commerce as "initiation, negotiation and implementation of business transactions via Internet" (Wirtz 2008; Heinemann and Schwarzl 2010). This definition identifies the transaction as the significant prerequisite for e-commerce, and is a key factor in its differentiation from other forms of e-business. General definitions and explanations of social commerce tend to emphasize that it contributes rather indirectly to sales and should not be interpreted as referring to direct sales (cf. Lückemeier 2012). Such an interpretation may be correct in many cases, but requires the opportunity for genuine "in-stream transactions", or quite different solutions, which take the entire buying process into account. However, if a consumer in the social network is unable to pay "in-stream", it does not constitute social commerce, but rather advertising or communication (cf. Chaney 2012a). As a second component alongside e-commerce, consideration should be given to social media, or at least social features used when shopping. The term "social" is already indicative of a natural characterization of people and their need for mutual coexistence and interaction (cf. Wikipedia 2013). Social behavior involves people interacting and communicating with one another, and a social network with existing friends is therefore of great importance. The social component is omnipresent and has a decisive impact on shopping activities. Whereas consumers are happy to communicate during offline shopping, and to receive recommendations and advice, shopping at brick-and-mortar stores also offers further, additional support options, if desired. And moreover, all social interactions during brick-and-mortar shopping take place in "real-time". However, what this means for social commerce needs to be clarified in further detail: given that consumers now expect their online shopping experience to be nothing less than perfect, opportunities for social interaction have become almost compulsory in the online shopping world. Social commerce therefore represents a kind of collective shopping experience (cf. Grabs and Bannour 2011, p. 332.). Consumers expect to be supported with social features, enabling them to connect with friends immediately, as for example in the case of chat programs. They might be provided with ratings and recommendations from other users, ideally with personalized advice. Chats and co-browsing functions, which consumers can use to share product experiences or opinions in real time, are highly valued, and ensure that consumers' shopping experience is not inferior to offline shopping in any way (cf. Weave 2012, p. 223). Such tools are designed and implemented to ensure that consumers enjoy smart and positive shopping experiences. In contrast, retailers are given the option of listening to and understanding customers, and providing them with customized solutions (cf. etailment.de 2012a). In addition to the offline shopping experience, specific characteristics of social media can also be used to define the parameters of social commerce more precisely. Based on the specifics of social media for example, where significant aspects are reflected in user-generated content (UGC), this is also indicative of a high level of interactivity. User-generated content can easily be used for community building in social commerce. Users should be capable of building a relationship with other consumers, which also requires leadership. Social commerce therefore represents more of a social science than a technological concept, although it naturally requires technological implementation in the back-end (cf. Mühlenbeck and Skibicki 2007, p. 198.). With regard to UGC, social media also enable users to act as producers, and thus allow buyers to also operate as vendors. In this respect, refocussing efforts should ensure that consumers can interact with the supplier and can participate. In turn, this requires a certain relevance to the store, i.e. extensive consideration of appropriate opportunities for customers to influence the business model. Social commerce is therefore associated with a new type of freedom, allowing users to select the role they would like to play within the transaction process. This role may relate to the prospects for the consumer, producer or advisor (ibid., p. 107). The opportunity for customers to sell actively on the platform may be regarded as the highest level of social commerce. Increase in "customer value" is a major element of social commerce. In particular through the extensive opportunities for customer involvement, this represents a completely new business form of retailing (cf. marketing-blog.biz 2012). Customer value can only be improved if the retailer provides new "social instruments" or Web 2.0 tools. Such instruments should let customers solve their own problems or help resolve other customer's problems (cf. Marsden 2012b). If this gives users the opportunity to utilize a certain social intelligence, they can also make better buying decisions, which increases customer satisfaction. It is not without reason that online retailers are now ranked among the top places for customer satisfaction (cf. OCC&C 2012). With reference to Marsden, social intelligence describes a human capacity to learn from others simply by observing (cf. Marsden 2012a). Social problems can be resolved by allowing for a certain social status, for example. Exclusive fan offers or limited conditions with restricted access can be cited as examples, but social connections arising from buying options, such as "group buying", online gifting or a "wish list", also give rise to special social positions (cf. Weave 2012, p. 224). These examples show that social commerce must be based on transaction options. Social marketing and social media are certainly relatively widespread in retailing,

Checklist for social commerce		
1. Commerce	yes	no
- Transaction must be completed without leaving the site		
- Revenues from current product sales; revenue streams from advertising activities or similar activities not included		
2. Social	yes	no
- Consumer must be supported in problem-solving or solving social problems		
- Users should be capable of actively participating in social media – freedom of choice and role		
3. Result	yes	no
- Individualized products and buying experiences for retailer		
- Social utility for the customer		

Fig. 2.4 Checklist for social commerce (Source: Haarhaus 2013)

but not many companies have realized that genuine commerce must also be integrated in social media portals. In addition to an "in-stream transaction", relevant "social tools" should also be provided. Moreover, active customer participation and a high degree of personalization and customization are required. The requirements of social commerce are depicted in Fig. 2.4. It should be pointed out here that social commerce is not just a topic for the online world only, but also goes beyond that. Modern social commerce factors should also be considered in brick-and-mortar retailing, which has become possible through the mobile Internet (cf. Weave, p. 224). This issue is also addressed in more detail in the empirical section.

2.2.1.1 Relevance of Social Commerce

Social media have turned into an Internet tool that we can no longer imagine living without, and have a great impact on online buying decisions. They enable users to communicate easily with one another in all areas. Today's customers check out their retailers' social media presence, ratings and recommendations, and share information about specific products and retailers in their social network (cf. Weave 2012, p. 224). As a result of the increasing level of communication and increased sharing of data through social media, retailers have become more transparent. Potential customers are now able to check on retailers' activities, offers and service commitments (cf. Peters 2011, p. 113). Such developments result in a change in the customer journey, away from a linear sequence of phases and towards a circular decision-making process with a constant feedback loop to the social network (cf. Marsden 2012a). A new buying environment has emerged for retailing here. In particular, new attitudes towards social networks are drivers of social commerce. In a world of social media and permanent feedback on products and services, new success factors have arisen for retailers. Web 2.0 has become a key driver for the Internet and the majority of all buying decisions, and thereby for the latest generation of online commerce (cf. Heinemann and Schwarzl 2010, p. 1). A study conducted by SteelHouse confirms that 64 % of all buyers read product ratings and recommendations before making purchases (cf. Chaney 2012a). In another study, conducted by market research institute Ipsos and the Hotwire agency, 56 % of German Internet users confirm that they would rather buy a product that has positive comments from other users. In any case, 30 % point out that they would not carry out any transaction on the basis of negative ratings. This confirms how important comments, ratings and rankings have become for the buying process (cf. Mühlenbeck and Skibicki 2007; Haug 2013; Mindwyse 2011). The relevance of such UGC increases the more the persons involved know each other personally. Accordingly, 75 % of users who are mutual friends indicated that they prefer to draw inspiration from friends, family members or colleagues before making a purchase. Therefore, it is not surprising that 68 % of customers prefer to use this – close – group as a source of information prior to making a buying decision (cf. Intertone 2010). Facebook, Twitter and community blogs in particular have essentially brought about new forms of "peer-to-peer" communication and information in commerce. A study by marketing agency SteelHouse from 2012 substantiates the leading role of social media websites, especially Facebook. Roughly half the respondents said they had bought a product or service rated or recommended on social media sites (cf. Chaney 2012a). Consumers trust such sources of information considerably more than promotional campaigns by established retail companies. One major reason is the fact that such traditional forms of advertising are regarded as less credible (cf. Mühlenbeck and Skibicki 2007, pp. 76 et seq.). Figure 2.5 illustrates in detail the extent to which customers trust different forms of advertising.

The facts indicate that there are fewer and fewer opportunities to influence buyer behavior through traditional advertising. In terms of their marketing activities, retailers are therefore required to give consideration to the more dynamic buying behavior of modern customers, as described in the customer journey for example. This fact applies all the more to sales-based advertising contents and emphasizes

To what extend you trust the following forms of adverising?	
Globale average	Trusted completely/ somewhat
Recommendations from people I know	92%
Customer opinions posted online	70%
Editorial content such as newspaper articles	58%
Branded Websites	58%
Emails I signed up for	50%
Ads in magazines	47%
Brand sponsorships	47%
Ads on TV	47%
Ads in newspapers	46%

Fig. 2.5 Global trust in advertising (Source: Own illustration with data source from Nielsen Global Online Survey 2011)

the growing importance of social filters in the buying process. In addition, many companies have realized that an increasing amount of customer traffic is generated on social media platforms, especially Facebook, on the basis of recommendations from Facebook friends. Customers arriving at websites via social networks already make up 1.3 % of the total online traffic and result in 1.9 % of all online sales as at Q2 2012 (cf. IBM 2012). As a result of this trend, several retailers have begun to search for ways to accommodate the development towards interactive forms of shopping and thereby exploit the potential of social commerce. The idea is that sharing product information in social networks has really paved the way for offering such products directly in the social network, with an option to buy. But if members are willing to come out as fans and collect or share information relevant to the purchase, why not integrate a direct buying option for offers wherever potential users discuss the subject of brands or retailers? Ultimately, it is in the supplier's interest to make maximum use of the potential for word-of-mouth advertising and therefore directly integrate social media activities into the buying process. In this respect, the fusion of social media and e-commerce appears promising. Use of Web 2.0 elements is already set as standard in marketing, with online marketing as a sub-function (cf. Mühlenbeck and Skibicki 2007, p. 87). A similar development could also be expected for their usage in e-commerce. Social commerce constitutes a natural further development of Web 2.0 in this respect. Helping customers get connected wherever they shop or initiate their purchase represents an effective tool for keeping pace with disruptive change. Online retailers which have already done so are regarded as modern and contemporary, in comparison with those with an "inflexible website" that does not include Web 2.0 elements. Polarization of outdated online concepts and new, modern online shops can therefore be increasingly observed (cf. Heinemann 2013b). In conclusion, it can be stated that online commerce has reached a new stage of evolution through social media and customers' usage of such media during the buying process. The social web has turned into a new kind of arena for modern shopping advice. The extent to which this endures and holds further potential is clarified below.

2.2.1.2 Potential of Social Commerce

Experts assume enormous potential for social commerce, provided the extensive usage of Web 2 tools on e-commerce platforms constitutes a form of social commerce. This results in a direct recommendation, to be used by every e-commerce website. Sooner or later, e-commerce will enter a new stage of evolution and mutate into social commerce: *"E-commerce is over. Long live social commerce"* (Marsden 2011a). A study by Econsultancy proves that 90 % of purchases are subject, to a greater or lesser extent, to a social impact, whether through recommendations from friends or visual inspiration. And precisely this level of socially-influenced purchasing reflects the volume and potential of social commerce (cf. ibid.). Business consulting firm Booz & Company estimates the future global market volume for e-commerce in social networks at around 30 billion US dollars for 2015 (cf. Internetworld.de 2012). Figure 2.6 depicts the relevant trend in social commerce sales revenues from 2011 to 2015. In 2011, approx. five

2.2 Social Commerce as a New Form of Commerce

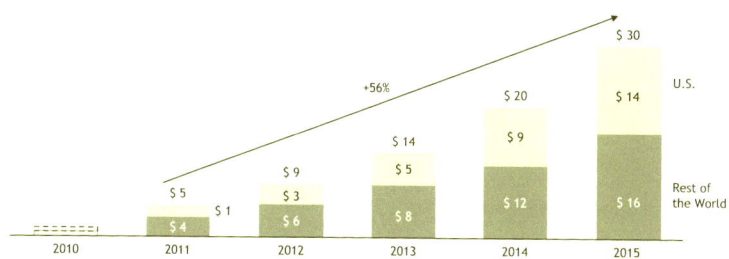

Fig. 2.6 Booz & Company estimated social commerce market size (Source: Grahampenrose 2011 based on Booz & Company)

billion US dollars was equivalent to roughly 0.8 % of worldwide e-commerce sales revenues, amounting to over 700 billion US dollars this year (cf. IMR 2011). By 2015, the share will increase to 2 % of the "e-commerce cake", with an estimated total of over 1,500 billion US dollars.

Facebook plays an important role in realizing the potential of social commerce, especially if the 1.15 billion users worldwide can be activated for this purpose, disregarding the fact that social commerce is also reflected in the retailer's P/L statement from a business management perspective (cf. Marsden 2012b). In view of the potential, the question should no longer be whether to start with social commerce, but rather when.

2.2.2 Stages of Development in Social Commerce

Social commerce has developed in several stages and has essentially been driven by technological progress and the resultant change in consumer behavior (cf. Haarhaus 2013). The first step has already been taken by introducing search functions and the opportunity to use price comparison sites (cf. Böge 2012; Haderlein 2012). Search engines make it easy for the customer to find products and information. However, strictly speaking, they do not network users, nor do price comparison sites. Neither of these tools fulfills the criteria for social commerce, but both have made significant contributions to its development, since they provide information to be shared by users on social networks. An isolated assessment should have changed, at least since the introduction of Google+.

According to expert opinion, social commerce, in its pure form, can be divided into three development phases (cf. Fig. 2.7):

- **First phase of social commerce – "pre-tool level".** The first phase of social commerce concerns the introduction of ratings and reviews. This phase – described as the "feature level" – involves customer reviews, expert opinions and sponsored reviews (cf. Lückemeier 2012). Customer reviews could now be one of the most important sources of information, especially as they are regarded as authentic and therefore most highly valued by users. Such reviews and

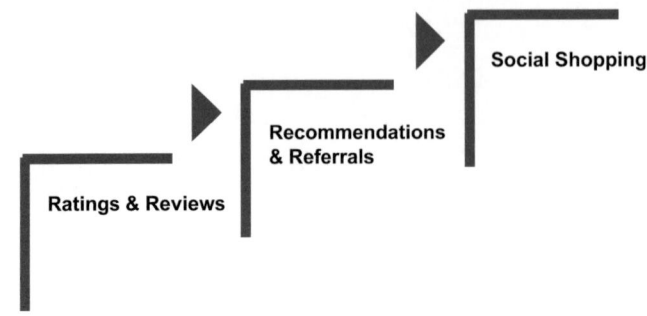

Fig. 2.7 Levels of social commerce (Source: Haarhaus 2013)

rankings can either be integrated on the website or found on special rating portals. The more ratings are listed in a shop, the better they match search engines and become a suitable SEO instrument for "search engine optimization" (cf. Mayer 2012). Reviews and ratings are not new. Major online players like Amazon and eBay have been offering these features for a long time. Such tools provide customers with decisive support in their buying process, especially as they provide reliable information and help to improve buying decisions. But they do not connect customers and completely ignore collaborative aspects. In this sense, they can only be regarded as the first phase or rather as an introduction into social commerce.

- **Second phase of social commerce – "tool level".** The second phase of social commerce is represented by advice and recommendations. This phase – described as the "tool level"– includes personal recommendations, advice programs (referrals) and social bookmarking (cf. Böge 2012). Personal recommendations are usually based on personal buying experiences or recommendations from friends. Customized offers make reference to personal preferences and make them all the more valuable. In particular, recommendations from friends have an enormous influence on contemporary buying decisions and add a considerably higher "degree of socialization". This second stage is primarily characterized by product-related information.
- **Third phase of social commerce – "conceptual level".** The third phase of social commerce constitutes the highest stage of evolution for social commerce and is also described as the "conceptual level". Whereas the first two stages were limited with regard to social interaction between customers and the mapping of offline buying decisions, the third stage also allows for these factors and involves "social shopping". This phrase is often used synonymously with the term "social commerce" in the literature. "Social shopping is a method of e-commerce where shoppers' friends become involved in the shopping experience. Social shopping attempts to use technology to mimic social interactions found in physical malls and stores" (Wikipedia 2012b). This definition reflects the synonymous use of social shopping and social commerce, and as a result is also viewed as the

highest evolution stage. Nevertheless, a distinction should be made between the two concepts. Social shopping represents more of a logical development.

Given that technological development is also progressing, it can be assumed that social commerce will continue to develop rapidly in the future and give rise to new tools. However, the situation will vary, depending on the prevailing form of social commerce.

2.2.3 Categorization of Social Commerce

The concept of social commerce offers numerous advantages to users and retailers. Social commerce enhances the online shopping experience. The offer of a social environment increases customer satisfaction, which in turn improves customer loyalty. At the same time the retailer offers genuine competitive advantages and added value, setting it apart from its competitors in a positive way. New sources of inspiration and personal recommendations increase the assumed benefit to the customer. In addition the customer is able to discover new and improved products, which would then find the right algorithm. In turn this has a positive impact on sales and turnover (cf. Chaney 2012c; Lückemeier 2012). Ratings, reviews and recommendations improve the relationship between customers and brands or retailers. Integrated information on "likes" from friends and purchases in an online shop also result in a greater probability of buying products. Furthermore, personalized and complementary recommendations contain high cross-selling potential. If retailers choose to sell on a social media platform, they have an additional sales channel, resulting in additional sales revenues. Impulse buys are primarily stimulated by the opportunity to shop in an environment in which potential customers already discuss relevant products and brands (cf. Steimel 2011). Social commerce is breaking down barriers between communication and commerce and facilitating immediate purchases, thereby increasing the number of impulse buys. Social media activities can also be measured by return-on-investment (ROI). Monitoring such activities objectively is also important in maintaining the right balance between income and expenditure (cf. Chaney 2012c). Another advantage of social commerce is achieved through an increased volume of customer data, based on personal interests and social interaction. Such data offer better insight into customers and create the opportunity for optimizing customer relationship management (CRM). In addition, information about customer preferences can be used to improve offers in the retailer's own online shop. This is relevant, for example, to product range or visual merchandising, which can be adjusted to preferences. Social commerce does not only serve to stimulate sales in this respect, but also helps retailers align sales strategies to their customers' needs. Users are highly integrated and thereby feel more than just part of a business and not just an external factor. Customers who have been persuaded tend to be willing to share their positive experiences, meaning that social commerce is also well-suited to viral marketing.

Fig. 2.8 Forms of social commerce (Source: Haarhaus 2013 based on Mücke, Sturm & Company)

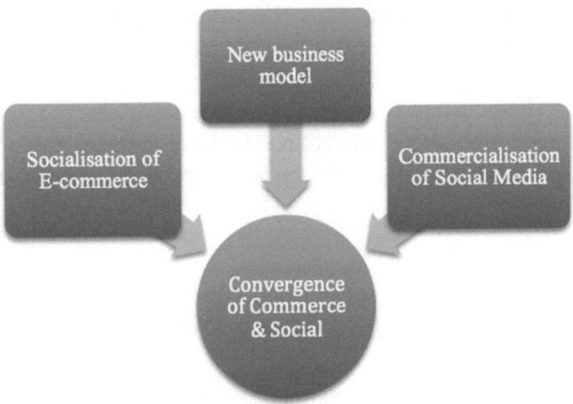

2.2.4 Future Prospects for Social Commerce

On the whole it is clear that social commerce has developed from the initial integration of social tools in existing online shops, through the further implementation of sales functions in social networks, and up to completely new business models. As a result of the development stages outlined above, three different forms of social commerce can be distinguished: socialization of e-commerce, commercialization of social media, and new social commerce business models (cf. Fig. 2.8).

- **Socialization of e-commerce** describes the transformation process from classic e-commerce into social commerce through the integration of social tools in existing online shops. Sharing ideas and opinions and acquiring recommendations improves the shopping experience from the customers' perspective. Customers are placed in a position to resolve problems better in a social environment, which includes the buying process. Such tools have been enhanced over the course of time. A mere presence in social networks, such as Facebook and Twitter, ultimately resulted in highly complex networking of the customer's "social graph" with his or her online shop. As a result of technological development, retailers were empowered to optimize personal offers, which then had a positive impact on target group marketing. Such personalization results in a genuine "added value" for customers and thereby a greater probability of buying (cf. Böge 2012). This could also be the reason why the majority of online retailers are usually linked to Facebook, Google+ and Pinterest (cf. Weave 2012, p. 224).
- **Commercialization of social media** refers to the opening of social media to e-commerce with a direct opportunity to sell products. Social media are turning into a new sales channel for retailers and no longer represent a mere communications platform (cf. Heinemann 2012b, p. 4), because when visiting the Internet, consumers spend most time on social media sites, where they are

connected with brands and retailers, and where an additional selling opportunity is directly offered. Facebook has turned into a mass phenomenon in recent years, which could offer enormous potential for e-commerce. The figures below, taken from the VendorShop report, illustrate the potential of Facebook as a sales channel (cf. Marsden 2011b): an average stay of 55 min on Facebook and 150 friends per Facebook user. At least 62 % of all users who "like" a shop would buy from there and 68 % of users who "like" a website receive promotions and discounts – these figures speak for themselves. The main focus of social media stores should be on Facebook in this respect. However, sales options on Twitter, YouTube and Pinterest should also be pursued. Since the enormous hype of social media has weakened slightly, social networks are being called upon to more strongly commercialize their business models (cf. BVDW 2011).

- **Social commerce business models:** As a supplement to the two forms of "e-commerce socialization" and "social media commercialization", some completely new business models have been established in the area of social media. They represent the highest evolution stage of social commerce and are mainly distinguished by an equal combination of e-commerce and social media.

2.3 Manifestations of Social Commerce

The forms of social commerce already categorized in the above chapter are described in greater detail below and corroborated with examples. Facebook commerce is addressed separately, given that it spans all forms of social commerce as a kind of "hybrid form".

2.3.1 Socialization of E-Commerce

With regard to the socialization of e-commerce, Facebook has certainly become a key factor. The following comments therefore primarily refer to Facebook, although Google+ and Pinterest also have great potential. By linking Facebook with conventional websites, the social user is transported to e-commerce, and users can shop with friends and receive personalized recommendations (cf. Marsden 2012c). The customer's individual social network may be used directly in the online shop, and vice versa.

Some products can be "liked" and shared in the social network, and customers can see which products have been liked and then recommend them to their friends in the network. However, Facebook tools extend far beyond this and along with the "like button" and "comment box", include "Facebook Connect" as well:

- **"Facebook Connect"** allows users to log onto an online shopping club or community via a Facebook account. If an online shop offers this opportunity, it is easier and quicker for customers to connect with Facebook. Instead of having to enter a large amount of personal data, users can employ the "single sign-on solution" to register on the website. With "Facebook Connect", retailers and shopping portal operators enjoy an advantage because conventional registration on a website is usually regarded as a major obstacle, but this is no longer the case (cf. Grabs and Bannour 2011, p. 234). "Facebook Connect" targets precisely the benefit offered by simplified registration. The incredible success of Facebook has certainly contributed to the high level of acceptance of social log-ins. Even if only 16 % of users currently use social log-ins, 49 % would consider doing so and would make use of the option of logging into a social network on an external website via an existing account (cf. Absatzwirtschaft 2012). Social log-ins normally increase session time and reduce the abandonment rate, thereby indirectly contributing to an increase in sales. In addition to the enhanced user experience, operators automatically receive profile information about users (cf. etailment.de 2012b). "Facebook Connect" also offers "Open Graph" and "Social Graph" on the retailer's website, which creates a diagram depicting connections between users, groups and organizations in the social network (cf. whatIs.com 2010). The opportunity to improve knowledge through and about customers also demonstrates the significant potential of Facebook with regard to social commerce. Facebook's "Open Graph" provides a large number of features, such as integration of the "like button" and "comment box".

- **"Like button" and "comment box"** are probably the most widely-known social plugins. Social plugins are tools which utilize other websites to support interested parties in respect of personalized and social aspects to shopping (cf. Facebook 2013). The "like box" is a small excerpt from the Facebook page, integrated onto the retailer's own website. The extent to which information from the Facebook page should be embedded can be selected. For example, a decision may be made to only mention the company name with regard to the like button or to integrate an additional "news feed" and/or photos of users who have liked the website on Facebook. The like button is independent of the retailer's existing Facebook page. If the user liked a product on the retailer's website, this fact is either shown in the retailer's online shop or in the user's individual profile. Customers can see whether a friend has already liked a supplier's product. While on Facebook, users are made aware of friends who have liked or even bought items. Using the "like box", retailers pick up Facebook functions on their website. If visitors like the page, they can receive additional information about the specific retailers in their individual "news feed" on Facebook (cf. Grabs and Bannour 2011, pp. 237 et seq.). Such use of Facebook enables retailers not only to obtain contact data, but also to receive a large quantity of additional information on specific interests, user habits or locations. This provides excellent insight into the wishes and attributes of their customers. The integration of social tools into existing e-commerce thereby produces a certain form of social commerce, relating to likes and comments, as well as other social media activities within the online shop. Support is provided here for referral marketing or "recommendation machines". The dissemination of generated information in social networks increases traffic on their own website, which in turn leads to increased sales.

2.3 Manifestations of Social Commerce

In this respect, social media activities can also become profitable and may be reflected in the return on investment (ROI).

The tools described above almost socialize e-commerce and help users to network more intensively, making it easier to share experiences and recommendations (cf. Grabs and Bannour 2011, pp. 332 et seqq.). To facilitate a clearer understanding of this subject area, selected examples of fashion providers are shown below, i.e. Levi's and Fab:

- **"Levi's Friend Store"**, which specifically features the individually aligned "digital storefront". Customers connected via Facebook see all "likes" first, but have the opportunity to switchto products preferred by their friends (cf. Grabs and Bannour 2011, pp. 334 et seq.). Levi's regards this form of buying as "like-minded shopping". On the "Friend Store" Levi's demonstrates impressively how "Facebook Connect" can be used to improve customers' shopping experience.
- **"Fab.com" online platform**, which is distinguished by inspiring shopping experiences for designer products, represents another example. Fab.com primarily focuses on heavy social media users, who network with one another, and on mobile commerce. Fab integrates a live feed, providing a real-time demonstration of what customers are buying and have added to their favorites (cf. Kolbrück 2012, p. 17). Moreover, users are able to view friends' recent likes and purchases. This allows for a collective shopping experience with friends if customers agree to having their favorite products published on the customer timeline, which can be done through "Facebook Connect". The new form of transparent commerce and the culture of sharing turn customers into ambassadors for Fab. Esty acts and thinks along similar lines (cf. etailment 2012c). The integration of social features has a direct impact on corporate success, since around 15 % of "live feed" visitors are converted into buyers (cf. etailment 2012d). Moreover, the lifetime value of customers who use social features while shopping on Fab is double that of other users. Recommendations from friends directly increase sales for Fab, which recognized the trend towards social commerce early on and implemented it as an essential differentiation factor (cf. Kolbrück 2012, p. 17).

In summary, socialization of online shops seems to be a relatively easy way to enter the world of social commerce. However, it is not advisable to merely provide "like buttons". Customers are becoming more demanding and all registers of social features should therefore be drawn on. The integration of a "Social Graph" for personalized recommendations and enhancement of the shopping experience should also be targeted. In addition, Facebook offers a relatively inexpensive opportunity to align the shop more socially, since no major investments are required. Social plugins may even result in sales increases of up to 10 % (cf. Weave 2012, p. 224). Retailers should therefore exercise such options even if they do not want to become a social commerce provider. In this respect, the socialization of e-commerce can be regarded as a must in modern e-commerce.

2.3.2 Commercialization of Social Media

From a social media perspective, the integration of sales activities shows great potential. On the one hand, established online retailers find it relatively easy to start selling in social networks, and, on the other hand, the social platforms themselves are in a position to launch their own e-commerce. Social media platforms receive a commission for each product sold or achieve higher margins through their own e-commerce. Depending on the social media platform however, the type and design of commercialization can vary greatly. In addition to Facebook commerce, there are other forms of social commerce which have emerged through the commercialization of social media, e.g. YouTube Commerce, Twitter Commerce and Pinterest Commerce.

- **Facebook commerce:** With reference to Facebook however, where a transaction takes place is also worth checking. If the Facebook transaction is carried out "off-site", it represents an e-commerce transaction supported by Facebook. In contrast, genuine Facebook commerce (F-Commerce) represents an "onsite" sale on Facebook. The differentiation is shown in detail in Fig. 2.9. Off-site sales, i.e. use of the Facebook network as a sales channel by online retailers, is the most common of the two forms of F-commerce. Recently however, Facebook launched its own e-commerce activities under the term Facebook Gifts, although the gift shop is presently only accessible on the US market (cf. Chaney 2012c). Until recently, Facebook only notified its members of birthdays, but now they are able to buy a gift directly on Facebook. Members are given recommendations based on their friend's profile. Notification of the gift may be accompanied by a message on the friend's pinboard. The recipient can decide whether to open the message or wait until the gift arrives. Facebook receives a commission for each gift sold (cf. Internetworld.de 2012). This concept has great potential for Facebook, since it connects members with a large number of friends and individual product recommendations are made directly.
- **Twitter commerce**: Although Twitter commerce is not very widespread, some brands and retailers still use Twitter to sell their own products. PC manufacturer Dell, for example, has created its own Twitter account as a "Dell Outlet", in order to promote its own products (cf. Twitter 2013). This account allows Twitter to implement Dell promotions (cf. CatalystMarketers.com 2010). Dell has so far made sales of 6.5 million US dollars through its presence on Twitter (cf. Grabs and Bannour 2011, p. 200). Twitter makes a social media platform available, which Dell uses as a "Dell Outlet" to sell its own products. However, genuine onsite transactions are not conducted on Twitter, instead, users are redirected to the partner company's external online shop. Although it has a

2.3 Manifestations of Social Commerce

Fig. 2.9 Direct versus indirect social-commerce (Source: Own illustration based on Thollot 2014)

positive impact on the partner's sales, this does not represent genuine social commerce as defined by the criteria. One major reason is certainly the fact that Twitter does not yet offer its own onsite fulfillment solution. This may also have something to do with the fact that the marketing potential for onsite sales on Twitter is seen as relatively low, since sharing of communications between Twitter members is considerably lower than on Facebook, and messages are still limited to 140 characters. Nevertheless, Twitter could be well suited to the sale of special offers or unproblematic basic goods.

- **YouTube Commerce:** Sales on **YouTube** can be regarded as another form of the commercialization of social media. YouTube is the second most frequently visited website around the world (cf. Marsden 2012d). YouTube shows great sales potential in this respect. In October 2011, for example, fashion retailer French Connection opened a "Youtique" (cf. French Connection 2013). Youtique is a combination of YouTube and Boutique. French Connection used YouTube exclusively to promote and sell its products for a short period of time. Fashion products were featured in videos, via which users received offers and product demonstrations. At the end of each video, users had the opportunity to order the displayed product via an integrated purchase button. Users were then redirected to the online shop (cf. Grabs and Bannour 2011, pp. 343 et seq.). However, this case also represented an "off-site sale", meaning that YouTube commerce does not represent social commerce in the stricter sense of the phrase. Moreover, social components have so far been rather limited on YouTube, since

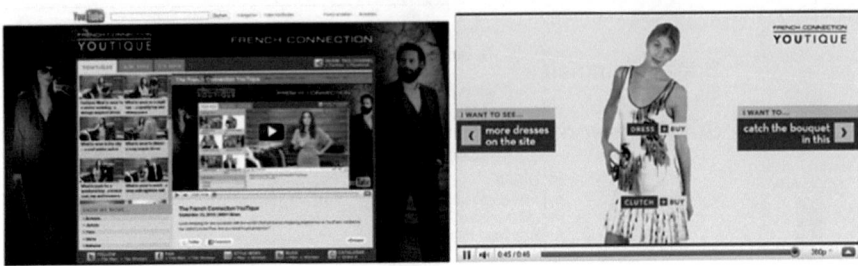

Fig. 2.10 Youtique – cooperation between YouTube & French Connection (Source: YouTube 2013 with permission from Google 2014)

neither social interaction with users nor participation is possible. Nevertheless, the nature of the visual presentation has a positive impact on the shopping experience. YouTube certainly represents more than just a marketing instrument in this respect. Through the integration of a purchase button, there is at least one bridge to e-commerce, which could certainly be upgraded towards "genuine social commerce" in future (Fig. 2.10).

- **Pinterest commerce:** Media platform Pinterest could boast enormous growth, especially in 2012. After ComScore, Pinterest is clearly the fastest-growing platform in the history of social media, with 11 million unique users as of January 2012 (cf. Werner 2012). Pinterest represents a visual platform, on which users are invited to create different pinboards. Users can pin images which they find on the web, and upload them accordingly onto their boards or even re-pin images already uploaded by other members. The concept can be described as a mixture of a catalog and lifestyle magazine. Although Pinterest is one of the youngest platforms, it has already become established and is now a dominant source of visual inspiration in social media (cf. Silver et al. 2012). Kurt Heinemann, Marketing Director of Monetate, a provider of cloud-based online technologies, points out that Pinterest is a platform which is ideally suited to creating awareness. It produces an enormous number of interactions and generates twice as much traffic as Facebook, in proportion to the number of users (cf. Werner 2012; Duryee 2012). Pinterest therefore represents a significant traffic generator for websites and has great potential for e-commerce activities. Online retailers are able to link individual product images on Pinterest to their shop. As a result, products can be presented in a new and extremely dynamic way. Moreover, they can easily be updated into different, inspiring images, and are particularly recommended for design, interior design, travel, and of course fashion. Pinterest is an expressive advertising medium in this respect (ibid.), which is well suited to promotions and product visualizations, as are required for fashion products in particular. "Style and fashion" is number three on the list of most favorite product groups, at 11.7 % (cf. etailment.de 2012e). Pinterest already largely embodies the future of social commerce. According to one study by Monetate, Pinterest is well on the way to becoming one of the most important drivers for social traffic on websites by the end of the year (cf. Duryee

2012). Nevertheless, a distinction should be made between Pinterest as a traffic driver and its suitability as a distribution channel. In any case, Pinterest is set to grow in importance for social commerce in the future, in view of the socialization of e-commerce (cf. Stambor 2012). Accounts have already been rolled out, which were specially designed for marketing specialists and feature a "verification badge" (ibid.). However, there is still some doubt as to whether Pinterest will be commercialized in terms of real shop solutions. But a large number of fashion retailers are already including Pinterest in their marketing strategy. Zalando is viewed as the leading German "Pinterest" company, as far as the number of pins is concerned (cf. Hengl 2012). The platform can also easily be combined with "gamification" approaches. The Guess "Color Me Inspired" campaign on Pinterest is deemed a good example. In order to win a pair of jeans, users are called upon to select one of the pinned trend colors and create a board with at least five "inspiration images" for one topic, e.g. spring. This campaign also lets Guess obtain information on its customers' preferences with regard to colors and inspiration sets. Both can be used as an ideal input for new collections and thereby for market research purposes (cf. Thaeler 2012). A similar approach to the one adopted at Guess can also be witnessed at Lands' End, which carried out the "Lands' End Pin it to Win it" campaign. Users were able to assemble the best boards from the Lands' End range, and were rewarded by winning assembled products. The primary focus here was on enhancing knowledge about the customers' mindset (cf. etailment.de 2012e).

Overall, it can be established that social commerce is still in its infancy. It is quite conceivable that users of social media might not want to shop in social networks, since they primarily like to use them as a communication and information platform, and have a negative view of their commercialization (cf. Wilhelm 2012, p. 50). In this respect, some experts do not regard Twitter and Facebook as suitable distribution platforms. This could be one reason for rather cautious investments in this area (cf. Steimel et al. 2012). Most retailers therefore tend to focus their social media activities on marketing rather than sales. Otto also sees social media as a major issue with respect to making purchase decisions and regards buying behavior as being greatly affected by social media, but does not currently see any potential for direct sales activities there (cf. Wilhelm 2012, p. 50).

2.3.3 Facebook Commerce as a Hybrid Form of Social Commerce

As previously mentioned, Facebook dominates the social commerce discussion. Nevertheless, most F-commerce is still conducted with external brands and retailers, which use Facebook as a marketing channel. There are three different options here, of which only the "onsite sales" variant represents genuine social commerce:

- **"Pure marketing"**, **as the first type of F-commerce,** merely features the integration of static shop elements for an online retailer, which are then linked to Facebook. Such links have essentially become an indispensable standard in e-commerce. Every online retailer should have a Facebook presence and set up a direct cross-link to its own shop. However, this relates purely to marketing activity, but not to e-commerce.
- **"Off-site sales", the second type of F-commerce**, which is rapidly growing in importance, involves setting up a sales function on an online retailer's Facebook page. The entire product range or only a selection may be provided. However, such a sales function is very rarely set up on Facebook. The user is generally redirected to the retailer's online shop when clicking on a product on the Facebook page (cf. Grabs and Bannour 2011, pp. 337 et seqq.). However, if a real transaction is not conducted on the Facebook page, it does not constitute social commerce.
- **"Onsite sales" as a third type of F-commerce** represents a self-contained shop solution, which allows for an onsite transaction, including the full buying process (cf. Weave 2012, p. 225). Purchase, payment and shipment are assured by the self-contained Facebook store itself. Special software is required to create this type of "real Facebook store". Companies providing the necessary shop software include Amazon, Ondango and Sellaround (cf. Internetworld.de 2012; Haarhaus 2013). German fashion retailer Lodenfrey has set up such a store on Facebook. This is a case of genuine social commerce.

Nevertheless, the situation seems rather promising, since little has been done in this area so far. Facebook stores have rarely focused on real e-commerce so far. Without real added value for customers however, e-commerce cannot work on social media. Sellaround and its CEO Adrian Thoma also point out that just offering products on Facebook and waiting for sales is not sufficient (cf. Internetworld.de 2012). The key question is how added value can be created in a social context. Facebook stores have to offer a new concept with a specific unique selling proposition (USP), which is differentiated from existing online shops, and have to give the customer a reason to buy directly on Facebook, instead of switching to a well-known online shop. The challenge for F-commerce will be to convert fans into buying customers. One definite option for successful social commerce could be the exclusive sale of products, i.e. special offers, to which fans and followers have exclusive access, or at least can access before anyone else. Pizza Hut, for example, offers this type of limited sale. Another example is Heinz Ketchup, which also installed a social media pop-up store to sell personalized soups (cf. Marsden 2012c; Chaney 2012d). Such concepts from the food sector could certainly be adapted to the fashion industry, especially since fashion products allow for greater exclusivity and epitomize greater involvement.

2.3.3.1 The Sellaround Widget for Selling a Product
The selling widget is offered as an app in order to sell individual products on the net. Customers can transact purchases without having to leave the site if the widget

is embedded on it as an advertising banner and shop (cf. von Kuhnhardt 2013). Social shop, promotion widget or social actions app are conceivable variants:

The social shop enables the sale of several products. The relevant app is suitable for e-commerce starters. But this function can also be used as a separate campaign shop, which is then embedded in the Facebook page. The social shop can be used as a stand-alone link or integrated in an existing website (cf. ibid.).

The promotion widget resembles the selling widget app, but does not contain any sales functions. The user is rerouted to an external product link, such as a web shop for the respective provider, via a click. It may be used to advertise specific products on Facebook, through embedding on the Facebook timeline. Analog integration of a YouTube video is also possible (cf. ibid.).

The social actions app represents a new form of onsite advertising. Based on the Facebook "like" button, Sellaround users can use appropriate buttons for the product, whether this is "I want", "I have", "I love", "I own", "I wish", or "I bought". If a user clicks on one of these buttons, a promotion widget appears in his or her Facebook timeline with images, texts and information from the target page. Similar to the "like button", buttons are made available as a code component, which users can include in their own websites.

This Sellaround idea is suitable for deal campaigns, in which a product is offered for a limited time or in a limited edition, and represents a kind of advertising banner and mini-shop in one. When the widget is opened, up to four images of the offer may appear, one of which is displayed in full size in each case. A description of the offer, a title, the vendor's name, price and a large "shopping cart" button can be displayed here. By clicking on "shopping cart", the widget is rotated and the user moves to the next stage of the purchase transaction, in which the shipping country and typical options can then be selected. Clicking on "checkout" activates the payment process, which takes place via PayPal. After checkout, the customer returns to where he or she first found the widget. The point of sale comes directly to the user here, in order to avoid media disruption.

2.3.4 Business Models for Social Commerce

As a supplement to the phenomena described above, completely new business models have become established in the area of social media. They represent the highest evolution stage of social commerce and are primarily characterized by an equal combination of e-commerce and social media. Examples of such business models are highlighted below, which certainly differ greatly in their specific unique selling proposition (USP) and form three categories: "Advice & Recommendation" or even "Advice & Referral", "Enabling & Infrastructure" and "Experience, Fun & Exclusivity" (cf. Haderlein 2012). In accordance with this categorization, the different social commerce business models are depicted in Fig. 2.11.

Advice & Recommendation	Enabling & Infrastructure	Experience, Fun & Live Shopping
Referral platform - Polyvore - Edeligt	Microeconomics: - Etsy - DaWanda	Club shops: - Vente Privee - Brands4Friends
Affiliate platform: - Smatch	Mass customization: - NikeiD - Threadless	Daily deals: - Groupon - LivingSocial
Curated shopping - Kaufmann Mercantile - Fab.com - Lyst and Blissany	Selling community: - Pippa & Jean - Stella & Dot	Live shopping: - Guut.de - zackzack

Fig. 2.11 Social commerce business models (Source: Haarhaus 2013)

- **"Advice and referral"**, the first category, is represented by recommendation platforms Edelight, Smatch and Polyvore. Of these three examples, Polyvore is the best-known and most important platform, as far as fashion is concerned at least. Polyvore can be regarded as the "mother of all social commerce platforms" (cf. Haderlein 2012). Tools are made available to users, enabling them to choose their own sets from a specified range of retailers and brands. Individual products are cross-linked to corresponding retailers. Polyvore represents a source of inspiration, which generates a large volume of traffic. Although Polyvore receives a commission for sold products, no "in-stream transaction" is conducted. Essentially, the basic requirements for social commerce are not fulfilled. Nevertheless, the platform is largely credited with giving recommendations and advice on a high level of social commerce, and is extremely well-suited to generating traffic as a marketing tool and acquiring new customers, particularly because it allows for visual recommendations, which are especially important for online fashion. It is not uncommon for other platforms and retailers to copy the mood board concept – a strategy employed in particular by Asos and Stylelight (ibid.). Curated shopping represents another trend which is very widespread in fashion e-commerce, and is frequently combined with "subscription commerce". Prominent examples here are Shoedazzle and BeachMint as well as Glossy-Box. Products are recommended to customers in their own showroom.
- **"Enabling and infrastructure"**, the second category, can be subdivided into mass customization, microeconomics and social selling communities. This trend is not necessarily new and innovative, but illustrates a reasonable degree of genuine social commerce for which it also has a certain level of significance.

Mass customization relates to product customization, which has only become economically viable through the use of Internet technology (cf. Haderlein 2012). Mass customization represents a concept that already existed before the age of social commerce. Nevertheless, it is an excellent example of customer participation and fulfills the social commerce criteria. In particular, the large sports equipment suppliers, such as Adidas and Nike, employ mass customization (cf. Faz.net 2012). Microeconomics stands for the generation of Web 2.0 portals that are primarily focused on communities. Etsy, for example, is a platform which enables customers to sell genuine handicraft products from the Third World to other members of the community. The platform tends to focus more on people than products (cf. Heinemann and Schwarzl 2010, p. 193). Social selling communities constitute a relatively new concept. Pippa & Jean or Stella & Dot can be cited as examples, which both operate based on the same principle. Customers are given the opportunity to set up their own business on the platform, therefore creating flexible business opportunities for users. In contrast to Etsy, users do not sell their own manufactured products here, but are based on users' individual preferences. The shopping platform Lyst makes the following comment: "(w)e didn't believe that one style could be distilled into an algorithm, rather we thought social curation was a far more effective way to personalize an experience to you" (cf. Stock 2012).

- "**Experience, fun and exclusivity**", the third category, is made up of club shops and daily deal platforms and currently has great potential, since customers are demanding more and more features (cf. Haderlein 2012). However, this involves a limited number of different concepts, which simply cannot exist in the current retail environment. Club shops are increasingly becoming obsolete. Elements should therefore be implemented to incentivize and revitalize concepts, based on limited access to exclusive offers. Daily deal sites, such as Groupon, are also representatives of this category and embody "social bonding" aspects.

2.4 Changes in the Buying Process Due to Internet and Social Media

2.4.1 The New Buying Process

Customers are not only increasingly using the Internet within their buying process, but also social networks (cf. Enderle and Voll 2011). They conduct research on the net in order to prepare for their purchases in brick-and-mortar stores. This includes both searches for product information and price comparisons. Prices are no longer compared sequentially, with the customer executing several brick-and-mortar store transactions one after the other. A parallel price comparison is now made through the Internet and price search engines, which reveal the products and prices of all retailers with one click. When customers are subsequently in the brick-and-mortar store, they compare the indicated retail price with the competition's online offer on their smartphone, and where appropriate order the best-value offer on the web

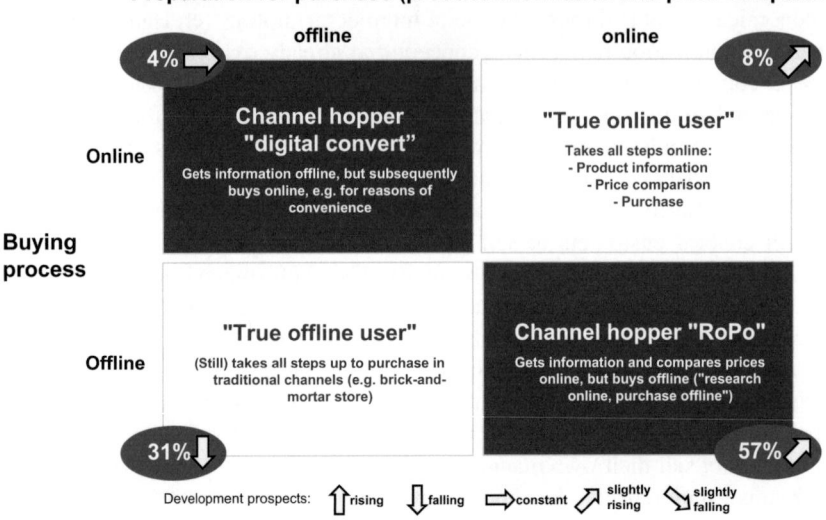

Fig. 2.12 Types of customers in online commerce (Source: Enderle and Voll 2011)

directly on site via the mobile Internet. Technological progress and changed buyer behavior result in unprecedented transparency in commerce, which increases price pressure for conventional business forms. At the same time, an increasing number of consumers buy their products and services from e-commerce companies or online retailers, which thereby register large gains in their market shares. Yet the number of "pure online buyers", who carry out all steps in their buying process online, still remains within limits (cf. Fig. 2.12). They make up 8 % of all customers. Another 4 % shop exclusively online, but search another store before buying. At 57 %, the most widespread group is constituted by channel hoppers, who prepare for shopping in a brick-and-mortar store on the Internet and follow the ROPO model. In any case, 31 % of customers are true offline users, who do not shop or conduct research on the Internet. Most of them could also be Internet-illiterate.

It is in each customer's interest to find a product during the buying process, in order to optimally satisfy his or her needs (cf. Boersma 2010, pp. 44 et seqq.). The behavioral principles of social commerce primarily relate to use of the Internet and mobile commerce, the rapid penetration of which certainly has a significant impact on consumer buying behavior. In order to understand this impact, the conventional buying process should first be depicted without Internet usage. This serves as a fundamental basis to present the new buying process, including Internet usage, and the "customer journey" before the buying process, which increasingly relies on social media tools.

2.4.1.1 Change to the Buying Process Due to Internet Usage

The central interest of each customer is to find a product during the buying process, which optimally satisfies his or her needs (cf. Boersma 2010, pp. 44 et seqq.). If a traditional retailer helps the customer to do so and offers an acceptable price, such a retailer then usually has high relevance for the customer. This was the original primary role of commerce for consumers. In the best-case scenario, retailers managed to optimize the benefit to their customers, having implemented the entire added value of the buying decision process. Procurement, pre-selection and consulting, etc. were remunerated accordingly. Retailers did not have to share the proceeds with anyone (cf. ibid.). The conventional buying process in brick-and-mortar retailing usually stipulates that the customer should start by selecting a supplier, and then choose the product which meets his or her needs at the point of sale. This requires the customer to get an overview of the products in the retailer's range, compare products based on product information, and ultimately make a product selection, followed by a subsequent purchase. The customer first selected one or more suppliers and then committed to a product on site. Conformity of the "point of decision" and "point of sale" was characteristic of the conventional buying process, as depicted in Fig. 2.13 (cf. ibid.).

The previous system for the buying decision process has been changed substantially by the Internet. In addition, competitive conditions have been redefined. In part, the Internet lets customers procure almost any product available around the world relatively quickly and easily. Customers can also find comprehensive information on the "World Wide Web" to support their search for the right product. The decision-making process is supported to a much greater extent by more detailed product information, additional test reports, and product ratings from other customers than is the case when receiving traditional advice from a retailer (cf. ibid.).

Customers can easily find their way around the Internet, not only in terms of rational buying, but also with regard to emotional motives for buying. Within a peer group in a social network, information can always be found about the acceptance and popularity of products. This provides security in the buying decision. Moreover, by purchasing a product, the customer can signal affiliation to a group and utilise social media tools to reach decisions. The buying decision process is therefore disengaged through the Internet, which is accompanied by the decoupling of value chains in retailing. Revenues are distributed to individual value-added stages and no longer fully collected by the retailer. The fact that the Internet shifts individual phases in the buying decision process and thereby separates the point of decision from the point of sale is emerging as a threat to commerce (cf. ibid.). The new (online) buying process is expressed by the customer first choosing a product on the Internet, which meets his or her needs. Customers get an overview of interesting products with the aid of price search engines, online marketplaces, social shopping services or communities. They then compare products based on product information, e.g. using manufacturer websites, test reports, opinion portals or social networks, before making a product selection. Only at the end of the process does the customer select what he or she views as the optimal supplier, and complete the purchase. Customers usually decide based on price, and relatively detached from online or offline channels. The importance of the individual retailer to customers is therefore greatly reduced. They are only perceived as a "point of

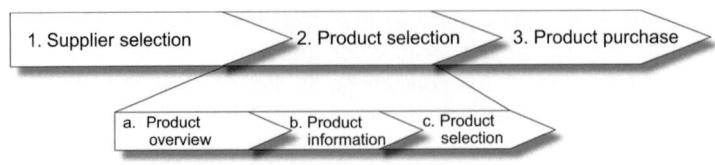

Fig. 2.13 Classic buying process (Source: Boersma 2010)

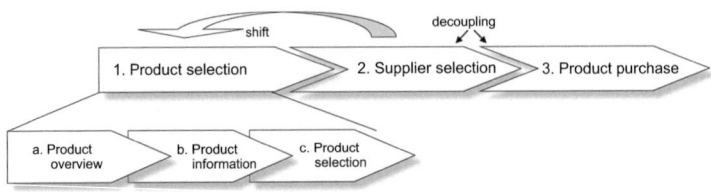

Fig. 2.14 New buying process (Source: Boersma 2010)

sale" in extreme cases, because there is a much greater volume of the information needed for a product selection available on the Internet. The "point of decision" is therefore gaining importance. Finding the right information provides the greatest benefit to customers and is thus becoming the most valuable part of the value chain (cf. ibid.; Stracke 2005, pp. 24 et seqq.). This new buying process is depicted in Fig. 2.14.

Even if the product is not purchased in an online shop, the Internet is the most credible medium for most users in connection with buying decisions. Studies show that 97 % of all German households with Internet access conduct research on the web before making a purchase decision (cf. Schneller 2009, p. 28). More than half of Internet users carry out price comparisons, acquire information on manufacturer's sites, read test reports on the Internet or give consideration to comments and contributions to discussions by other users (cf. Schneller 2008, p. 28). With the increasing transfer of communication onto the net, the relevance of individual sources of information is also shifting as far as Internet users are concerned: ratings by other users are now among the most trusted sources. Such ratings play a major role, in particular when preparing to make purchases. Focusing on the customer's last action before entering the buying process – usually Googling – cannot mask the "customer journey" (cf. Internet World Business 2011c, p. 16; Heinemann 2012a).

2.4.1.2 Customer Journey in the Buying Process

The "customer journey" in the buying process describes a series of stages between the idea of purchase and clicking. It is not uncommon for advertising banners or email newsletters to trigger the impulse to buy. The process leading to the final purchase can last several weeks, and includes searches, discussions in review platforms, sharing experiences or research on price comparison portals (cf. ibid.). Usage of social media tools plays a major role here. The customer journey approach

2.4 Changes in the Buying Process Due to Internet and Social Media

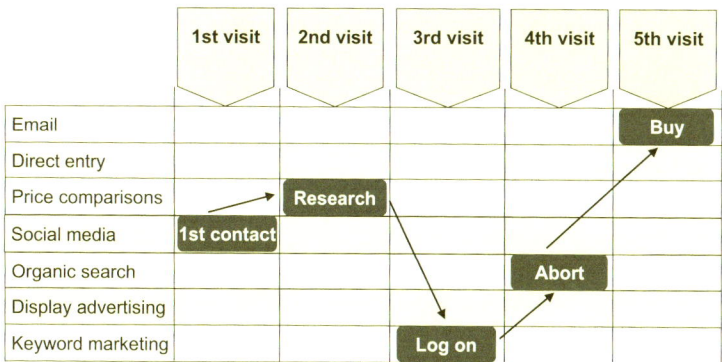

Fig. 2.15 Typical customer journey (Source: Own illustration based on Internet World Business 2011c, d, No. 10/11, p. 16)

also considers long-term effects and includes two dimensions. The first dimension represents buying impulses. The second dimension gives a weighting to the contribution of certain touchpoints during the customer journey to conversion ("conversion attribution").

It is difficult to show dependencies between different advertising media contacts because not everything on the customer journey to the buying decision can be measured. The effect of social networks on the customer journey cannot be underestimated, particularly at the start of the conversion chain. In this regard, Facebook represents a specific challenge, since Facebook campaigns cannot be tracked as easily as banner or adwords campaigns, for example. The same applies to advertising media contacts from the offline area, such as TV advertising, newspaper ads, or poster advertising (cf. Internet World Business 2011c, p. 16; Heinemann 2012a). The customer journey approach should always bring the online and offline world together here, which requires qualified data collection. A typical customer journey is shown in Fig. 2.15. In many cases, this provides for the usage of social media tools.

2.4.2 Customer Involvement in the Buying Process

Customer participation is practiced by best-in-class companies in various sectors. In addition to conventional customer product reviews, many online shops integrate user-generated product images and videos supplied by customers. Another example is the subject of "fitting": due to the lack of opportunity to try on or test something in advance, this has long been a problem for customers in distance selling.

In order to avoid a high rate of product returns, it is helpful to compile as much information as possible on fitting and size advice. If a large volume of such data is collected and made available to other customers, the conversion rate (share of customers completing purchase) may be increased and the rate of returns substantially reduced (cf. Haug and Küper 2010, pp. 119 et seqq.). Customers are often

Application areas for UGC	Best-in-class examples
Product rating	amazon.com, americanapparel.com
Product display	zazzle.co.uk, spreadshirt.net, expotv.com
Fitting	revolveclothing.com, shoes.com
Marketing	
Advertising	ikea.com, burgerking.com
Referral/Recommendation	polyvore.com, mydeco.com
Distribution	
Widgets	lemonade.com, cartfly.com
e-shops	zlio.de, amazonstore.com
Communication/branding	nikeplus.com
Product range	myfab.com, factory.lego.com
Customization	mymuesli.de, tastebook.com, cafepress.com, chocri.de

Fig. 2.16 Areas of application for user-generated content in mobile commerce (Source: Haug and Küpers 2010, p. 119)

integrated into advertising and marketing campaigns. Burger King's customers for example were called upon to delete friends on Facebook in a large viral campaign ("Whopper Sacrifice") and were rewarded with a burger. In addition, companies make entire shops or widgets available to their customers, meaning customers act as marketing staff for the company and offer products to their friends and acquaintances. Different examples of customer integration are shown in Fig. 2.16. However, before potential customer potential can be assessed and "societing" effectively commenced, online market segmentation is required in order to secure transparency about online target groups.

2.4.2.1 Consumer-Generated Advertising

The term "digital native" describes a generation of Internet users, who act with new technologies in a natural way that even many qualified "media designers" are unable to achieve. Such "nets" and others with an affinity for technology are increasingly evolving from consumers into "prosumers", i.e. customers involved in the creative processes. Through Internet shopping and in particular product configuration, consumers voluntary reveal information about their preferences, which form the basis for creating the product. The boundary between consumer and producer is becoming blurred. Through Internet shopping and in particular product configuration, consumers voluntary reveal information about their preferences, which form the basis for creating the product. The boundary between consumer and producer is becoming blurred. Accordingly, user-generated content is handled as an elementary good on the web, as demonstrated impressively by YouTube, Flickr, and Facebook. Most of the more than seven billion online videos viewed each month include public user-generated content (cf. Unterberg 2008, p. 205). Online retailers can no longer avoid interactive discussions on consumer experiences. Consumers have been emancipated through the Internet and are increasingly making decisions on when, where and how media are used and advertising thus "consumed".

The passive recipient consumer is increasingly becoming a thing of the past. It is becoming more and more important for advertisers to participate in consumer discussions or organize such discussions. The associated activation of customers forms part of consumer-generated advertising (CGA). This term describes all contents generated by the consumer that are promotional in character. If a company initiates the generation of advertising content for consumers, this represents a consumer-generated advertising campaign, which, as experience shows, is perceived by other consumers as more honest and credible. For example, participants in CGA campaigns are frequently also opinion leaders in their consumer worlds, or even the first users of the advertised product (cf. Unterberg 2008, pp. 208 et seqq.).

As the first step in a CGA campaign, consumers are invited – in a briefing – to submit their ideas in the form of photo or video material. As many consumers as possible should be motivated to participate through a competition of ideas, with prizes offered as an incentive. Briefings are key to success here, but often underestimated by companies, since they trust too much in the "power" of their own brands and products. The submitted ideas are also evaluated, coordinated and commented on by participants. This ensures that the best ideas do not disappear and that additional attention and community are generated. CGA campaigns can also be supported by other community-building measures. If a platform is made available to the campaign, for example, it is easier to track discussions between participating community members and use them for market research purposes (cf. Unterberg 2008, p. 210).

There have been several examples of successful CGA campaigns. Mozilla, provider of the Firefox browser, first practiced this new form of interactive advertising design. But BMW is also increasingly using CGA campaigns for its Mini lifestyle brand. Zappos can be cited as an example of CGA in online commerce, since users can directly access YouTube videos from customers, which reflect their shopping experiences on the website.

2.4.3 "Always-on" in Omni-Channel Use

Customers "channel hop" in the majority of cases, both in the new buying process and in the customer journey to the buying process, during the course of which they jump between buying and communications channels, either sequentially or in parallel. Within the scope of channel hopping, for example, consumers may notice a product in a printed catalog and subsequently obtain further information via the Internet. It is conceivable that the consumer may subsequently seek out the retailer's shop, in order to place an order for the desired product. Similarly, it is possible for the customer to order the product on the Internet and have it delivered to his or her home by parcel post. If customers are given the option to "channel hop", experience shows that it has a positive impact on the core business (cf. Heinemann 2011a, pp. 14 et seqq.). However, in the case of non-integrated channels, if a customer visits a store after an online purchase to complain about or exchange his or her product, it might well not be possible to replace a product ordered online in the store. Lack of customer information and inadequate integration of ERP systems within different marketing channels make such a scenario appear unlikely. In such cases, it is not possible to cater to the customer as a channel hopper. Additional problems are inevitable here, e.g. if customers in the retailer's various channels encounter ranges of products which are uncoordinated or not identified as channel-specific. If a multi-channel strategy is used, there is a great risk of customers transferring their negative experiences to other marketing channels. In order to share in the potential offered by increasing channel hopping, in particular for brick-and-mortar retailers, there is no longer any way to bypass an integrated multi-channel system. The integration of channels then requires professional cross-channel management, which holds a key position in the performance-based focus of multi-channel systems.

The reasons for channel hopping are depicted in Fig. 2.17. Instead of jumping backwards and forwards "sequentially" between channels – which is a feature of channel hopping – an increasing number of customers use different channels in parallel (cf. ohne tüte 2012, p. 1). If the retailer's objective is to establish separate, unconnected marketing channels, and thereby provide a channel-specific range of products, the range of products should not then be presented to the customer under uniform branding (cf. Ahlert et al. 2003, pp. 11 et seqq.). The opportunity for online retailers to benefit from customers' channel hopping through supplementary or support channels then becomes irrelevant. On the other hand, there are various options for a multi-channel strategy. An integrated multi-channel system in which different channels are equally important does not necessarily have to be established. It is also conceivable that additional channels could play different roles. As far as pure online retailers are concerned, it is quite reasonable for the Internet channel (initially) to become the "lead channel" and have brand supremacy over all channels, which are then subordinate to and realign the online channel. The Internet channel is then able to dominate as lead channel and assign more of a support role for online business to the brick-and-mortar retailing channel. However, in order to share in the potential offered by increasing channel hopping, in particular for brick-and-mortar retailers, an integrated multi-channel system is essential. But the integration of channels requires professional cross-channel management, which thereby has a key position for the performance-based focus of multi-channel systems. This applies primarily to omni-channel usage as an emerging new trend in consumer behavior, with the simultaneous use of media and distribution channels.

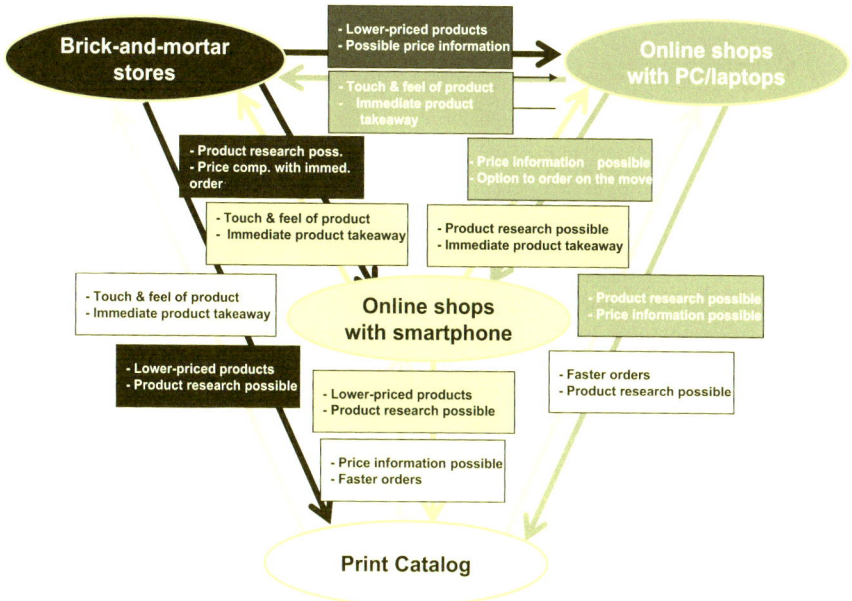

Fig. 2.17 Reasons for channel hopping (Source: Eckstein 2013)

2.4.3.1 Omni-Channel Use

Parallel usage of channels, termed "omni-channel use", is on the increase and fueled by smartphone usage during the buying process. Within the scope of omni-channel use, an increasing number of consumers no longer buy online or offline only, but effectively in both channels at the same time, as enabled by new smartphone technology and the mobile Internet. Buyers are increasingly obtaining information before buying a product, not only in stationary form on the Internet, but also directly at the POS via mobile devices. It is not without reason that the Harvard Business Review also devoted an article to this subject in the March 2012 edition (cf. ohne tüte 2012). Under the title "Selling the new form of art", the trend towards omni-channeling is primarily explained from a business perspective, but also provides important information on changes in consumer behavior. Experts make the assumption that many customers are already omni-channel users today, i.e. they utilize several channels at the same time when shopping. Whether they do it consciously or subconsciously, it is still considered omni-channel use (cf. ohne tüte 2012). However, it also underscores the need for multi-channel retailers not only to (re-)launch their online shop for the purpose of optimization, but also to link this more closely to their brick-and-mortar store. The following advantages are produced for consumers, which should also be paid for (cf. ibid.):

- **Flexibility:** A customer buys online and tries items on at home. Customers preferring a dress in a different color or size search for the nearest store on the

way to work and exchange the article there. They thus make use of the gradual amalgamation of different marketing channels.
- **Experience:** Customers can have their photographs taken by an interactive mirror, as in the adidas neo-store in Hamburg, and involve their friends in the buying decision on Facebook.
- **Simplicity:** Visitors to the store no longer find only limited product information on price tags or labels, but can request all necessary information either directly with the potential product or online with a smartphone.

These examples already seem perfectly natural to many Internet users, since consumers are quickly getting used to new buying behavior and require the existence of such services.

2.4.4 Smartphone Usage and Smart Natives

The key drivers of omni-channel use are smartphones, which make it possible to access the mobile Internet virtually anywhere. In two years' time, almost one in four Germans will use a smartphone and view it as a natural component of their buying processes (cf. Go-Smart study 2012, p. 31). They expect a far greater range of services on their smartphone than they are familiar with through stationary Internet usage. Local functions and social networks in particular will play an even greater role than today. In 2013, the number of mobile Internet users, at around 1.6 billion, already exceeds the number of desktop users. One in three of them has already bought something using a mobile device, as shown by a representative study conducted by VERBRAUCHER INITIATIVE e.V. and eBay entitled "Smart shopping", in which the author was involved (cf. eBay 2012a). Mobile commerce is a growing market, which places new challenges on infrastructure providers. The increasing usage of smartphones also allows simple price comparisons on the Internet to be used for assessing offline prices. Products in brick-and-mortar retailing can very quickly be identified through a product image or barcode and compared with mobile commerce offers. Roughly half of "smart natives" already use a smartphone to obtain additional product information. Price information is also requested very frequently, as shown in Fig. 2.18.

The constantly available price information on the mobile Internet is also enhancing customers' self-confidence. If customers find a lower price on a mobile device, over half are willing to directly ask for a discount (cf. IDC Retail Insights 2010). In the course of this development, an adjustment and resultant additional price squeeze can be assumed. The same should apply to reference prices, which are used for assessing prices (cf. Diller 2008; Schleusener 2012, p. 170). Phases including price campaigns could also be affected, since customers are less reliant on retailers' external reference prices, but are then able to determine actual savings by comparison with online prices (cf. Schleusener 2012, p. 170). Users are already doing this (cf. Socialbakers 2012; von Kunhardt 2012). At the same time, the mobile Internet is upgrading the cellphone from a communication to an interaction

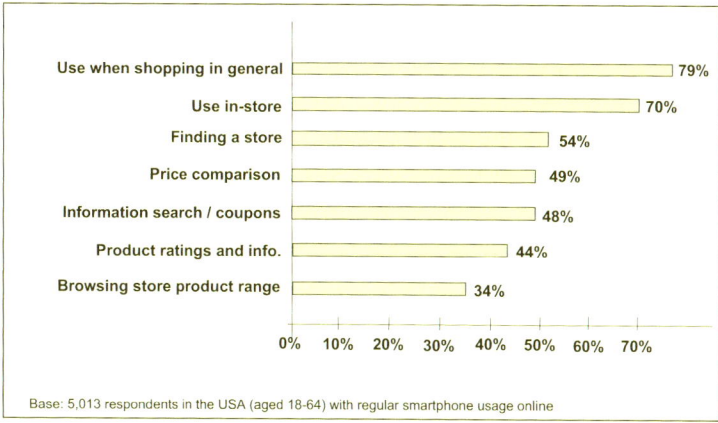

Fig. 2.18 Use of smartphones in brick-and-mortar buying process (Source: Google and Imposes OTX MediaCT 2012)

medium and turning it into a central point of the "digital lifestyle" (cf. Go-Smart study 2012, p. 18), whereby online offers are available at any time. Fourty-nine percent of users already primarily acquire useful information for everyday life, such as traffic data, timetable information, etc., via their smartphone (cf. ibid.). The "instant-on character" of the mobile device turns the Internet into a secondary medium, whereby the device is adjusted to user preferences and can easily be integrated into everyday routines. Situational and lifestyle-related adaptation of offers to customers' individual buying habits represents the master class of mobile commerce. The new "SoLoMo synergies" can therefore be played out, which result from social, local and mobile networking (SoLoMo). These include customizable virtual shelves and the use of augmented reality in all conceivable facets. Mobile 2.0, i.e. mobile-based implementation of social media tools with networking to Facebook, Twitter and the like is standard. Twitter accounts do not only function as a service tool to reply to customer questions, as practiced at Best Buy with Twelpforce. They can also sustainably fuel other sales channels, as demonstrated by Whole Foods Market (WFM) (cf. Heinemann 2012a, p. 91). Situational usability largely constitutes mobile added value for users and changes their demands and usage habits at the same time.

2.4.4.1 Smart Natives

As with digital natives, who can almost be described as "heavy users" of the Internet, trend-setting smartphone users are described as smart natives (cf. Go Smart 2012). Significant attributes of smart natives include heavy use, and affinity for technology and the web. As far as smart natives are concerned, it is no problem to use all functions of the latest smartphone, and thereby usefully integrate the device into their everyday lives. For example, they access useful information on an ongoing basis, often incidentally, or fill their spare time by using the device. Smart natives have above-average education, and tend to be young and employed. They are able to find exactly what they need online on their iPhone in an app-based form. In general, smart natives can no longer imagine having to forego mobile added value (cf. Go Smart 2012).

From the perspective of smart natives, the iPhone primarily meets their device requirements. This can be attributed to established and intuitive touchscreen control. However, the Samsung Galaxy has rapidly caught up and the IV model has even surpassed the performance of the iPhone. In addition, there is a whole generation of new devices from China waiting in the wings, which will cover the lower price segment. Google's Android has already outsold Apple's iPhone (cf. ZDNet 2013). Among smart natives, a preference is already emerging in which smartphone usage produces benefits in terms of real-time, responsiveness and whereabouts (e.g. local search) (cf. Go-Smart 2012).

The opportunity to access any type of information at any time represents a particular incentive for smart natives, because they ease and enrich everyday life through the availability of the mobile Internet. Three factors are especially important to smart natives: their search behavior, primary search content and social media linking (cf. Go-Smart 2012).

- **Search:** Smart natives still primarily use search functions on a stationary computer. But roughly one in four smart natives already use local search and wikis in equal shares on the smartphone and PC (cf. Go-Smart 2012). More than half, i.e. Fifty-five percent, say they use search engines on mobile devices just as heavily as they do on the stationary PC. Around one third (31 %) already use smartphones for local searches. Geo-localization seems to be very popular here in particular (Go-Smart).
- **Content:** With respect to useful information in everyday life (e.g. weather reports, traffic info, road conditions, timetables, stock prices, etc.) and news, smart natives recognize the smartphone's added value. They access such information almost exclusively on their mobile device. Around one in two smart natives prefer the smartphone for this reason. This is more than the number of those who access information in equal shares on the smartphone and stationary PC. One in three smartphone users access useful information equally as often on mobile and stationary devices (cf. Go-Smart 2012).
- **Social media:** Social media functions in particular have the potential to attain far-reaching and exclusive usage via smartphones, especially when it concerns appointments and maintaining contacts. Around one fifth of smart natives today (already) prefer this kind of personal communication and for 30 % of non-users who plan to purchase a smartphone, the use of social media is an essential reason for buying a device later on (cf. Go Smart 2012).

Smartphones and stationary computers have tended to be used in a complementary manner so far. However, parallel media usage is emerging among smart natives. Internet users can no longer be assigned to a specific type of device, but use different formats in different situations, or even in parallel. This trend has recently been described as "multi-screening" and indicates that flexible format solutions will increasingly be in demand. "Mobile commerce is couch commerce" (DDV Dialogue 2013, p. 22) perfectly describes parallel media usage, now also termed "omni-channeling". Studies by Google on the subject show that 65 % of online purchases are already initiated via an information search with the smartphone and 61 % are finalized on the desktop (cf. Google 2012). Mobile devices play a leading role here as a "feeder function" for the online shop. The big topic now, following the large smartphone wave, is the tablet. No other technology market is growing faster than the tablet computer market. Whether Amazon, Microsoft or Google, all of the big players on the market are currently moving full steam ahead on the issue of tablets. The driver of this trend is the transfer of computer output from stationary to mobile devices. With the iPad, Apple currently controls around three quarters of the rapidly-growing tablet market. However, "only" half of the forecast sales of 280 million tablet computers for 2015 are allotted to Apple, while the second-largest supplier, Samsung, is set to catch up strongly (cf. Heinemann 2012a, p. 77). The use of tablet PCs does not apply to mobile commerce based on the current definitions. However, given that the tablet PC constitutes a kind of hybrid between smartphone and notebook, which also allows for a telephone option on additional devices, the distinction from mobile commerce does not hold up. Smartphones and tablet PCs are frequently used in a dual function and with a dual twin card for use on the move. In addition, changeovers between mobile devices and tablets are increasingly fluid and provide diverse formats, which are frequently used in parallel to television.

2.5 "Always-in-Touch": The SoLoMo Mindset

The smartphone is turning into a "cross-technology platform", which creates new sales prospects by sending local information in combination with innovative services and technologies (cf. Heinemann 2012b). Such "location-based services" are increasingly combined with attractive discount offers, which can attract customers to brick-and-mortar stores. Furthermore, they allow for a new dimension in price transparency through local price comparison options and immediate availability of digital services, called "OTA (over the air) deliveries". The smartphone will increasingly take on a payment function and replace the credit card in the future (cf. BV Capitals 2011; cf. Heinemann 2012a, p. 10). Simple access to constantly available online offers enriches the everyday life of smart natives and offers a new form of user-related efficiency. Driven by the growing importance of social networks and constant connection with friends and acquaintances, communication is becoming significantly more open. "Always-on" forms the technical basis, and "always-in-touch" the social consequence of the SoLoMo mindset (cf. Go-Smart study 2012, p. 17). This is shown in Fig. 2.19 and includes four components: SoLoMo usability, SoLoMo efficiency, SoLoMo communication and SoLoMo convergence (cf. ibid., pp. 17 et seqq.; Heinemann 2012b). These components are addressed by the Go-Smart study as a result of a representative study on mobile usage in Germany from 2012 (cf. ibid.).

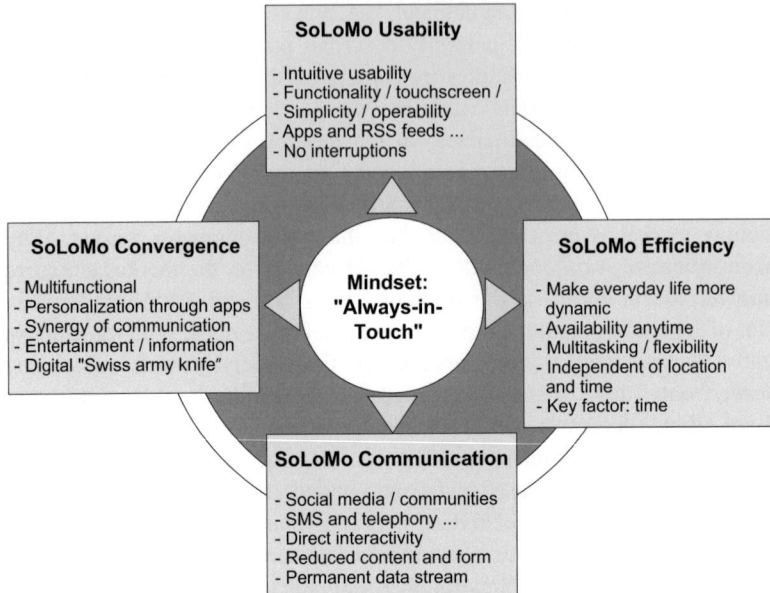

Fig. 2.19 SoLoMo mindset "always-in-touch" (Source: Based on Go-Smart study 2012, p. 17)

2.5.1 SoLoMo Usability

Smart natives are distinguished by heavy usage and a high affinity to technology and the web. They comprehensively integrate the intrinsic potential of the mobile Internet into their everyday life. The term "remote control of life" encapsulates this lifestyle (cf. Kerkau 2012). In this respect, intuitive usability and personalization options increase the fascination for technical devices. They are largely responsible for the rapidly growing numbers of smartphone users. In particular, the introduction of touchscreens and touch-sensitive displays and apps make devices easy to use in mobile form. The device allows users to focus on content because it is easy to operate. Apps offer simplified access to functions and contents here. They compensate for technical deficits, such as low screen size and small keyboards (cf. Heinemann 2012b). Access to the mobile Internet is seamlessly integrated into everyday routines on such devices. As a result, almost half of smartphone users already acquire useful everyday information on their smartphone (cf. ibid., p. 18; Mindwyse 2011; Heinemann 2012b).

2.5.2 SoLoMo Efficiency

Regardless of location and time, smartphones enable their users to deliver digital services immediately, in the form of the OTA deliveries mentioned above. They effectively serve as "enablers" and "catalysts". Accessing information, communication, entertainment and shopping are possible at any time. In many cases, such offers are used in parallel, in the form of "omni-channeling" (cf. Heinemann 2012b). Constant availability induces new behavioral patterns. Ad-hoc decisions can increasingly replace advance planning, since the acquired mobility allows for greater flexibility. Situational information is permanently available and can be quickly and reliably accessed. Access to knowledge is just as important as the knowledge of facts. At the same time, media-free islands of time become dynamic, allowing idle periods to be bridged. Eighty-two percent of smart natives already use their device for amusement during breaks. They are increasingly using the smartphone instead of the desktop at home, since they value their instant-on functions (cf. ibid., p. 19; Mindwyse 2011; Heinemann 2012b).

2.5.3 SoLoMo Communication

In particular, written forms of Internet communication, e.g. email or instant messaging, are increasingly supplementing or replacing classical telephony, which only makes up 22 % of usage. VoIP, chat, status updates, pin board entries, and social networks take priority with a 29 % utilization rate. Ten percent of all used smartphone functions are already allocated to social networks. The volume of mobile data services therefore already exceeded the volume of SMS (text messages) and MMS back in 2010 (cf. Go-Smart study 2012). Around 77 % of smart natives use social networks, and 18 % of them primarily on their smartphone. Open communication is preferred, since it generates feedback and highlights the social role of the user. At the same time, constant connection with friends and communication in virtual real-time reduce the amount of verbal interactions. Response times are getting faster because, in addition to communication contents, constant exchange is also stimulated. Smart natives are therefore almost in a continuous data stream, but also emphasize their own private sphere and control. Fourty-nine percent of smart natives worry about missing something when the device is switched off, and are therefore "always on" (cf. Go-Smart study 2012, pp. 19–20; Mindwyse 2011; Heinemann 2012b).

2.5.4 SoLoMo Convergence

Convergence as a concept describes the amalgamation of various functions, contents and channels in one single device. Around 33 % of all smartphone users still primarily use their device for telephony, but only 22 % of smart natives do so. Fourty-four percent prefer to use their smartphone for Internet functions. In this regard, devices are used for organization, photography and films and videos, or for computer tasks. In addition, information on the weather (92 % of smart natives), local search information (74 %), and price comparison sites (39 %) are accessed on the mobile Internet. Sixty-three percent of smart natives already use classic search engines on their mobile device. Entertainment offers are also increasingly used.

YouTube fills break times, amusing apps encourage entertainment, and computer games increase the entertainment value. As a digital "Swiss army knife", the smartphone offers its users barely imaginable functions. There is a mixture of private and professional usage, since 43 % of smart natives also use their professional smartphone privately. In any case, 45 % of all smartphone users and 60 % of smart natives say they don't mind doing work-related tasks in their spare time (cf. Go-Smart study 2012, pp. 20–21; Mindwyse 2011; Heinemann 2012b).

2.6 The Role of SoLoMo in Brick-and-Mortar Retailing

The SoLoMo phenomenon is also fueled by the fact that users want to stay informed online. The same applies today to smart natives, for whom permanent access to the digital data stream is normal. They demand mobile offers, which they can continuously keep up-to-date and share with their network. In this regard, local real-time offers with geo-location, increasing response speeds, real-time information and augmented reality create interesting mobile added value for SoLoMo users. Added value is certainly provided by online buying (cf. Go-Smart study 2012, pp. 30–31; Mindwyse 2011; Heinemann 2012b), which is convenient and varied, and can be done 24 h a day, regardless of location. Nevertheless, experts do not make the assumption that brick-and-mortar stores will disappear completely (cf. eBay 2012a). Consumers do not want to buy everything online, but nor do they have to forego the advantages of one channel just because they happen to use another channel. Some companies therefore let their customers shop in parallel. However, this should not lead to an exodus of customers. As a result, some retailers are currently working on no-line strategies (cf. Heinemann 2012b). Most customers can no longer imagine a world without online shopping. That is exactly why brick-and-mortar retailing should not get left behind, especially since the Internet has become a central part of many people's lives (cf. ibid.). A targeted social media budget is key to the success of brick-and-mortar retailers in this respect. However, it is not uncommon for this to be disregarded. The online marketing budget alone is often not aligned with the usage intensity of digital media (cf. Wirtz 2008, p. 81; Wolter 2012). In 2011, the total share of Internet advertising in the media mix, at 19.6 %, amounted to one fifth of the total advertising budget (cf. OVK 2012), which is equivalent to an increase of 2.1 % from 2010 (cf. OVK 2012). Whereas online advertising enjoys a prolonged upward trend, print advertising is continually becoming less important. The share of Internet advertising in the advertising budget has more than doubled since 2006. In contrast, the share of the "gross advertising cake" for newspapers, magazines and trade journals fell around 17 % during this period (cf. webhelps 2011). With regard to Internet advertising segments, it is noticeable that traditional online advertising, including pop-ups, advertising banners and layer ads, benefited the most from this trend (cf. ibid.). In this respect, classic Internet advertising will exceed the 3.6 billion threshold for the first time, with a growth rate of approx. 12 % in 2012 (cf. ibid.). Expenditure on social media is not included in the online marketing figures, although it is forecast to increase

2.6 The Role of SoLoMo in Brick-and-Mortar Retailing

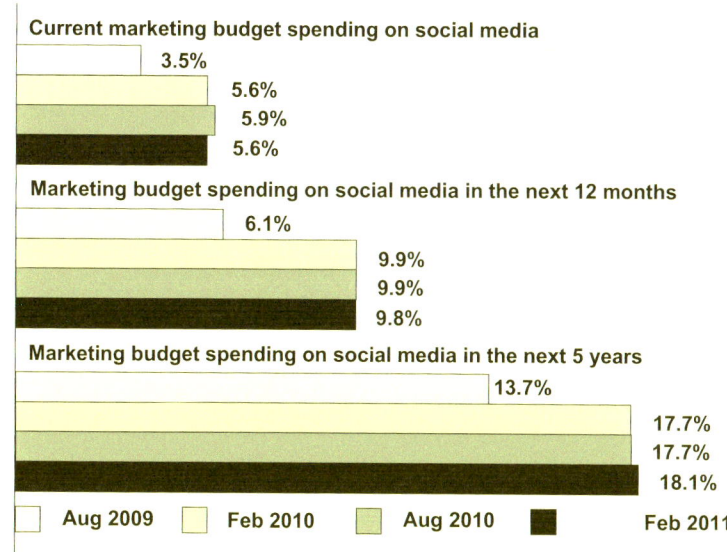

Fig. 2.20 Social media shares of US marketing budget (2009–2011) (Source: Own illustration based on SEO-united 2011)

significantly. This is also shown by the results, published on emarketer.com in 2011, of a survey of current social media marketing expenditure in the USA. As the surveyed employees with responsibility for marketing from 400 US companies point out, social media expenditure is set to multiply in the next few years (cf. - SEO-united 2011).

As shown in Fig. 2.20, social media expenditure in the USA amounted to 5.6 % of the total budget on average in 2011. In contrast, US marketing managers intended to increase expenditure in 2012 to around 10 %, and even to 20 % in the next 5 years. At the same time, the survey respondents admitted that they still have major problems with successfully integrating social media into their company's marketing concept. Almost half the participants indicated that they had not yet managed, or barely managed to coordinate their activities correctly. The result of the study illustrates a problem which is typical of social media. Whereas, on the one hand, several companies are now intent on increasing their spending on social media, there is a lack of opportunity to include social activities in a feasible concept. Activities on Facebook, Twitter and the like are hardly comparable with conventional marketing measures. In particular, many companies find it difficult to set up an ongoing dialogue with the general public, as is necessary for social media (cf. SEO-united 2011). US companies are much further ahead in this area than those in Germany. An increase in the social media budget is on the agenda for American companies. In the next 5 years, this should break the 19.5 % mark of the overall marketing budget, although the figure is currently around 7.4 %. But German retailers do not have to go that far in the first stage. As far as many retail companies are concerned, this initially involves making a start in the social media world, which is really quite manageable.

As shown by the Adzine magazine for online marketing, on average only around 50,000 euros a year are required to include social media functions in the website and update them for 1 year. Optimal social media integration consists of the following three elements (cf. Adzine 2012).

- All relevant social networks must be separately linked with their own website in each case.
- The website must be optimized in terms of functionality and usability to ensure that all the advantages of social networks can be utilized.
- User data from social networks should be appropriately collected and evaluated, in order to faciliate their use in internal online marketing.

The first two elements can take up to 60 developer hours per network. On the other hand, integration costs may be reduced by up to 80 % with a single interface or application programming interface (API) (cf. ibid.).

Location-based services as Base Factor No. 2 for SoLoMo

3.1 Mobile Applications with Local Relevance

It is increasingly becoming clear that smartphone usage provides great opportunities for brick-and-mortar retailing (cf. Haug 2013). Its (as yet) unchallenged strengths, such as immediate availability of purchased products, the opportunity for a real tactile and visual product inspection and a brick-and-mortar shopping experience, can now be connected – through use of the mobile Internet – with the benefits of digital channels. This primarily relates to "search & browse" opportunities, preparations for buying, and the virtually unlimited choice of products. Furthermore, detailed product information, recommendations and product ratings for making purchase decisions in brick-and-mortar stores can also be made available to customers in digital form. Customers can also be reached in "transfer spaces" while they are on the move, which is a good option if potential buyers have a contextual relationship – e.g. at a sporting event – or local proximity to the product offer. The penetration of smartphones also results in decoupling of the buying process, which can now be implemented independently of specific stores and/or buying situations. This process is accelerated by mobile applications, which can be subdivided into three areas: "optimization of local search", "aggregation platforms and offer bundling" and "local referral marketing on social networks" (cf. Haug 2013).

3.1.1 Local Search Optimization

Preparations for purchases increasingly take place on the mobile Internet, where buying intentions often originate. Whether with a smartphone on the train, en route to the office, at the supermarket checkout, or during a discussion with friends, a prior search on the net during waiting times is becoming customary for an ever larger number of users. Sometimes this is due to an interesting product recommendation. Purchase-related results of a digital search on the net often also yield leading pure plays, such as Amazon or Zalando, given that they usually have a very extensive range and still conduct professional online marketing (cf. Haug 2013). The continuously improving delivery capacity of online retailers and the first steps towards "same day delivery" make it increasingly likely that customers will buy on the Internet. However, it would be much more attractive for those with an interest in buying if the availability of the required product in a nearby store could be displayed. The customer would then be able to make a targeted search for relevant suppliers and immediately take the product with him or her. For brick-and-mortar retailers, it is therefore advisable to ensure that their available products are found during digital searches. This gives them a good profiling opportunity, especially if their range also has local relevance. Against this background, they should fully exploit all of the traceability and placement options provided by Google (cf. Haug 2013).

3.1.1.1 Google Applications for Brick-and-Mortar Retailers

As a search engine, Google serves customers – based on experience about their needs – who initiate a search with a specific purchase request. If customers already have an idea about a product, it is not uncommon for them to use Google services, in order to obtain extensive information about alternative offers and finally obtain a concrete purchase recommendation. Such services are usually augmented by local and contextual information. Google thereby responds to the exploding number of mobile search queries, which often have local relevance (cf. Haug 2013). At the end of 2012, around 25 % of clicks on SEM ads in the USA were already executed via mobile devices (cf. Marine Software 2012, pp. 6 et seq.). Various Google products, such as Google+, Google Places and Google Shopping, interact to improve the local offer of the search engine provider. As a result, shops can market their online presence with a few hand movements on Google+, Google Places and Adwords Express. Registering the local store on Google Places and displaying address, opening times and photos is recommended. By integrating Google+, customers can rate the shop, share with friends, or make recommendations. They can even interact with owners and employees on site. A combination of Google Places and Google Local, and the Google Maps app lets customers gain access to opening times and ratings while they are on the move. The app functions on both iOS and Android and thus covers most mobile devices. Brick-and-mortar retailers can also take out locally-based ads on Adwords Express, which are then displayed during search queries in the vicinity of a store. As a result, the customer can be reached in a situation of acute need, thereby increasing the probability of conversion (cf. Haug 2013). Eighty-two percent of smartphone owners already search for local information via mobile devices. Eighty percent of such search queries lead to a direct response to search results, in which customers search for a shop, for example (cf. Haug 2013; Google 2012, p. 22).

The presence of local retailers can be improved through integration in Google Shopping, i.e. the search engine's product search function. Retailers can promote their products with the help of "product listing ads". In this case, a relevant product data feed has to be prepared and processed for the products available in the brick-

3.1 Mobile Applications with Local Relevance

and-mortar store, and a regular in-feed provided for via the Google Merchant Center. When customers search for a product, they are also advised that they can buy the product in a nearby store. All retailers can be displayed on the smartphone, including the contact data for where the desired item is available. Given that the retailer profile is linked with retailer data from Google Places and ratings on Google+, the customer is quickly able to make a buying decision, which allows him or her to acquire the product immediately from the local retailer of his/her choice (cf. Haug 2013).

By merging various products for mobile consumers, Google is positioning itself as a practical "assistant", enhanced with local relevant information and social recommendations. Through the combination of Google Shopping and Google Places or Google+, Google transfers online mechanisms to brick-and-mortar shopping (cf. Fig. 3.1). The question of whether local retailers offer a truly relevant service for preparing for a purchase crucially depends on the real-time availability of their data feeds. At present, brick-and-mortar retailers are rarely able to convey product availability correctly and automatically.

But this should only be a matter of time, because today's consumers are increasingly shaped by the shopping experience on the Internet and value the efficient finding and comparison of products (cf. Haug 2013).

The display of product availability is a key factor in ensuring the added value of the product search. It is only worth making a quick trip to pick up the desired product on site from the brick-and-mortar retailer if the customer can be certain that the product is in stock. The more products from brick-and-mortar suppliers that can be found through a digital search or aggregator platforms, the better access the customers will have to the products they are searching for. The potential could be so great here that even large marketplace suppliers like Amazon, with its online shop,

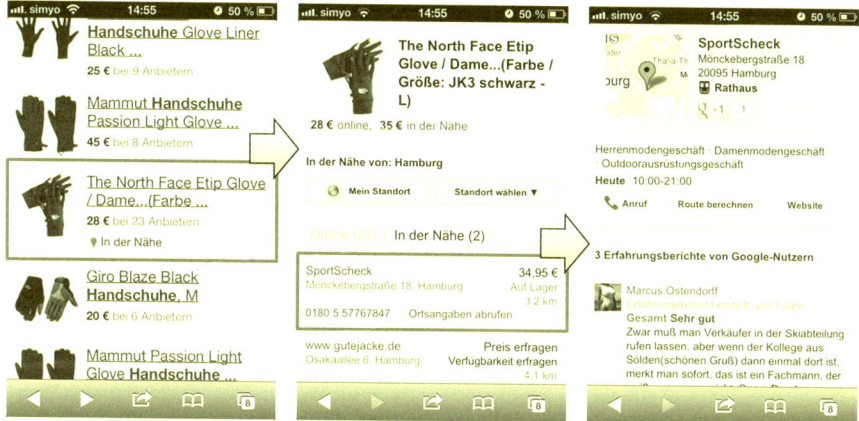

Fig. 3.1 Mobile Google search with information about offers at brick-and-mortar stores (Source: Haug 2013 with permission from Google 2014)

can no longer keep up. In addition, there is the advantage that customers can immediately try out the products physically and take them with them.

3.1.2 Bundling and Aggregation Platforms

A large number of major online players are developing appropriate concepts. This shows how relevant this issue will be in terms of competitive positioning in future. One such player is eBay. Bridgeheads into brick-and-mortar retailing are currently being established through targeted acquisitions, such as RedLaser, Milo, Where and GiftsNearby.

3.1.2.1 Local eBay Applications with Milo

As an aggregator platform, Milo accesses local inventories and makes local product ranges available online. The young platform is positioned as a local shopping guide. It lists products from brick-and-mortar retailers, along with their price and availability. Consumers can research products online or in mobile form. It is also possible to access additional purchase-relevant information on product ratings and make the purchase the same day, at the best possible conditions. In addition, the app is fitted with a barcode scanner, meaning that prices of nearby retailers can be compared with one another. The advantage for retailers is that the app provides them with more customers with targeted buying interests. They can influence the consumer's supplier selection via Milo by displaying coupons. Following a takeover in 2010, eBay integrated the search results for Milo into its RedLaser price comparison app and utilized the data feed for the local gift finder GiftsNearby, now called eBay Local. The service has since cooperated with more than 140 brick-and-mortar retailers, including Target, RadioShack, Best Buy, Toys-R-Us, and Sears (cf. Haug 2013). Overall, Milo therefore has access to the inventory management of 50,000 stores in the USA (cf. Kessler 2011). In contrast to Google, Milo currently already offers a reservation option for participating retailers. Furthermore, payments can be made through Paypal over the telephone. In the future, however, payments could also be possible via Google Wallet (cf. Haug 2013).

Marketplace operator eBay uses the real-time inventories of local retailers in various strategic local shopping products. The company is currently testing the integration of its local search service and same-day delivery model called "eBay Now". During initial experiments in San Francisco, products from retailers' brick-and-mortar stores, whose real-time inventories are retrieved via Milo, could be ordered on the eBay Now app. Such products were subsequently delivered to the customer within one hour (cf. Internetworld 2012). If the search and purchase preparation phase can be efficiently implemented via digital channels, this is an ideal solution for many modern consumers. They can thus execute the concrete buying process – with tactile and visual inspection of products, personal specialist advice, and direct pick-up at a brick-and-mortar store nearby (cf. Haug 2013).

3.1 Mobile Applications with Local Relevance

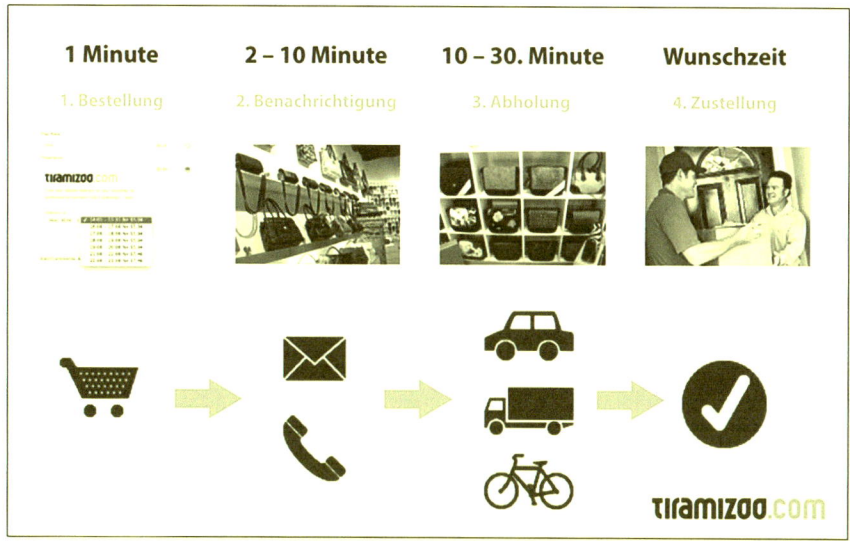

Fig. 3.2 Processes at tiramizoo (Source: Haug 2013 with permission from Google 2014)

3.1.2.2 Local Supplier Services with Geo-Location Technology

Locally available products can also be shipped by innovative logistics and goods suppliers within a very short time. This has become possible due to startups such as Shutl, Postmates from San Francisco, and tiramizoo from Munich. Figure 3.2 depicts the processes at tiramizoo for local immediate delivery as an example (cf. Haug 2013). London-based company Shutl operates an innovative platform, which offers a marketplace for local delivery services and product suppliers, using intelligent technology. Appropriate subcontractors are selected for deliveries, which collect the products from the supplier and can deliver them to customers as quickly as possible. Both the price and required service standards are considered in the selection. In addition, the platform is compatible with all current inventory control and ERP systems. Shutl makes it possible for brick-and-mortar retailers, such as Argos, to deliver products to customers within a few hours, or even minutes. As a result, it is a direct affront to the next-day delivery standard of the major online pure plays.

3.1.2.3 Mobile Addressing of Customers to Create Demand

At least in theory, consumers can be addressed on their smartphones at any time. Ideally, a relationship is established with the customer's current situation, based on time, location or cause. If a customer is located near the store, addressing him or her with a personalized offer by SMS (text message), email or voice message is recommended, preferably with a discount offer for a relevant product category. It should be possible for customers to search for the store based on product availability and proximity. This activation method is also known as geo-fencing and requires a prior opt-in process, in which the customer releases his data for mobile contact. If customers have not given consent to being contacted directly, mobile local advertising can be placed. This option is offered by Radcarpet for example. However, experience shows that suppliers can only be successful with their strategies to create demand if they formulate relevant and target group-specific offers. Coupons, discounts, special products or service offers, such as specialist consulting, are recommended here. Offers that are very closely connected to the concrete requirements of the customer could also be used with this approach, such as offers related to vacation preparations or a pregnancy.

3.1.2.4 Locally-Based Advertising with Radcarpet

Locally-based advertising – "mobile advertising" – makes it possible to reach customers on their mobile devices and thus display advertising messages contextually. It allows the retailer to precisely target customers in its vicinity, using GPS data. Radcarpet is one such advertising platform. The advertising service provider is currently building a network of wide-reach publishers, through which mobile offers for locally-based ads can be placed. These publishers include Springer Verlag with the Bild app. For example, a banner is displayed for the reader, on which Starbucks promotes the purchase of a drink in a nearby store. If the customer clicks on the banner, he or she is redirected to a landing page with a clear request for action, which is customized for the campaign. The user may be requested to retrieve a map, request a callback, or write an SMS or email. Advertisers only pay for the ad if one of these actions is completed. Companies acquire available advertising space in a real-time auction process, using real-time bidding, based on the Google model (cf. Haug 2013).

According to Radcarpet's own information, the company can accurately adjust the relevant magnitude of ads up to 10 m. The local relevance of the advertisement significantly improves its impact. In a test conducted with eight million advertising media contacts, the interaction rate increased by 50 % when the advertising material contained the statement "just 200 meters away" (Eisenbrand 2012). Using the Radcarpet solution, companies are offered the opportunity to call customers' attention to their offers in "transfer spaces", and provide a context-based incentive to visit. If not only location, but also the content of the mobile offer is taken into consideration when designing the ad, the relevance of such advertisements can even be increased. Accordingly, the Blue Moon Brewing Company in the USA, for example, used the mobile offer from cinema operator Fandango to make moviegoers aware of the opportunity to visit the bar before they go to see the film (cf. Haug 2013; Johnson 2012). In the future, context and proximity will be important tools for addressing customers, particularly spontaneous shoppers.

3.1.3 Local and Social Referral Marketing

Recommendations from other consumers have the greatest credibility in the buying process. It therefore makes sense to intensively use rating and social media platforms to address customers (cf. Haug 2013). In addition to the authenticity of users' opinions, the attractiveness of social networks is also founded on the digital diffusion mechanism, which did not previously exist. Users posting an opinion, photo, video or product recommendation thus reach their entire network, which creates the opportunity for the viral spread of information within a very short timeframe. With regard to local retailers, Qype currently represents the largest rating portal in Germany. Qype registers around 7.5 million visitors a month and provides ratings for any type of service, including restaurants, bars, stores, local services and doctors (cf. Qype 2012; Haug 2013). Qype lets people update and supplement their own profile with additional data, and respond to ratings. Data may include photos, opening times or directions. Furthermore, incentives may be provided for customers to submit ratings for brick-and-mortar services. Information on sales receipts or stickers or tags in the salesroom might be offered for example. If attractive customer retention schemes and loyalty benefit programs succeed in getting customers' email addresses registered, an extra impetus for ratings and reviews in social networks can be provided by means of email marketing.

For smartphone users, in addition to review and rating platforms such as Qype, an increasing number of new location-based networks are emerging. Customers can check in on these sites, as on Facebook, Twitter, Instagram, Google+ and Foursquare. They all offer their users the opportunity to check in directly or supply published content with a geo-tag (specification of location). An ever increasing number of users are utilizing such features (cf. Firsching 2012; Haug 2013). By checking in, users can display their location to their network. They can also supplement such information with comments, ratings or photos of the locality. Check-ins can be submitted more quickly and thus a greater number of check-ins collected than is the case with reviews and ratings. Foursquare, for example, has one billion check-ins worldwide and offers highly differentiated instruments to address customers locally or retain them through incentive systems and rewards (cf. Haug 2013). The local service has over 20 million users worldwide and approx. 750,000 affiliated companies, demonstrating rapid growth, given that it had seven million registered users in 2011 (cf. Schott 2012). Foursquare integrates a large amount of additional attractive content in its products through open system interfaces. On the basis of collected data, it creates applications which raise geo-social and local searches to a higher evolution stage. Foursquare Explore, for example, is a web-based, personalized search engine, which lets users search for any supplier of their choosing, including tips, photos, reviews and ratings at any location. Relatively few business offers are available on Foursquare in Germany. There are some isolated check-in deals, but even in large cities only a few Foursquare Specials are available. In addition, offers are usually not very attractive (cf. Haug 2013).

"Geo-tags", which relay the geographical position, are primarily very popular among younger users. They will play an even greater role in the future if retailers are involved in location-based campaigns. This could increase the prospects for smartphone usage in-store. In particular, the distribution and geo-tagging of photos on location-based networks show large growth rates. The leaders here are Foodspotting and Instagram. Instagram was sold to Facebook for one billion dollars last year and has approx. 100 million registered users worldwide. Roughly 11 million of them are active every day (cf. Haug 2013). Campaigns on Facebook are also relevant, at least for Germany. Facebook has around 1.2 billion users worldwide, almost 26 million of whom are in Germany. Roughly half are active every day (cf. Buggisch 2013; Haug 2013). In this respect, actions on Facebook are suited to users who provide information on their whereabouts and, where applicable, report on their shopping experience or product purchase.

3.1.4 Local Real-time Offers

Mobile addressing of customers allows for the placement of offers, improves the current utilization and reduces stockpiles. This approach is used by Groupon, for example, with its mobile app, Groupon Now.

3.1.4.1 Groupon Now

Groupon markets up-to-date and location-based offers with discounts of 50–70 %. The marketing specialist supplies local retailers with a high-reach online platform, in order to address a local target group and acquire them as new customers through introductory offers. Deals are given high visibility through the large email distribution list of Groupon and diffusion in social networks. Groupon launched Groupon Now in the USA in 2011, thereby expanding its service with a mobile deal platform using a location-based service approach. Users of the Groupon Now app receive location-based real-time offers, which are advertised nearby (cf. Fig. 3.3). The app creates inspiration for occasions, such as shopping, wellness, dining and sports. Although Groupon is repeatedly subjected to criticism, the business model offers new opportunities in local marketing for brick-and-mortar retailing, even if it is associated with poor implementation of deals and high commissions. Local retailers are given the opportunity to expand their classic target group through a mobile location-based couponing offer and thereby address other customers, and not just passing trade. People in more remote urban districts can be reached through the mobile couponing service, and are provided with an incentive to visit the store. Due to the real-time aspect, retailers have the option to adjust offers ad hoc and only for a few hours a day. This allows them to optimize their utilization or yield management. For example, if a nail salon has open appointments in the afternoon, it can use the app to spontaneously address customers who have time and are in the area. Mobile offers have high strategic relevance for Groupon in this respect. Over half of traffic in the USA takes place on mobile devices. Thirty percent of transactions were carried out in mobile form by Groupon in April 2012 (cf. Walsh 2012). Groupon is increasing the range of its real-time offers, including through cooperation with the location-based service platform Foursquare. Offers on Groupon Now are also displayed on Foursquare in what are referred to there as specials. The real-time service has not yet officially gone live in Germany. However, retailers can already place real-time offers via the merchant center, which, according to Groupon, can be controlled down to the minute. By means of a strategic partnership with Telekom, the mobile reach of the platform is also set to be enlarged in Germany (cf. Telekom 2013; Haug 2013). Real-time offers have a future and the opportunities for utilization-based pricing might well be implemented in innovative business models or marketing tools by additional suppliers in the future. Thus, for example, Hoteltonight and Jetsetter provide attractive solutions for hotel customers, in which hotels booked at the last minute are offered at extremely low prices. The social reservation system *resmio* enables yield management for restaurants in the gastronomy sector. For example, more guests can be acquired during times of low occupancy and revenues can be improved (cf. Haug 2013).

3.2 Digital In-store Applications

"The customer is online in-store" (cf. Heinemann 2011a). The change in buying behavior cannot be encapsulated in any other way. However, brick-and-mortar retailers frequently leave customers in the lurch. A ban on cellphones in the store, poor Internet connection, and lack of WLAN or even jammers are the exact opposite of what the modern customer should expect today. "Online goes online" primarily involves "digital in-store applications" responding appropriately to digital progress in-store. However, digital in-store applications are only used if and when the concept is adapted to the customer's specific problem. The following issues should therefore be clarified before starting to use such applications (cf. Crossretail 2013):

1. **Target group relevance:** Identification of specific buying behavior, decision-making structures and requirements of the target group in the relevant product category.
2. **Touchpoint relevance:** Knowledge of all online and offline touchpoints that customers encounter during their search for the optimal offer and use within the scope of their buying process.
3. **Buying phase relevance:** Knowing which buying phase of the customer journey the customer is in when he or she enters the brick-and-mortar store.

The necessary information can be generated both online and offline. Web analytics and e-reputation tools are provided online. Sales personnel at the PoS or a consumer survey can be used offline. It is advisable not to satisfy all target groups in parallel and at the same time, but to initially focus on an in-store goal (cf. Crossretail 2013).

3.2.1 Reinforcing Brick-and-Mortar Benefits as a Basic Approach

Addressing customers and making local product ranges available via mobile devices may increase the frequency of store visits. However, the resultant potential can only be exploited if local retailers fulfil customer expectations as far as possible at the point of sale. Therefore, they should create inspiring multi-channel shopping experiences with good advice provision and smooth processes (cf. Haug 2013). Globetrotter is currently compiling best practices for in-store applications in Germany. The multi-channel retailer illustrates how a balanced multi-channel strategy can leverage and combine the strengths of individual channels. Globetrotter customers are encouraged to scan barcodes with the supplier's mobile app, in order to access detailed product information or customer reviews. The smartphone is turning into a digital customer adviser. The Globetrotter catalogue, with a print run of around 1.2 million copies, is available online and on the mobile app. Furthermore, product ratings and additional detailed descriptions from the browser display are intuitively available, like browsing the app. The same applies to the connection to social networks (cf. Haug 2013). Moreover, products from transmissions by Web TV broadcaster 4-seasons.tv, which operates Globetrotter, can also be placed directly from videos into the shopping basket at Globetrotter. Furthermore, through its own outdoor community on 4-seasons.de, Globetrotter offers a comprehensive portal on which customers can communicate with one another, or even with experts (cf. dgroup 2012b; Haug 2013).

Smartphone usage in-store is supported by Globetrotter through mobile apps via which product information can be accessed. This represents an integrated alternative to external price comparison apps. Globetrotter thus retains customers within its own eco-system. This prevents "advice theft" and thereby the migration of customers to other suppliers. Lowe's also pursues the same strategy. The world's second-largest DIY chain, with over 1,700 stores in the USA and Canada, serves more than 14 million customers every week. Lowe's mobile app lets users scan the product barcode while in the DIY store. As a result it delivers product information, application tips, customer ratings and even cross-selling offers with products from surrounding shops. The result is a strong customer commitment to their own products, meaning they conduct mobile searches at Amazon or Google much less often (cf. Reilly 2012; Haug 2013).

In addition, skilful channel-linking can resolve one of the biggest problems in brick-and-mortar retailing, i.e. restricted product selection due to limited space capacities. A digital shelf extension may therefore be implemented in stores, in which larger product ranges are presented from the internal online shop via terminals or tablet applications. Leading suppliers, such as Apple and Nordstrom, which equip their sales personnel with iPads and thereby considerably improve the service for customers, have so far had good experience with this shelf extension strategy. Store employees, e.g. by using such digital devices, can search for other sizes, colors and additional products, which can then be delivered to the store or directly to the customer's home. The payment process can also be transacted on the device. Lines at store checkouts are therefore consigned to history, and customer satisfaction is increasing as a result. Other similar technological innovations will no doubt find their way into brick-and-mortar retailing in the future, in order to design the shopping experience in a way that makes it even more convenient and easy (cf. Haug 2013).

3.2.2 Gamification for Enhancing Experience

Apart from music titles, which are largely downloaded in digital form from the mobile network, the games industry, along with the book industry, is particularly affected by the digitalization trend and mobile commerce. Over ten million Germans already play games online (cf. BITKOM 2009). Around 1.86 billion euros were spent on computer and video games software in Germany in 2010 (cf. Die Welt dated April 27, 2011h, p. 14). Based on a recent market analysis, social games in combination with Facebook show above-average development and already constitute a global market of four billion US dollars (cf. Mücke Sturm 2011). Digitalization accommodates the desire for "immediate gratification", i.e. immediate availability and delivery of mobile services (cf. BV Capitals 2011). The trend towards e-games is also spreading to new business models. The integration of game mechanisms into non game-related actions can be observed. This will fundamentally change the buying behavior of mobile users in relation to mobile commerce. The following three aspects are conceivable here (cf. Tollmien 2011):

- **Shopping for games online:** The shopping platform "deutschlandklickt.de" encourages users who want to buy online, including through a click box, in a playful atmosphere. It offers users opportunities to obtain free clicks, free samples, coupons and instant prizes. A campaign is launched every 3 days with 15 free clicks, which are part of the gaming concept. Players therefore have five free clicks a day to try their luck, with the click box changing every day.
- **Real (physical) buying of games:** The American start-up Checkpoints has developed a mobile shopping app which enables customers to collect loyalty points with each purchase, which can later be exchanged for coupons or services. Customers entering the store are automatically notified about all nearby products included in the loyalty scheme. By scanning the barcode with a cellphone, customers can collect valuable points for their user account, and add to them at their discretion by participating in additional interactive games, which open up when the barcode is scanned.
- **Gaming promoted:** BBDO Argentina, a subsidiary of the global advertising agency, designed the Nike Air Race in conjunction with Castro Innovation House. This game can be played on site in the Nike store in Buenos Aires, but also at home. Two Nike Air-Max shoes hover roughly two centimeters above a magnetic bar. The player can move the shoes forward, by blowing into a microphone (which requires installation of a microphone or – via the mobile Internet – a flash interface). Promotion at the point of sale is combined with an interactive advergame on the net.

Facebook credits represent a special aspect of the gamification trend: the credits are essentially the site's own virtual currency, which can be used effectively in social games, such as Farmville, Cityville, or Restaurant City. This confirms the close connection between games and social interaction. Social networks play a large role in the use of gamification. Customers seek out verbal confirmation and attention through activity in social networks, such as Facebook and Twitter. No doubt this is partly related to the opportunity to share and disseminate information quickly. However, it can also be used for customer retention purposes. Sharing photos taken at the PoS generates recognition effects. As a result, customers identify more strongly with the brand and products. Examples include the Jimmy Choo label and the social game "retail therapy" (cf. Intertone 2010; Konrad 2013; Haarhaus 2013).

3.2.2.1 Jimmy Choo Case Study

Fashion label Jimmy Choo launched the "CatchaChoo" campaign in London in April 2010. The campaign involved a treasure hunt, using Twitter and Foursquare. The concept envisaged addressing users' sense of fun, games and performance. Jimmy Choo placed a pair of sneakers worth 500 US dollars at a suitable site and posted a photo on the CatchaChoo Twitter account. An employee then checked in at Foursquare to share the sneakers' position. It was then up to the users to find the sneakers and the Jimmy Choo employee. The first user to do so and say the sentence "I followed you" without being prompted was given a pair of sneakers as a present. Participants had to follow both the Twitter and Foursquare accounts of the brand in order to win. The credibility and success of the campaign was also corroborated by the fact that the winners shared their photos on the Jimmy Choo Facebook page. By linking various social networks, the brand made skilful use of their respective qualities (cf. Salt 2012 pp. 119 et seqq.; Konrad 2013). The positive outcome of the campaign is illustrated by the following figures: one out of every 17 people contacted in London searched for Jimmy Choo sneakers in the city, as a result of which approximately 6 % of addressed contacts were activated. 4,000 participants were registered online on Facebook, Twitter and Foursquare, which can certainly also be largely attributed to word-of-mouth advertising. Due to the enormous spread of the CatchaChoo campaign, the label's sales figures subsequently increased markedly (cf. Konrad 2013).

3.2.2.2 Retail Therapy Case Study

The social game Retail Therapy can also be cited as an example. Social games are online games with low complexity and are relatively not very demanding. They are normally embedded in social networks, such as Facebook (cf. Informatik und Gesellschaft der Universität Köln 2011; Konrad 2013). In this regard, "Retail Therapy" represents a social game for Facebook and combines game activities and e-commerce functions. Fans of fashion become owners and managers of virtual boutiques in this game. They play at being retailers and design their own virtual store concept (cf. Weiss 2010; Konrad 2013). They equip the store with virtual products and recruit staff. The special feature of Retail Therapy is that virtual products are equivalent to real products that are currently offered in brick-and-mortar stores. This makes it possible to link the virtual and real shopping world, which is enabled through brand cooperation schemes with fashion labels, such as

3.2 Digital In-store Applications

Diane von Furstenberg, Gap and Top-Shop. The goal is to make the store public and successful on Facebook. The player is "paid" with coins for each sold product, and thereby gains access to "new levels". In turn, each new level represents the key to new products, which the player can offer. Furthermore, each player can also shop in other players' boutiques. Players also have the opportunity to purchase additional game options at any time (cf. Rusli 2010; Konrad 2013). The core target group for the game are women, who gain practical experience of how to manage a boutique. Self-fulfillment, trend research and social skills are important here. The advantage for partner companies is that they can test out new product lines and present new collections. Furthermore, real experiences are created and emotions generated by the sale of virtual products. This produces positive associations with the brand (cf. Konrad 2013), whose products can be bought immediately. By clicking on a depicted clothing item, the user is redirected through ShopStyle, an international social shopping portal for fashion, to the relevant retailer's website (cf. Sugar Publishing 2010; Konrad 2013). Given that there is the option to shop during the game, Retail Therapy therefore also becomes a marketing channel.

Linking a social game with customer retention programs, e.g. where suppliers load their store cards with virtual game currencies, would be a new factor. Customers could then be given game points for every purchase, regardless of whether online or in stationary format, which would be useful for upgrading their virtual store (cf. Konrad 2013). "Multiscreen gaming" is also innovative. This could be seen in the latest Gamescom games, which run simultaneously on TV, PC monitor, tablet and smartphone (cf. Welt am Sonntag (WAMS) No. 33 dated August 18, 2013, p. 50).

3.2.3 QR Scan Retail and Showrooming

This form of no-line commerce is QR code-based. The virtual store is the most prominent representative of these innovative formats. Furthermore, posters with QR codes are on the increase, enabling immediate purchase of the promoted product.

- **Virtual store:** Tesco opened its first virtual store in South Korea a few months ago, the Tesco Homeplus subway store (cf. Fig. 3.3). In order to make practical use of waiting time in the subway, customers can now shop "on site online" in Seoul using their smartphones, where product photos in original size induce customers to buy on billboards. Buyers only have to scan in the QR code to purchase items online. South Korean media report that over 200,000 people use the virtual shop in Seoul every day. Probably the first best-in-class example comes from South Korea, where adaptation to omni-channel behavior seems well-advanced among consumers and results in relevant no-line formats (cf. ohne tüte 2012, p. 1). Virtual shops or shelf space can also serve as a supplement to the real store, especially if there is a shortage of shelf space.

Fig. 3.3 Tesco's Homeplus subway store (Source: ohne-tüte 2012)

- **Posters with QR codes** combine classic print advertising with a concrete buying option. Customers receive a corresponding marketing component on their mobile device. OBI's 2012 spring campaign uses exactly this concept, by hanging posters with an integrated QR code at bus stops, e.g. on the topic of garden ponds. While customers are waiting for the bus, they have a few minutes to scan the QR code. It is important for companies to offer the customer added value with the code, as in the case of OBI, which offers DIY instructions for the garden pond (cf. ohne tüte 2012, p. 1). Another good example is represented by the virtual fan shops of Hertha BSC. The club is expanding its fan shop offer in the Berlin underground through posters with QR codes at all 400 Berlin subway stations (cf. von Kuhnhardt 2012).
- **Showrooms with QR codes** also constitute a form of QR scan store. As a result of online-related declines in sales volumes, future shop formats will probably get smaller or showrooms will replace current shops. For cost reasons, stores as we presently know them, with an attached warehouse, will probably no longer exist in their current form in the future. Brick-and-mortar shop space will increasingly be converted into pure showrooms, in which the customer then has a touch & feel experience: all products are exhibited, but each one only once. The customer can test, try out and try on at his own discretion. If the customer chooses a product, he or she can buy it directly in the showroom without any problem and without waiting, using his smartphone, for example via a QR code. A new version is then delivered directly to the customer – in the store, at home or at any other location of his choosing. This form of purchase has essentially worked in traditional furniture commerce for a long time, not with a QR code, but with home delivery and relatively long delivery times (cf. eBay 2012a).

3.2 Digital In-store Applications

The customer receives further information through identification of the product by a barcode scanner or relevant object recognition software. This may comprise product information, usage instructions or product ratings by other customers. Moreover, the customer can reserve his product directly with the retailer (cf. Negele 2011). The mobilized store card is another option for optimizing the buying process. The mobile customer can call up such a card using an app and since it can be accessed via the smartphone, it is always at hand. The customer thus regularly calls up the application and acquires information about new offers. The payment process can be simplified and accelerated with mobile applications. By means of a self-checkout app, the customer can already scan in all products, which he or she would later like to buy, while visiting the store. Payment is made directly via the application at the end of the buying process. The customer only has to submit a receipt to the retailer to complete the purchase (cf. ibid.).

3.2.4 AR App Retail and In-store Navigation

Another form of no-line commerce relies on "augmented reality technology". Initially, augmented reality can be employed in-store, for example as a navigation aid. Another usage option combines this technology with print media as a magalog. In both cases, an augmented reality browser implemented in a mobile app is activated.

- **Augmented reality in-store** is founded on smartphone technology, which connects the real environment with virtual elements in real-time. This may also be described as "computerized upgrade of the perception of reality". The use of augmented reality in mobile commerce assumes an integrated camera in the smartphone, which is able to record the environment. This can then be superimposed onto the smartphone display with virtual elements. Virtual elements can be geocoded so that they are available at specific locations. However, such elements may also allow for automatic recognition of objects on the smartphone camera. In the clothing trade, augmented reality is already used for virtual dressing rooms in online shops. The user's body is recorded by a webcam in real-time, meaning that items of clothing can be superimposed or virtually placed on them. Built-in cameras on smartphones also make this technology applicable in the mobile format. Primarily in combination with location-based services, this creates opportunities to address consumers in innovative forms and make them aware of augmented reality in the vicinity, through notifications on the smartphone. One example of the use of augmented reality is provided by Hennes & Mauritz. By means of the augmented reality app GoldRun, customers are also given the option to search for selected virtual items of clothing in New York and then obtain a discount through further interactive actions. The campaign is similar to a treasure hunt and was launched to support the autumn/winter collection in 2010 (cf. Chami 2012, pp. 37 et seqq.). Augmented reality can also be employed directly at the point-of-sale.

Fig. 3.4 Magalog (Source: ohne-tüte 2012)

LEGO, for example, has introduced an innovative form of product presentation using augmented reality. LEGO installed terminals in several toy shops in 2008, allowing customers to assemble and view the still packaged LEGO building sets. All they had to do was to hold the building set package in the camera at the terminal, in order to see the assembled content on the screen. Geocoded information was not used, but rather product recognition via the camera. This type of product presentation can also be used in modified form in brick-and-mortar fashion retailing. In addition to the physical presence and tactile feel of the products (touch & feel), another positive experience factor can be created at the point-of-sale (cf. ibid.).

- **Magalogs** (a combination of the words "magazine" and "catalog") are essentially based on catalogs, which have already been buried as a sales channel by many marketing gurus (cf. Fig. 3.4). However, thanks to augmented reality, it has become possible to use the conventional catalog and the online channel in combination. The latest example is the Dutch magalog from Vtwonen. The company has developed a new version of an old classic, in cooperation with Layar: the magalog is visually attractive due to its magazine and lookbook style and the purchase button is displayed on the smartphone via augmented reality. This is a must-have for all catalog aficionados (cf. ohne tüte 2012, p. 1; Schürmann 2012). Bogner Homeshopping provided evidence quite early on and long before the smartphone that premium products can also be sold through content with high-quality magazines. Bogner Homeshopping (www.bogner-homeshopping.de) represents an outstanding supplement to its own lifestyle stores and retail partner shops. With the goal of content enrichment, a "lifestyle magazine catalog" was published, communicating the latest lifestyle info and providing detailed product descriptions for premium products, which can be ordered "on all channels". In close alignment with the magazine catalog, exclusive offers are also presented in the online lifestyle shop with 3-D animation. For example, Bogner succeeded in positioning women's jackets as a "money-spinner" in the elite premium segment over 8,000 euros and can be regarded as an excellent example of a "lifestyle multi-channel" approach, which has also been successful in terms of business figures.

- **In-store navigation applications** can help customers find their way around in large stores with a large number of diverse products. This may be implemented through RFID chips (radio frequency identification system). In this application, RFID chips are affixed to the product, allowing customers to locate it on the mobile Internet. In addition, customers can retrieve information on product features and availability, which has been stored on the RFID chip (cf. Rio mobile 2010, p. 19). This lets customers browse the entire range in-store and access information on availability and location via the product site (cf. Negele 2011).

The shopping experience can also be enhanced with applications for product interactions, if customers engage more intensively with products as a result.

3.3 New Formats with Digital In-store Applications

The best examples of digital in-store applications can be found in the new offline concepts of the pure plays. Online retailers are increasingly creating brick-and-mortar offline concepts, which, however, can be differentiated. The temporary opening of pop-up stores is popular, as first practiced by eBay Germany in Berlin in the 2012 Christmas season (cf. eBay 2012b). In addition however, permanent flagship store concepts are also being utilized by online retailers, as practiced by Shoepassion or Notebooksbilliger, but without extensive implementation of digital in-store applications. This is currently being done in particular by vertical multi-channel retailers, such as Burberrys, which are joining in the best practices of digital in-store applications. But the most popular form of "online goes offline" could be showrooming, with the Butlers online shop for furniture or "Wohnstücke" ("home items") as best practice. Successful examples of the three "online goes offline" categories are shown below, some of which were collected within the scope of a seminar paper supervised by the author at the Niederrhein University of Applied Sciences (cf. Seidenberg 2013).

3.3.1 Pop-up Stores by Online Retailers

Pop-up stores have enjoyed relatively large popularity in recent years, as they have managed to generate a high number of visitors and large media interest at comparatively low expense and cost. Moreover, they can be used to effectively test new brands and markets (cf. Baumgarth and Kastner 2012, p. 5). Japanese fashion label Comme de Garons opened the first pop-up store in Germany in 2004, with the primary goals of strategic branding and customer retention (cf. Baumgarth and Kastner 2012, p. 5). The focus is on young, urban and open target groups, with an affinity for the Internet, who can also serve as a basis for viral communication. Two additional objectives are pursued in particular, long-term and strategic communication and brand objectives, as well as short-term or operational sales targets. The inspiration and enthusiasm of store visitors can be regarded as long-term communication and brand objectives, which can produce increased involvement and emotional brand loyalty. Furthermore, a pop-up store represents an additional marketing channel, to generate large media interest at relatively low expense. On the operational side, the goal is to temporarily increase turnover through direct sales and the sale of past collections, which are usually discounted. Moreover, future new customers can be approached (cf. Baumgarth and Kastner 2012). By comparison with other commercial forms, such as flagship stores, the pop-up store should be differentiated by its unique nature, scarcity and viral marketing activities (cf. Baumgarth and Kastner 2012, p. 7). But above all, the testing of innovations, concepts, shop formats and locations are important factors in favor of pop-up stores. Well-known examples of the pop-up store concept are the FrontlineShop stores in 2009 and 2011, as well as the Tommy Hilfiger "Prep World Pop-Up-Store-Tournee" in 2011 and the Zalando pop-up store from 2012 (cf. Baumgarth and Kastner 2012; Zalando 2012). The latest example is the eBay showroom, already discussed in detail, from 2012 (cf. eBay 2012a, b). eBay has 18 million users in Germany and – as a platform – cooperates with several brick-and-mortar retailers. In conjunction with PayPal, eBay also wanted to illustrate a piece of the future in the form of the "eBay showroom" (cf. eBay 2012a, b). eBay UK had already opened the first pop-up store in 2011, with the eBay Christmas Boutique in London (cf. eBay UK 2011). The eBay store in Berlin provided the opportunity to purchase exhibited products directly and in mobile form, but only through a smartphone scan app or eBay app. The actual purchase was made on the eBay homepage, when the customer scanned the QR code for the product and was taken directly to the relevant eBay website with the desired product. In addition to this first area, there were some "PayPal innovations" in the form of a coffee shop in the eBay showroom, where payment was made conveniently via the PayPal-QR-Shopping app. Based on other examples, e.g. mStore, smobsh and Emmas Enkel, a demonstration was also provided of how payments can be made conveniently on an app basis in the future. The eBay showroom is presented in Fig. 3.5.

In a third area, there was also a demonstration that used various "future scenarios" to show what payment by PayPal and shopping on eBay could look

Fig. 3.5 eBay showroom (Source: with permission from eBay 2012b)

like in the future. This included scanning articles directly from shop windows, using the eBay app, allowing products to be purchased even after the shop has closed. Moreover, visitors could get advice from professionals on the subject of private selling on eBay and get rid of undesired Christmas presents on site or even offer them for sale. Given that eBay – with its eBay app – is one of the leading mobile commerce retailers, the company sees great potential in linking local, brick-and-mortar retailing and mobile commerce. The Head of eBay in Germany is certain that "it is increasingly becoming vital for retailers to pursue a sophisticated multi-channel strategy [...]. Online should not be understood as another store in the retail business, but rather viewed as a completely new sales channel" (eBay 2012a, b). The eBay showroom could also implement a long-term showrooming concept, which is examined in greater detail below.

3.3.2 Flagship Brick-and-Mortar Stores with Digital In-store Fittings

A flagship store is a "brand's exclusive and unique store in a big city, which manages an extensive range of products" (*Gabler Wirtschaftslexikon* 2013). It is usually a brick-and-mortar flagship store of a company, which is generally situated in a preferential location and specially equipped. There are normally only a small number of flagship stores, or just one such store. Given that flagship stores mainly serve to retain customers and promote the company's image, they may be less profitable or even completely unprofitable (cf. Wikipedia 2012c). As a result, flagship stores are often viewed merely as a marketing tool, without a focus on earnings targets. High rents for top locations are therefore frequently accepted (cf. Ahlert et al. 2009, p. 228). One of the best known flagship stores is the New York branch of Tiffany & Co., which also came to prominence through the film "Breakfast at Tiffanys" (cf. Wikipedia 2013). Other well-known flagship stores include Prada stores, Faber-Castell and Montblanc stores, as well as Nivea Haus in Hamburg, Germany (cf. Nivea 2013; *Gabler Wirtschaftslexikon* 2013). An important aspect of a flagship store is customer experience and customer retention. The crucial factor here is that the customer should feel properly addressed. The brand must come alive. Successful customer interaction plays a large role in this respect. But within the scope of international expansion of premium brands, great importance is often attached to flagship stores. An initial flagship store in a country makes it easy to assess local customer requirements, meaning that a company generally gains insight into the local market (cf. Ahlert et al. 2009, p. 865). The flagship store also serves as an in-house market research tool with a view to new products or services. Technologies, products and services can therefore essentially be tested on customers in the flagship store. For example, fashion provider s. Oliver recently tested the link between the brick-and-mortar store and the mobile commerce channel in its flagship store in Würzburg, Germany. For example, customers can get recommendations for accessories from an electronic style assistant, and purchase relevant products directly in the online shop. Flagship stores may contribute to consolidating a brand, not least through the opportunity to generate important information for the company. This could also be one of the objectives of Burberry, which can be regarded as an outstanding example of a vertical multi-channel retailer for a brick-and-mortar flagship store. Premium provider Burberry is therefore seen as the best practice in the area of the digitalized POS. The new Burberry flagship store, which recently opened on London's High Street, may be regarded as an absolute benchmark for a brick-and-mortar format in the future. The latest technologies of digital in-store applications are integrated into the physical shopping world.

"Walk into Burberry's flagship store in London and you will find a temple dedicated not only to the brand, but also to Digital POS technology" (Syzygy 2013, p. 19). A large number of digital aids are offered to customers, which make shopping easier and help them make better and quicker purchase decisions. Shop personnel are equipped with tablets and other digital tools. Burberry ensures the digital adequacy of the salesroom with today's virtual world. The flagship store concept is not only deemed innovative, but also presents brand values and the DNA of Burberry in the most contemporary way. In this interactive environment, visitors are involved in a unique brand and shopping experience. Burberry views the flagship store as an opportunity to revive the online shop: "seamlessly blurring physical and digital world" (Burberry 2013). The flagship store therefore uses interactive mirrors on the basis of augmented reality. Such mirrors can be converted into personalized screens and provide additional product information if the desired item is held up to the mirror. The digital mirrors also show videos from the production process or deliver personalized recommendations (cf. Pointsmith.com 2013). Sales personnel are equipped with tablet apps, which have access to the customer's buying history and help them make appropriate recommendations. In total, over 100 screens can be found in the Burberry store for product information and fashion shows, which are activated by tags. The store is not only considered technically outstanding, but also a prime example of personal shopping. "This luxury retailer has set the pace for creating a truly interactive and engaging shopping environment" (Pointsmith.com 2013).

3.3.3 Showrooming with Mobile Shopping Option

A showroom usually constitutes an exhibition space in which customers can view a company's latest products or product groups. Products are presented to customers, in order to help potential buyers make a selection. Visitors to the showroom have the opportunity to perceive the feel, quality, form and colors of products with their own senses. This opportunity represents a decisive factor in the buying decision, and accordingly, online pure plays are increasingly opening showrooms. One such example is furniture start-up Fab.com (cf. fab.com 2013). Well-known examples of showrooming are Sitzfeldt's locations in Hamburg and Cologne, Germany (cf. Sitzfeldt 2013) and the showrooms of online furniture retailer Fashion for Home (cf. Fashion for Home 2013). This online shop for designer fittings, which now operates internationally, is founded on a vertical business model. As a result, customers do not need to wait longer for their order than in a traditional furniture store. The online furniture retailer opened a 400 m² "offline" showroom in central Berlin in August 2012, which now offers customers the opportunity to "touch & feel". This includes professional advice, test options, and digitally-supported shopping experiences. The multi-channel strategy is set to be expanded in the future and the business model extended to include an omni-channel strategy. Mobile devices certainly play a leading role here (cf. Fashion for Home 2013). Probably the best current example of showrooming in Germany is demonstrated by multi-channel retailer Butlers. Home accessories supplier Butlers opened its first showroom for furniture in Berlin in July 2013. According to the company, customers can now experience the entire range of the Butlers furniture collection "live and in color" for the first time, in an area spanning around 650 square meters (cf. Der Handel 2013). The furniture range is primarily offered in the online shop or annual catalogue due to limited sales space in stores. Only a few selected items are displayed in the stores, yet furniture is clearly Butlers' fastest-growing product group. Given that the range of furniture is more or less a purely online range, the Butlers showroom can also be cited as an example of "online goes offline". Furniture is placed on stages specially made for the showroom, as in the online shop and catalogue. The web shop should also benefit from the presence of a brick-and-mortar store. Sales personnel in the Berlin showroom will not only offer advice on site, but also provide customers with information on products in the online shop by video chat. Employees are therefore furnished with headsets and cameras, as can be seen in Fig. 3.6. If requested, staff will film the surface of a nearby table or sit on a sofa to try it out for customers. The webcam in the Butlers showroom does not only allow for a 360° view of the item of furniture. Various product functions can also be presented in detail. At the same time, an online demonstration of the product allows for a much "more tactile" product experience than the online shop alone. If requested, the user can also make eye contact with the sales employee using his or her own webcam. Customers in the showroom can test Butlers' "augmented reality app" on the smartphone on site, or later at home, to see whether the items of furniture match each other (cf. Shopanbieter 2013).

Fig. 3.6 Butlers' showroom (Source: With permission from Butlers 2013)

3.3.3.1 Showrooms as New Stand-Alone Formats

Smartphone technology also allows for the development of completely new brick-and-mortar formats, which were previously not feasible. For example, US retailer Hointer designed the first fully-automated fashion stores based on a showroom in which customers are able to shop with their smartphones using the QR scan retail method. The first Hointer store was opened as a jeans store for men in October 2012. At first glance, the shop looks like a completely normal showroom, with one reference piece displayed for each product. Each pair of jeans is furnished with a QR code which can be scanned by customers. This requires visitors to download a mobile app from Hointer in advance, which, however, has only been available for iPhones up to now. After scanning the QR code, the required size and preferred color can be selected. If the customer pushes the "try-on" button, a check is made to determine whether the requested product is in stock. The customer is then told which vacant changing room his jeans will be brought to. In the meantime, the desired product is taken from the fully-automated warehouse by a robot or self-driving cart and placed directly into a box in the reserved changing room. After trying on the jeans, the customer can take them with him, or – if he doesn't like them – put them back in the box, in which they are returned to the warehouse (cf. etailment 2013, Hointer). The Hointer concept highlights a completely new and innovative shopping experience at the POS, which changes established behavioral patterns. The customer has the opportunity to shop quickly and autonomously and at a lower price than in a store with service personnel (cf. Hointer 2013). This is made possible through smartphone technology in combination with showrooming.

The concept leaves room for further developments, particularly in combination with social commerce. In order to improve customer service at the POS, other applications are conceivable as well. For example, an app linked with all feasible social media functions could be used to share images of products with friends and ask them for advice. Customized data could also be transferred to the retailer, which would be instrumental in decision-making. US fashion retailer Neiman Marcus, which uses apps to enhance sales, already operates in a similar way.

3.3.4 Renovation of Existing Formats with In-store Apps

US fashion provider Neiman Marcus has developed an "in-store app" with a social media application to support its sales team. This is not so much a matter of integrating social media elements into shop fittings as developing an iPhone app to be used by staff and referred to as NM service. The app, which is based on localization of customers, provides sales personnel with information on customer preferences. Localized customers have to download a customer app and can choose between two options. First, there is an option for sales staff to be informed when the customer enters the shop. Second, there are variants in which the customer actively enters a check-in if he or she wants to receive advice in person. In this case, the sales adviser is informed of the customer's interests and inclinations, shares and likes, as well as his or her purchasing history.

3.4 Relevance to Situational and Real Environment as a Success Factor

Fig. 3.7 Neiman Marcus mobile app (Source: Based on Schürmann 2012)

The customer's social graph is made available directly at the POS. This makes the question of which staff are available, or can be reserved for a sales consultation in the near future, transparent to the customer. Moreover, by means of QR codes, customers can access special product information and obtain information on trends or new products. At the same time such information is also made available to sales personnel, who can then make customer-specific recommendations and give customized advice. This example shows how brick-and-mortar retailers in particular can use the SoLoMo approach as a profiling option. The Neiman Marcus mobile app is shown in Fig. 3.7 (cf. Mashable.com 2013).

3.4 Relevance to Situational and Real Environment as a Success Factor

Situational adequacy is critical to success in social mobile marketing. This involves correctly recording all significant features of a user's situation and implementing them in situation-related offers. The success of such offers then depends on the economic potential of the situation, which has to be assessed. Based on the assessed potential of the situation, the mobile shop can be customized and used to offer context-sensitive services and location-based services.

3.4.1 Situational Adequacy and Potential in Mobile Marketing

The mobile Internet allows the individual customer's specific situation to be addressed. This goes beyond the mobile one-to-one approach, which – as a direct marketing approach – merely allows consideration of the special characteristics of the individual customer. The situation is characterized by a different macro- and

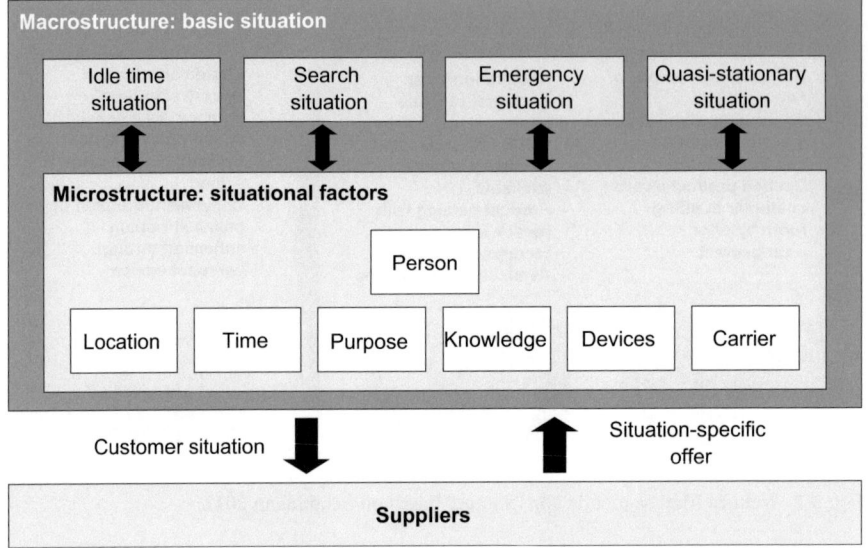

Fig. 3.8 Classification of situations (Source: Link and Seidl 2008, p. 54)

microstructure in each case. Whereas the macrostructure assesses the idle time, search, emergency and quasi-stationary situations, the microstructure – in the sense of localization – refers to current whereabouts and time. Both factors determine situational adequacy, which is added to the usual direct marketing measures for customer adequacy (i.e. meeting the needs and requirements of customers) (cf. Link and Seidl 2008, p. 52). The correlations between the macro- and microstructure of situations are explained in Fig. 3.8.

3.4.1.1 Macrostructure of Situations

The macrostructure identifies the basic situation. This is characterized by the fact that communication and transaction can exclusively take place for the customer via a mobile channel and features the following situation types (cf. ibid., pp. 54 et seqq.):

- In this regard, the **idle time situation** refers to unproductive times during transport. Essentially these result in opportunity costs within the context of lost enjoyment from leisure activities. The use of cellphones allows such idle periods to be used productively, e.g. for phone calls, information or entertainment (mobile entertainment). All types of transactions that are usually possible over the Internet, can also be completed during a trip with mobile devices, e.g. mobile shopping.
- The **search situation** describes a situation-dependent information or service requirement, which leads to the user conducting a search with the use of electronic aids. Typical examples are navigational functions, local information

services, or price comparisons in a defined distance from the user's whereabouts. Determining geographical position plays a key role here.
- The **emergency situation** represents an unplanned and involuntary requirement for information and services, which is automatically reported via the user's pushbutton system or the evaluation of measurement data. Examples include assaults, medical emergencies, break-ins, theft, car accidents, breakdowns and other emergency situations.
- The **quasi-stationary situation** describes a special circumstance in which two options for Internet access are available to customers, i.e. mobile or stationary access. The user's choice depends on specific context variables, such as person, product and situation characteristics (e.g. time pressure and/or convenience).

3.4.1.2 Microstructure of Situations

The microstructure identifies relevant individual situational factors within the specific basic situation (cf. Kriewald 2007, pp. 10 et seqq.). Such factors are considered if the mobile commerce provider approaches the customer with an individualized and situation-based offer. An expanded customization concept is utilized here, which in addition to the person, also includes the location, time, purpose, knowledge, devices and carriers (cf. Link and Seidl 2008, pp. 58 et seqq.) (Fig. 3.9):

- The **person** certainly has special importance as a situational factor. First, sociodemographic features are relevant, such as gender, age, occupation,

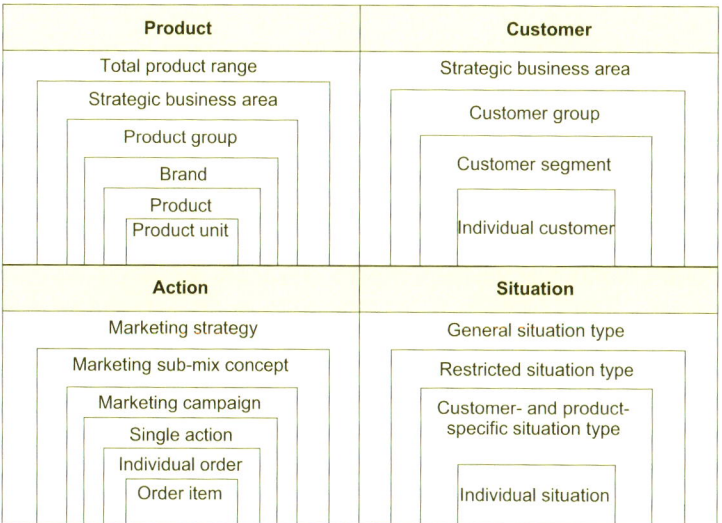

Fig. 3.9 Reference object hierarchies in situational marketing statement (Source: Link and Seidl 2008, p. 65)

household size and marital status. Psychographic criteria are also important in the context of preferences and personality profile.
- **Location** describes the local situation of the person and can refer to the static place of residence as well as the dynamic whereabouts. The dynamic location allows the consumer relationship with stores to be established through the geographical proximity of a customer and lets the store use this information to satisfy the customer's requirements.
- **Time** may refer to a date, timeframe or season, and allows the time context of the mobile user to be determined and an action context derived for marketing policy measures.
- The **purpose** defines the intent of an action emanating from the customer, and may involve destinations/goals, occasions or causes.
- **Knowledge** or prior knowledge is relevant to problem-solving options. The less knowledge that exists, the more auxiliary services must be provided.
- The user's **device** generates the usage requirements and configuration for offers. Technological compatibilities, bandwidths and network conditions are partly decisive for the situation-specific offer.
- The **carrier** describes the vehicle, which produces different requirements. Whereas a car driver is interested in traffic information, flight schedules are more relevant to airline passengers.

The interaction of all situational factors determines the customer situation and enables the compilation of situation-specific offers. A large number of individual profiles can be collected over the period of a customer relationship, eventually yielding a meaningful overall profile. When creating profiles, consideration should be given to data privacy factors, of course (cf. ibid., p. 61).

3.4.1.3 Situation Potential in Mobile Marketing

Correct evaluation of the situation is determined via the marketing statement. The risk of incorrect decisions is reduced with the greater level of precision with which the real structure of the decision-making situation and potential courses of action are presented. This may be described as mapping accuracy, where all decision-relevant parameters are included in the decision-making model. Parameters subject to attribution factors may relate to objects which are the subject of operational decisions, i.e. reference objects. Reference objects, in the conventional sense, may be service bundles (e.g. products, brands, orders), service recipients (e.g. customers, markets, regions), service providers (e.g. staff, departments, systems, sales channels) or actions (individual measures, campaigns, strategies) (cf. Link and Seidl 2008, p. 64).

The potential of a situation is calculated based on reference object hierarchies. A situational statement is drawn up with the focus on the situation as a new reference object (cf. Link and Seidl 2008, p. 66; Link and Weiser 2006, p. 214). This statement reveals the overall earnings potential associated with a specific situation and might consist of the following components:

3.4 Relevance to Situational and Real Environment as a Success Factor

	1 product	Several / all products
1 customer	**Concrete customer- and product-specific individual situation** (e.g. passenger XY with a specific catering need), concrete location, time, carrier	**Restricted customer-specific situation type** (e.g. passenger XY with specific catering, accommodation, entertainment and wellness needs), typical location, time, carrier
Several / all customers	**Restricted product-specific situation type** (e.g. average passenger with catering need)	**General situation type** (e.g. average passenger with catering, accommodation, entertainment and wellness needs)

Fig. 3.10 Levels of situational statements (Source: Link and Seidl 2008, p. 65)

1. The revenue potential of an individual customer for an individual product group, minus costs.
2. Cross-selling revenue potential of this customer with regard to other product groups, minus costs.
3. Revenue potential of other customers who are likely to be in the same situation, minus costs.
4. Cross-selling potential of other customers who are likely to be in the same situation, minus costs.

The different levels of the situational statement are shown in Fig. 3.10 and described based on the example of a trip (cf. Link and Weiser 2006, p. 214).

Situational statements may become particularly interesting in mobile commerce if situations such as trips are typical mobile situations. Two variants are feasible. In addition to calculating the earnings potential for different types of travel situations, in which customer-specific offers can be relayed on a display, the earnings potential could also be recalculated, with the inclusion of customized information. The example shown in Fig. 3.10 is also relevant to basic earnings potential of tourism customers outside of mobile commerce. Such situational statements may be drafted either as short-term (operational) and accrued, or long-term (strategic) for longer periods (cf. Kriewald 2007, pp. 10 et seqq.; Link and Seidl 2008, p. 68).

3.4.2 Situation-Oriented CRM

The mobile commerce channel represents just one of many potential customer touchpoints. However, particularly with regard to customization, omnipresence and multimedia processes, mobile commerce offers outstanding opportunities to establish competitive advantages. This is illustrated by placing two central aspects of mobile commerce, i.e. the mobile channel and situational relevance of marketing

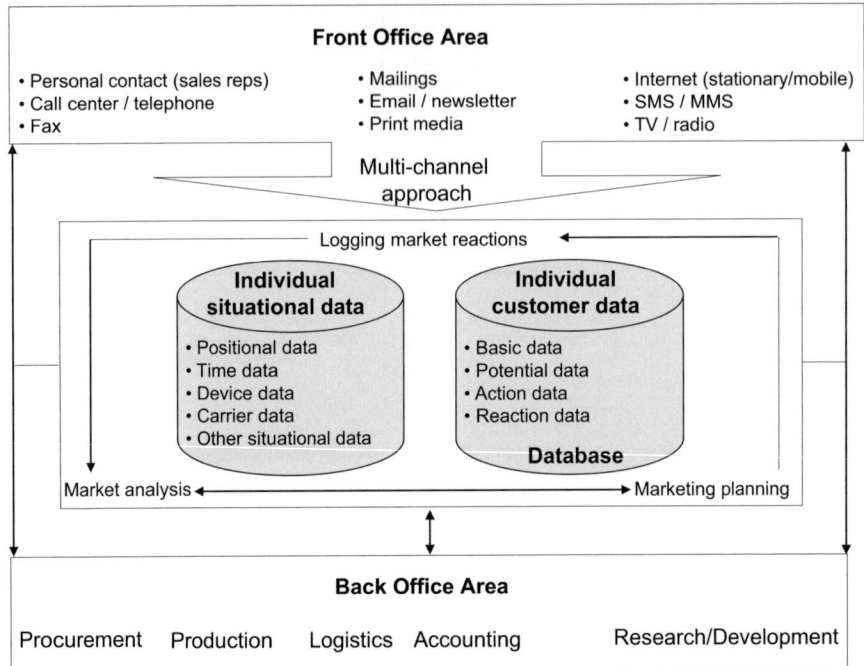

Fig. 3.11 Integrated situation-oriented CRM system (Source: Link and Seidl 2008, p. 62.)

measures, in an overall context (cf. Link and Seidl 2008, p. 61; Link and Weiser 2006, p. 90). An integrated situation-oriented customer relationship management system is depicted in Fig. 3.11. This takes account of the fact that companies require more and more precise and detailed customer and situation profiles, but on the other hand, as in the case of "one face to the customer", all marketing-based measures must increasingly be coordinated. This approach primarily relates to front-office operations as an interface to the customer (cf. Heinemann 2011a, p. 145). "Forward together and backward apart" is the prevalent conclusion among retail experts. Multi-channel therefore requires consistent behavior towards customers in all "front-office" functions, in order to avoid uncertainty on the customer side, but separate management in the back office, in order to account for different skills requirements. As a result, channels should be managed compatibly, but separately. Separate management must be implemented uniformly, to guarantee maximum realization of potential back-office synergies between channels. Incentive and management systems should be ensured with separate responsibility for the performance of channels, to prevent them working against one another (no "channel selfishness"). Customer relationship management and associated customer data management should in particular be "jointly" managed, i.e. across channels (cf. ibid.). The alarmingly widespread phenomenon among many multi-channel companies is prevented by collecting identical or similar information on customers (e.g. demography of users) in different channels.

3.4 Relevance to Situational and Real Environment as a Success Factor

Otherwise, the consequence is huge redundancy of customer data, the reconciliation of which involves immense system complexity. But customer requirements also require systematic integration of customer data, because – when channel hopping within one buying process or between different buying processes – consumers expect the contact person at the company (e.g. call center, brick-and-mortar store, delivery agent, etc.) to be "up-to-date". Only the integrative design of all customer touchpoints makes it possible for customers to contact the company on any channel of their choosing, at any time. The multi-channel retailer should ideally be capable of restarting dialogue with the customer exactly where they left off (cf. Link and Seidl 2008, p. 62). The entire content of all discussions should be stored on a situational database during and after contact and essentially be available at the push of a button. Any submitted information should be available to each contact point or included in customer communications (cf. Wegener 2004, p. 216).

Customer Interaction Centers (CIC), which have increased greatly in importance in recent years within the scope of multi-channel strategies, have proven useful. They represent an enhanced version of conventional call centers, which coordinate and combine telephony and additional media, such as fax, SMS, Internet and email, in one organizational unit, for the customer (cf. Kantsperger and Meyer 2006, p. 26). Given that all informational, consulting, buying and post-buying processes in B2C distance retailing usually now operate with media support, customer interaction centers are particularly important, especially in multi-channel commerce. However, all communications channels should be coordinated and harmonized. Customer requirements must be identified early in order to be able to proactively present appropriate offers. Moreover, contact persons should be able to access the entire customer history, so that employees are therefore aware of whether customers have already written several letters or emails on the matter (cf. Kantsperger and Meyer 2006, p. 26).

In many cases, the implementation of a multimedia interaction center is a logical response to changed customer requirements, since, as already stated, customers increasingly want to make their own decisions on when and through which channel to contact their multi-channel retailer. In addition to goals related to effectiveness, interaction centers should increasingly be measured against efficiency-related benchmarks, with the priority being on relevant costs and customer value. In addition, CICs are more often being managed as profit centers rather than cost centers, as was formerly the case with call centers. Moreover, an efficiency-driven trend towards outsourcing to external service providers can be observed, but this should be examined critically in terms of image and customer satisfaction aspects.

A prerequisite for situation-oriented mCRM and the functioning of a CIC is the existence of a customer database and a – supplementary – situational database. Both represent central integration platforms for all customer-oriented information systems and all other customer touchpoints in the front-office area (cf. Link and Seidl 2008, p. 62).

In respect of individual customer data stored in the database, a distinction should be made between basic, potential, action and reaction data, which are continually recorded and stored in the form of customer and situation profiles. These data form the basis for mobile marketing measures, e.g. in the form of personalized and situation-specific offers, through push mechanisms. In any case, all files in both databases should be capable of being combined at any time. Additional linking with action and reaction data allows certain success patterns to be deduced.

3.4.3 Context-Sensitive Services and Localization Functions

Customer relationships can also be improved through the provision of useful services (cf. Silberer and Schulz 2008, p. 154). Suppliers' external sales staff can be provided with useful services through mobile communications, providing the opportunity to communicate with the customer in person while he or she is on the move. Such services relate to possible measures for "mobile CRM", including optimized knowledge about customers through analytical mCRM. With regard to situation-oriented CRM, as outlined in the previous chapter, context-sensitive offers are primarily useful in the form of communications services, information offers, navigational aids, tracking services, entertainment offers and transaction services (as an order or buying option). A service may be regarded as context-sensitive if it allows for information on whereabouts in the context of the user (cf. Silberer and Schulz 2008, p. 154; Kaspar et al. 2007).

Examples of mobile and context-sensitive services are depicted in Fig. 3.12. Reference is made here to possible starting points for marketing events, approaches to regional and marketing activities, and operational and usage options for the automotive industry and external sales force. With regard to the examples presented here, two aspects will be covered in greater depth below, i.e. "local-based content distribution via Bluetooth" and "mobile information and multimedia delivery via GSM and UMTS" (cf. Silberer and Schulz 2008, p. 154).

3.4.3.1 Local-Based Content Distribution via Bluetooth

Information and entertainment services are increasingly utilizing Bluetooth technology. For example, British company Qwikker, regarded as the market leader in this area, uses the fixed-location network, which transmits mobile services to devices via Bluetooth. However, a client must have been installed on the cellphone in advance, in the form of Java application software. Such software, in addition to access to contents via Bluetooth, also enables access to GSM and UMTS networks. Qwikker has more than 1,000 Bluetooth distribution stations, called "content distribution points", in the USA and Europe (cf. ibid., p. 155).

3.4.3.2 Mobile Information and Multimedia Delivery via GSM and UMTS

Users can access WAP content and mobile services within GSM or UMTS mobile communication networks through browser software at any time. USA-based ShoZU lets users enter content they are interested in into profiles, following installation of client software onto the device. The need to open the browser as well as waiting times for connections are therefore omitted. Furthermore, preferred contents are

	Event marketing	Regional and city marketing	Mobile context	Mobile connection
Tracking services	Geo-location at events	Geo-location on city sightseeing tours	Geo-location of vehicles	Geo-location of staff
Navigation services	Route to the event (e.g. stadium)	Routing on city sightseeing tours	Route to the nearest service station	Route to nearest customer
Information services	Information about artists	Information about places of interest	Traffic information	Information on order processing status
Communication services	Chat between user groups	Mobile contact to city information	Contact to technical support	Coordination between employees
Entertainment	Distribution of video clips	Mobile city quiz game	Offer of interactive game	Provision of latest advertising clips
Transaction services	Purchase of ring tones	Overview, selection, execution	City information for a fee	Mobile order acceptance

Fig. 3.12 Examples of context-sensitive services (Source: Silberer and Schulz 2008, p. 155)

constantly updated and made available. Given that this requires a permanent mobile connection, a flat rate is definitely recommended (cf. ibid., p. 156).

3.4.3.3 Localization Functions

Localization functions form a central pillar of location-based services (LBS), since they are mobile services which access location-based and situation-based data. These functions are of key importance, in particular within the scope of situational adequacy of mobile commerce offers, and require localization of the mobile Internet user. Different methods can be used in this regard, and are divided into "network-based procedures" and mobile subscriber-based methods. In the network-based approach, relevant data are measured to determine the position of the mobile network. This has the advantage of enabling rapid market penetration for providing LBS provision, since geo-location is feasible on existing devices, including older generations. However, the downside is a certain lack of precision. The use of mobile subscriber-based ("MT-based") procedures is therefore indispensable if it becomes necessary to determine exact positions. Such a procedure requires new-generation smartphones, or at least alterations to existing cellphones, which is relatively cost-intensive (cf. Logara 2008, p. 81). The following applications are already currently possible (cf. ibid.):

- Localization of persons, objects or locations at exact times.
- Search for positions in the vicinity, such as shops or restaurants.
- Routing or directions.
- Information on the traffic situation during localization (e.g. congestion).
- Advertising and incentives for visits to specific locations.

The key here is combining the social, local and mobile net, and this also has a great impact on existing commercial structures, since the mobile Internet is increasingly becoming a disruptive technology, which redefines overall commerce and significantly fuels the trend towards no-line systems (cf. Heinemann 2013a).

3.4.4 Bargaining and Couponing

Situation-based offers produce various ideas for bargaining approaches, which can be provided for "normal business operations and product range". The following business model innovations place the emphasis on best price in business policy and deliver inputs for corresponding bargaining ideas in mobile commerce (cf. Wieschowski 2008, p. 47; FAZ 2008, No. 156, p. 19):

- **Live shopping – just one product and one price:** "One day, one product, one aggressive price" sums up the business model of live shops, such as "guut.de". With a manageable product range, and sometimes just one single product at competitive prices (e.g. bright red slides), live shops are increasingly competing with conventional Internet stores.
- **Club sale – shopping only after registration and logon:** Only customers who have previously registered and logged on, or been invited to do so by other club members, are allowed to shop in club sales. High price reductions on attractive goods are at the forefront of the concept, with the focus of the offer on brands, fashion and lifestyle products (e.g. Diesel, Swatch, Dolce & Gabbana, Armani or Converse). Five promotional actions a week, which club members are notified about by email, are common and usually run for 1 or 2 days.
- **Shopping exchange – buy if the price is right:** The Gimahhot business model functions similarly to the Frankfurt Stock Exchange. Buyers and sellers suggest desired prices for a certain product (e.g. iPodNano or the latest Motorola cellphone) on shopping exchanges. To start with, the retailer enters its product at a specific price, while all product suppliers are listed in a table. Once the customer has entered his or her desired price, the negotiation begins, with all retailers receiving the price proposal and having several days to decide whether to sell the product at the desired price. If they agree to do so, the customer will be notified by email of retailers which are willing to sell. However, the transaction is exclusively conducted via Gimahhot.
- **Flea market – handicraft instead of bulk goods:** In contrast to conventional flea markets, small companies that focus on handicrafts now offer their products on Internet platforms, such as Dawanda. Bulk goods are not offered, but rather

"products with love", i.e. handmade, unique items or limited editions from small manufacturers. Roughly 15,000 manufacturers with over 200,000 products at Dawanda also provide an insight into their work and exchange information with colleagues and customers. Such transitions to cooperating and verticalized online commerce are fluent.

- **New auction form – eBay for gamblers:** Telebild.de has recently started offering a combination of auction, gambling and bargain hunting. Each bid costs 50 cents and increases the price by 10 cents. The winner is the last bidder. The winner can grab a bargain, with technology products primarily being auctioned (e.g. cellphones, computers, game consoles, household appliances, cars and even cash vouchers). By comparison with the shop price, winners save 65 % on average. But there is always only one winner, while all other bidders are losers and still have to pay for their bids. Nevertheless, in the three countries where Sofina GmbH operates Telebild – Germany, Great Britain and Spain – 3,000 new users register every day. Goods with a total value of well over 30,000 euros are sold every day.

In addition to these new "best-price" business ideas, couponing is another price tool, which can easily generate a bargain and is outstandingly suited to mobile commerce. In particular in multi-channel systems, couponing can be used to fuel brick-and-mortar sales channels via mobile offers, which can be converted in stores. But conversely, it is also feasible for a couponing promotional campaign in the brick-and-mortar store to support the online channel. For example, the customer may be given a voucher – following in-store consultation – allowing for a reduction of the mobile commerce or online price within a limited time frame. However, this should be linked with additional product policy or service-based measures. Inputting the voucher code could result directly in the item relevant to the buyer being displayed. If an item is unavailable, there is also the option for the customer to order the required item himself on the Internet, having been invited to do so through a personalized email. Conversely, following an Internet search, the customer could be offered a voucher for a discount on an offline purchase. It is important that such vouchers are only valid for a limited time, which should be very short. Vouchers should primarily reach price-sensitive customers. The customer's previous search behavior on the mobile net could shed light on this matter (cf. Schleusener 2012).

Couponing is also increasingly used by mobile commerce providers, because it is capable of being measured, protects shelf prices and boosts marketing and sales. Furthermore, tracking may provide information on who has viewed which coupon when, who requested it, and who redeemed it at which point of sale (cf. Hermes 2010, p. 86). Couponing is still much more widespread in the USA than in Germany, given that 87 % of US consumers use coupons. Five billion coupons a year are redeemed in the USA and at least 8 % of advertising budgets in the USA are spent on couponing (cf. Heinemann 2008, p. 65). A similar trend is becoming increasingly apparent in Germany. One in two consumers is willing to use coupons. The repurchase rate among those who redeem vouchers is already 64 % and sales volume in relation to coupons is 30–60 % higher than prices for special offers. Sectors in which customers use coupons are food (64 %), CD/DVDs (59 %), refueling (45 %) and clothing (44 %). Individualized couponing and emails are regarded as an ideal route to the customer.

Tchibo and Bonusnet can be cited as examples of couponing being practiced in Germany. Tchibo combines couponing with the "Privat-Programm" club approach, whereby customers receive 4 coupons worth 3 euros each, which can be redeemed per quarter, for an annual fee of 10 euros. This is accompanied by a monthly "Privat-Magazin", which provides private customers with early information about offers. Moreover, there are additional coupons for coffee and TCM products, exclusive events, special discounts, contests and travel offers. The fundamental approach of Bonusnet, on the other hand, is a discount club on the Internet, in which customers are essentially given the opportunity – for a monthly fee of 5 euros – to shop at 350 online partners at discount rates and receive rebates by bank transfer (e.g. 30 % of fixed-network calls). In addition, they are given monthly coupons worth up to 100 euros. On the whole, customers are increasingly seen as receptive to such offers. 67 % of consumers are interested in coupon promotions via mobile phone (cf. Schleusener 2012, p. 176). The fashion industry is also deemed relevant in this context. Above all, linking between channels is almost natural for consumers when they name the Internet and email newsletters as the most important touchpoints for acquiring coupons (cf. ibid.).

3.5 Dynamic Pricing and E-Payment with Local Relevance

Price is extremely important in relation to location-based services. But this does not mean having to put a squeeze on every price in the mobile channel. Rather, it is a question of employing channel-specific mobile commerce price tools in such a way that all channels benefit and that the specific characteristics of the mobile price world are also taken into account. This partly relates to bargaining and couponing, but also to virtual coupons and virtual bonus cards. In the future, this will be connected more frequently with mobile e-payment methods.

3.5.1 Special Characteristics of Dynamic Pricing with Local Relevance

Compared with the offline price world, the pricing policy in mobile commerce looks completely different. As in online commerce, the competition's offers are only a click away (cf. Kollmann 2009). Transaction costs are low if customers switch providers. A large number of search engines (agents) help to find the provider with the lowest price, such as Google Shopping (cf. Simon and Fassnacht 2009; Schleusener 2012, p. 165). Search costs are thereby kept low for the customer and aggressive price behavior is induced on the supplier side. However, with regard to price comparison in mobile commerce, a distinction is made between brands and

3.5 Dynamic Pricing and E-Payment with Local Relevance

private labels in retailing, which are difficult to compare. On the other hand, generic products can easily be compared. Inevitably, this results in a price squeeze, which should be consolidated on a low level due to greater market transparency. Nevertheless, large price heterogeneity can also be identified in the online channel, which may be attributed to differentiation of mobile shops in terms of their recognition, brand and other services (cf. Clement and Schreiber 2010; Schleusener 2012, pp. 165 et seqq.). In respect of price changes, the prevailing dynamic is much greater in mobile commerce, and could even be higher than in "normal" online commerce because price changes can be implemented very quickly and at very low marginal cost, or "menu costs" (cf. Clement and Schreiber 2010, p. 95). These produce much quicker responses on the customer side due to the mobility and permanent availability of devices and, moreover, to price comparisons in brick-and-mortar stores as well. This results in frequent and sometimes very small price changes. A mobile commerce provider is therefore able to respond much more quickly to competitors and fluctuations in demand than is the case for offline and "normal online". Amazon has led the way here, ahead of Media Markt, for photography and electronics. Amazon decreased prices for selected items during exactly the same period in which certain special offer prices were in effect at Media Markt. Immediately after the end of Media Markt sales promotions, prices were increased again. This is unimaginable in brick-and-mortar retailing, where costs and duration are particularly relevant to any new markup (cf. Schleusener 2012, p. 168).

Price reductions are not only used in isolation in mobile commerce, but also in combination with other parameters. Shopping clubs like Brands4Friends or Vente Priveé, for example, operate through an artificial shortage of goods at significantly reduced prices for highly emotional brands, thereby creating a great desire and willingness to buy (cf. Heitmeier and Naveenthirarajah 2010; Schleusener 2012). Ultimately, customers then purchase regardless of actual need, allowing providers to earn a quantity bonus. The available technical capabilities have led to the development of a large number of new and sometimes interactive forms of pricing in Internet and mobile commerce (cf. Clement and Schreiber 2010; Schleusener 2012, p. 168). Reference should be made to variants of customer-controlled pricing, such as power shopping, auctions and reverse auctions, which, as interactive forms of pricing, can hardly be coordinated with fixed, brick-and-mortar prices. If retailers employ several such formats in parallel alongside the mobile channel, pricing requirements will increase further (cf. ibid.). The special features of mobile pricing in comparison with offline pricing are depicted in Fig. 3.13. By virtue of such special features, the best price is regarded as an absolute success factor in mobile commerce. A killer price can also be procured through one-off bargain offers, like those made by club shops for a limited period of between 1 and 3 days. Such bargain prices represent an example of bargaining, which includes couponing.

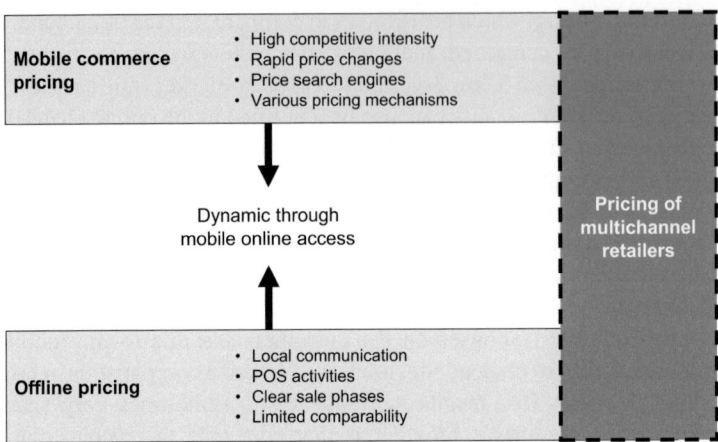

Fig. 3.13 Special characteristics of mobile commerce pricing (Source: based on Schleusener 2012, p. 169)

3.5.2 Virtual Coupons and Bonus Cards

Programs which deliver rebate vouchers to the customer by mobile phone or smartphone pursue a different approach as compared to couponing. This is increasingly being practiced by large rebate systems, such as Payback. But individual retailers like Netto Marken-Discount also do the same. Such offers become especially interesting in mobile commerce when implemented based on location, e.g. Placecast's ShopAlerts (www.placecast.net). Customers are given individual, customized offers here, regardless of their location. This naturally requires localization of relevant users, as with the following location-based service: users find a product online during a search on the mobile Internet. They are subsequently notified of nearby stores, and can submit a price proposal to them (for example MAKEaDEAL, at www.spreezio.com).

Online and offline channels are therefore ideally linked. In addition to virtual coupons, which can easily be used to fuel offline channels, there is also an opportunity to employ virtual bonus systems. The customer can already acquire bonus points just by entering shops or scanning barcodes on articles (www.checkpoints.com). In particular, as far as a multi-channel retailer is concerned, it is conceivable for virtual bonus points to be collected from brick-and-mortar or mobile commerce ("earn") and then exchanged in the other channel ("spend"). Consideration could also be given to providing selected customers with access to rebates before other consumers, which would have been granted a few days later in any case. This makes it possible to promote seasonal sales (preference for the reduced-price phase). In respect of virtual vouchers, overall, it should be noted that the period leading up to possible encashment could be too long and under certain circumstances, the channel-linking function of this instrument may be lost. Such a risk arises in particular in the case of regular low rebates. Moreover, it should be borne in mind that price reductions for linking different channels are relatively expensive in terms of profit margin. Potential substitution effects should also be assessed as accurately as possible. A strict time limit on such promotional actions may be helpful in this respect. The abundance of reduced phases, however, offers many opportunities to implement creative and comparatively favorable linking options (cf. Schleusener 2012, pp. 176 et seqq.).

3.5.3 Mobile E-Payment in Brick-and-Mortar Retailing

With regard to the "best price and bargaining" success factor, it is very important for the payment transaction to function smoothly and securely via the mobile channel. Someday, NFC will no doubt allow for mobile payment and mobile ticketing. This would certainly simplify the payment process considerably, given that NFC means it is sufficient to hold the cellphone at the point-of-sale terminal's touchpoint for internal authentication and authorization of the payment process. Furthermore, it would allow the short range to ensure a clear classification of application and user, and simultaneously offer inherent protection against operating errors or manipulation.

Nevertheless, mobile commerce providers should be clear about the fact that NFC technology is still in its infancy, and Deutsche Bahn (German Railways) is only launching NFC as a test on November 1, 2011, and therefore a breakthrough or wide-ranging penetration of NFC is not expected before 2015. Sweden, for example, has set itself the goal of definitively eliminating cash by 2018 or 2020. From the state's perspective, this also has the advantage of making illicit earnings and money laundering practically impossible. Whereas Sweden and Finland are clearly playing a pioneering role here, other countries, such as Italy or Portugal, will take significantly longer (cf. Internet World Business 2011d, f, No. 13/11, p. 12).

iPhone and iPad apps have recently been offered, which are intended to replace credit card terminals for brick-and-mortar retailers or suppliers. Such an app is available from payment service provider "Ogone" under the name "m-Terminal", and from competitor "ConCardis", called the "ePayment App". Both offers are aimed at companies that account for location-dependent card payments, such as craftsmen, taxi companies and delivery services. Employees start up the app, enter the card data, confirm the transaction with a personal PIN and complete the payment process following authorization (cf. Internet World Business 2011a, d, No. 6/11, p. 36)

Established online retailers usually provide different payment methods in their mobile commerce channel, as requested by Internet customers. According to the latest ECC study, around 20 % of customers prefer purchase on account over payment by direct debit, at 17.4 %. This is followed by PayPal (16.1 %), cash in advance (14.3 %) and credit card, at 11.7 % (cf. ECC 2011; Siebers 2011, pp. 1–2). In order to avoid risk, various types of risk assessments are offered by service providers in order to identify and prevent potential reasons for payment difficulties or non-payment. At-risk customers can then be offered secure payment methods, such as cash in advance, in order to control the payment method used. In the event of positive results arising from such controls, however, additional payment options can then be offered (cf. Internet World Business 2011b, d, No. 9/11, p. 26).

Money is credited, almost in real-time, for the Giropay, Firstgate or Paypal payment methods, and the product is thereby paid for and can be sent directly. Such payment systems are secure, fast and trustworthy from the customer's perspective. Google is also developing its own payment systems ("One Pass") and, like Amazon ("Simple Pay"), is now competing with eBay subsidiary PayPal. However, it is not yet clear which players will dominate the payment market in future. Various initiatives are centered on the virtual wallet. There are three conceivable scenarios in this regard (cf. Internet World Business 2011d, f, No. 13/11, p. 12; Internet World Business 2011g, No. 15, p. 36).

- **Scenario 1:** The large US Internet companies, such as Amazon, Apple, Google and eBay/Paypal prevail. On the US market, Google is pushing the issue strongly as the preferred mobile payment platform for Android phone users, e.g. with "Google Wallet". Payment network partners in this Google initiative are Citi, Mastercard, First Data and Sprint.
- **Scenario 2:** Telecommunication companies penetrate the market through their payment systems. Isis is a mobile initiative from AT&T, Verizon Wireless and T-Mobile, and has Discover, Mastercard and Visa on board as network partners.
- **Scenario 3:** The banking industry manages to hold its ground, as represented in two initiatives. "Serve" exclusively addresses American Express (Amex) customers, while Visa should be open to various payment providers through the "Visa Wallet". Accordingly, 14 other banks and financial service providers should be affiliated partners of the initiative. Increasingly however, market participants which do not include mobile phone providers are starting to dominate (cf. Internet World Business 2011a, No. 6, p. 36).

Whichever scenario prevails, the time is ripe for mobile payment: more than half of Germans are interested in payment by cellphone. As GfK Customer Research identified in a global study (cf. Internet World Business 2011d No. 11, p. 28), 62 % of the 8,700 respondents find mobile payment appealing. Whereas Germany is slightly below average at 56 %, China, at 82 %, and Brazil, at 73 %, hold the top places. At 72 %, Spain also ranks high, while France only comes in at 42 % (cf. ibid.).

Out of all respondents, younger men seem particularly receptive to the issue. While only around one in four smartphone owners presently use their device for shopping, most purchases – around 45 % – are still settled in traditional fashion by credit card or invoice (cf. Fig. 3.14). However, 38 % of mobile buyers already indicate that they have paid for their purchases through mobile payment providers, such as Paypal or Sofortüberweisung.de (cf. Internet World Business 2011d, g, No. 11/11, p. 28).

3.5 Dynamic Pricing and E-Payment with Local Relevance

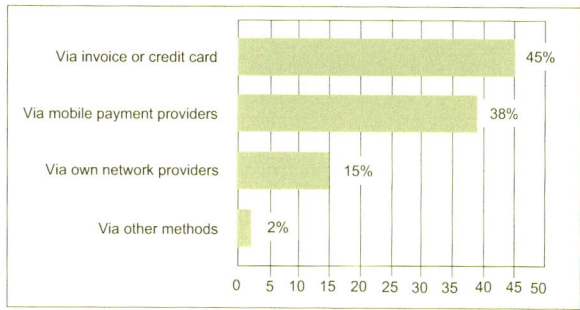

Fig. 3.14 Payments in mobile commerce (Source: Siebers 2011; Internet World Business 2011d No. 11/11, p. 28)

Mobile payment involves the digital wallet and, in addition to the payment method, includes store cards, business cards, invoices, insurance cards, IDs, subway tickets, other tickets, etc. (cf. Internet World Business 2011d No. 15/11, p. 36).

- **Payment method:** This core function of the digital wallet will essentially have a decisive influence on the success of a solution and must be capable of prevailing over established alternatives, such as EC and credit cards. NFC technology is seen as the most promising candidate here.
- **Financial services:** Intelligent applications are also conceivable with regard to private financial management, with recommendations for financial providers depending on the current financial situation of the mobile phone owner.
- **Coupons:** Voucher and check-in services, such as Groupon.com or Foursquare.com, can secure access to incentives and rebates for the user.
- **Price comparison services:** The user can save money and the retailer has a mobile marketing platform. Barcode readers help in the price comparison between providers and between sales channels.
- **Tickets and IDs:** The barcode ticket systems of Deutsche Bahn and airlines Lufthansa and Air Berlin are currently being tested with NFC tickets and show great potential.

Mobile e-payment is not only of interest to mobile commerce providers due to access to users' personal data. Future transaction volume is also interesting, given that experts assume a 20 % turnover share in total e-commerce turnover by 2015, which quickly adds up to 20 billion euros or more. As a result, it is also essential to integrate the issue of mobile payment into the multi-channel environment and develop solutions for the different regulation of online and offline worlds and their integration.

3.5.4 Integration of Mobile Pricing in the Multi-channel Environment

The special characteristics of mobile commerce pricing raise the intriguing question of how pricing policy for the mobile channel is consistent with other channels.

Product	Samsung R 730 Niel		Toshiba Satellite Pro A200-008	
Dispatch center for online and mobile	+ shipping costs = total price	449.00 € 10.00 € 459.00 €	+ shipping costs = total price	777.00 € 12.50 € 789.50 €
Möhnesee branch (pick-up at store)		444.51 €		784.77 €
Aachen branch (pick-up at store)		449.00 €		784.77 €

Fig. 3.15 Differentiated channel prices, using Atelco as an example (Source: Schleusener 2011)

Giving unrestricted consideration to these special features would mean offering different prices in the channels and responding accordingly to resultant challenges. This does not have to signify a problem, since a large number of retailers already offer different prices on the website (www.ikea.com, www.atelco.de). The necessary selection in a store should therefore be implemented either automatically using cookies or through location-based services (cf. Schleusener 2012, pp. 174 et seqq). Differentiation of prices between online and offline environments continues if the management of shipping costs is considered. When ordering products in-store, frequently no shipping costs are incurred, but the relevant store price is then payable (cf. Fig. 3.15). If a provider's prices can be researched on the Internet, such information is already available when visiting a brick-and-mortar competitor, which could intensify price competition. Price differences for the same products in different channels may result in an erosion of the total price level. This risk arises in particular when price guarantees are provided which cover different channels – and particularly the mobile commerce channel. This is the case at BestBuy for example. If the customer finds a lower price after making a purchase, he or she is refunded the difference between the paid price and the lower price. However, this is only valid for as long as the product could in any case be returned. In the course of price differentiation, it should be ensured that different prices do not constitute a problem, including when returning items. There is no problem if the price paid has to be verified before being refunded accordingly (cf. Schleusener 2012, p. 175).

3.5.4.1 Merger of Online and Offline Pricing

Differences between the offline and online world are increasingly being diluted, including in terms of pricing policy. Key drivers of this development are smartphones, which make access to the mobile Internet possible at practically any location. This results in the possibility of using simple price comparison options, which exist on the Internet, to assess offline prices. Products in brick-and-mortar retailing can quickly be identified through product images or barcodes and compared with mobile commerce offers. Around half of "smart natives" already use the smartphone to obtain additional product information. Price information is also very often requested (cf. Otto Group and Google 2012).

Price information which is constantly available anywhere on the mobile Internet also increases the self-confidence of customers. If customers have found a lower price via a mobile device, over half of them are willing to directly ask for a discount (cf. IDC Retail Insights 2010). As part of this trend, an adjustment and resultant additional price squeeze can be assumed. The same could be true of reference prices, which are used to assess prices (cf. Diller 2008; Schleusener 2012, p. 170). Phases with price campaigns could also be affected, since customers are less reliant on retailers' external reference prices, but can then determine actual savings themselves by comparison with online prices (cf. Schleusener 2012, p. 170).

3.6 Prospects for Brick-and-Mortar Stores and Potential of Location-Based Services

Brick-and-mortar retailing is still by far the largest marketing channel even if online commerce is growing strongly (cf. Gerling 2012; Haug 2013). It has great advantages, in particular for customers who want immediate availability of goods, feel and touch, qualified personal advice and a real shopping environment. Furthermore, there is the opportunity to transport the potential of e-commerce into the brick-and-mortar store by means of a multi-channel concept. Accordingly, new technologies and formats provide additional services and interaction options in stores. This is possible via mobile apps or in-store terminals example (cf. Haug 2013). Cross-channel services, such as online information on branch stocks, compilation of individual product ranges, pick-up and return options in-store, primarily offer the customer real added value, compared with pure online competition. Cross-channel customer management may allow the retailer to improve its utilization of customer potential. Retailers can use couponing, cross-promotions or online store cards for example (cf. Haug 2013). Mobile activities in brick-and-mortar retailing are depicted in Fig. 3.16.

New technologies allow for an improvement in service and experience while simultaneously decreasing expenditure. Customer loyalty and the formation of a regular clientele may be increased as a result. Studies prove that multi-channel customers are much more satisfied with their company if it allows for channel hopping (cf. OC&C 2011). In addition, willingness to buy is greater among multi-channel customers. At Sainsbury's for example, shoppers spend more than twice as much money if they can shop online and offline (cf. InternetRetailing 2012a; Haug 2013). Suppliers from the USA and UK are dominant among best practices in multi-channel commerce. US retailers invest up to 30 % of their total expenditure in the necessary reorganization and realignment of processes. Nordstrom, for example, planned e-commerce investments of over 140 million US dollars for 2012 (cf. Brohan 2012; Haug 2013). Such high investments in the expansion of online activities usually pay off. Macy's has managed to increase turnover growth in e-commerce by more than 30 % in the last 2 years. Moreover, traditional retailers are ranked first in the prestigious L2 Digital IQ Index for specialist retailing (L2 2012) – closely followed by Nordstrom (cf. Haug 2013). Fifty-one percent of

Fig. 3.16 Mobile activities and applications for brick-and-mortar retailing (Source: Haug 2013)

total revenues are already said to come from multi-channel sales revenue at British multi-channel retailer Argos. 30 % of sales come directly from the "Check & Reserve" offer, in which customers reserve items online and can pick them up in the store. Investments are therefore being phased out in the shop network and stores closed or relocated (cf. InternetRetailing 2012b; Haug 2013).

Modern and technology-savvy customers are "always on" with their smartphone. They can move onto the Internet at any time, access all information and interact with friends. As a consequence, social networking and recommendation processes become important factors influencing customer decisions. Customers are searching more intensively for personalized, apposite information and products. One reason for this is the almost unimaginable variety of alternative offers. Based on such developments, the following requirements and opportunities are derived for brick-and-mortar retailing (cf. Haug 2013):

- **New communications or transaction sites** with local relevance: web-enabled mobile devices let customers conduct product research or complete a purchase anytime and anywhere. Suppliers will therefore increasingly be available in "transfer spaces" offline, including subway stations, bus stops or concert arenas. They will offer their products for purchase on posters or billboards with QR codes. Other suppliers will follow the prime example of Tesco from South Korea, with subway supermarket walls.
- **Efficient mobile marketing:** In the future, brick-and-mortar retailers will increasingly address customers via mobile applications, like apps or aggregator platforms. This allows for contextual and local relevance, which in turn results in less wastage when addressing target groups.

- **Local product ranges:** Product groups with local relevance are made available online through marketplace applications, e.g. Milo and eBay. Google could also play a large role here in future, by systematically integrating product availability data into the local search. Brick-and-mortar retailing will also be capable of providing attractive mobile and brick-and-mortar offers for digital consumers.
- **Attractive real-time offers:** Coupons and rebates are made available to the general public in mobile form via apps or platforms, such as KaufDA and Groupon. Technological solutions, e.g. Shopkick, also offer the opportunity to send personalized offers in-store to the customer's smartphones.
- **Systematic customer data recording:** Customer data can be systematically recorded in all channels, in order to establish modern and integrated customer retention systems. These are no longer channel-centered in an age of channel hopping and multi-screening, but have a customer-centered design and thereby allow for a personalized customer experience.
- **Social relevance:** Social media are included across channels. Product ratings and recommendations are also made available in brick-and-mortar form, as C&A already does in Brazil with the latest numbers of "likes" for products. Retailers are creating new incentive systems for their customers, in order to obtain wider distribution in social networks – whether Facebook, Qype or Foursquare.
- **More attractive, comfortable and convenient shopping experiences:** Shopping experiences in brick-and-mortar stores are becoming more attractive through the inclusion of digital in-store services. Stores are also becoming event and activity areas with highly-qualified specialist and style advisers. Technical innovations enhance the comfort and convenience of brick-and-mortar shopping through digital information displays, mobile payment options or in-store navigation applications.
- **Smart channel synergies:** Multi-channel retailers will also have to link their channels more intensively, enhance their specific advantages, and offer the customer an integrated, accessible, multi-channel experience. Smart channel linking also makes online advantages available at the POS, e.g. through the use of tablets, info terminals, QR codes on shelves and/or in-store apps. This relates to a large product selection, additional and more extensive product information, or customer recommendations.
- **Competition on delivery times:** Established and innovative logistics providers, such as Shutl and tiramizoo, also make it possible for brick-and-mortar retailing to deliver products to customers within the shortest timeframe. This constitutes an important profiling opportunity for brick-and-mortar retailers, allowing them to hold their ground with large online pure players. Amazon is currently building additional logistics centers, in order to further reduce delivery time and offer same-day delivery. This trend will favor the development of online commerce.

Positive multi-channel approaches are also becoming increasingly apparent in German commerce, although still at an early stage of development. With Click & Collect, a greater number of chain stores are currently introducing store pick-up concepts, for example Media Markt, Douglas, C&A and Karstadt (cf. dgroup 2012a; Haug 2013). This could improve their customers' shopping and service experience across channels and thereby considerably increase utilization of digital channel potential, since the channel benefits of online commerce are relevant to many customers and it is no longer possible to imagine life without them. The transparency of the market has increased expectations in all channels and made service and convenience requirements standard, illustrating the necessity for all providers to develop new, differentiated service commitments (cf. Haug 2013).

In addition to location-based services, appropriate digital in-store technologies are also required. Such technologies are only sensible if they provide customers with concrete added value. The content and functions of the digital in-store concept should therefore be closely coordinated. The following contents and functions offer benefits to customers (cf. Crossretail 2013):

1. **Service quality:** Rapid and simple payment has a positive impact on service quality. Value is increasingly placed on multi-channel services, such as ordering options for items and delivery options to any location. Pickup, exchange and online collect – i.e. items can be placed in an online shopping cart – as well as loyalty programs, voucher redemption and newsletter registration also form part of the standard modern shopping service.
2. **Brand content:** Every brand has a history. Digital in-store applications can offer interesting opportunities to draw attention to the brand and enhance it with content and narratives.
3. **Entertainment:** The point-of-sale continues to offer outstanding opportunities for a positive enrichment of the shopping experience (cf. Heinemann 1989). In particular, the salesroom offers numerous entertainment opportunities: contests or connection with social networks, in order to share buys with friends, are just two examples.

In addition to this added value, the mechanism for applications must ensure that an application is not only of interest to the customer, but also contributes to achieving marketing goals. This means it is important for an in-store application to be enriched through gamification. Games mechanisms and opportunities for interactivity, which are fun for the customer to try out and use, should be in place. The adventure factor as well as the motivation and receptiveness of users are thereby increased (cf. Crossretail 2013). Furthermore, digital in-store operation should also support the multi-channel concept. A multi-channel presence and the connection of offline and online channels accommodate consumers' current buying and search behavior. Moreover, such an approach may prevent customers from switching providers when channel hopping, but also allows for the collection of important data, which can be utilized in performance marketing if the concept is designed as a useful information system (cf. Crossretail 2013). Whatever the format in which digital in-store applications are used, it is certain that brick-and-mortar retail formats will look different in the future – either as showrooms or with showroom areas, pop-up areas, partly automated, or even scaled down. The first fully-automated store with robots is already in place, see clothing retailer Hointer in the USA (www.hointer.com).

Mobile Commerce as Base Factor No. 3 for SoLoMo 4

4.1 Development and Future Prospects for Mobile Commerce

4.1.1 Development and Status of Mobile Commerce

The number of mobile phone connections worldwide also illustrates that the mobile web is growing enormously and will soon overtake the laptop and PC as the primary device for Internet usage. Notebook sales figures have also caught up with the PC market. According to forecasts from investment bank Morgan Stanley, there should be more mobile Internet users than desktop users around the world by 2014, with a relevant mobility impact on customers and retailers. More than one billion UMTS (Universal Mobile Telecommunications System) users are already registered around the world (cf. Fig. 4.1). This generates new expectations and requirements among customers, which, from their perspective, should also be fulfilled by traditional retailers. No doubt, "the new-generation of mobile commerce" will play a key role here in the future of online commerce, since it consistently allows for simultaneous purchase on all channels, i.e. with the smartphone in-store. However, the question of the manner in which retailers can make best use of the disruptive technology of mobile Internet for their brick-and-mortar stores can no longer be answered separately from the issue of "SoLoMo".

Above all, a combination of the web with the camera function of a cellphone gives rise to new applications, which use augmented reality or gamification. Such services also offer benefits through customized product recommendations, which is facilitated, for example, by m-commerce pioneer Stylight. This provider's iPhone app enables users to take a photo of a passerby and subsequently initiate a search for the items of clothing they are wearing: representing a kind of shopping inspiration on the street, with a direct buying option. Mobile is thereby becoming established as an additional information and marketing channel (cf. Bruce 2011, pp. 50 et seqq.).

However, any retailer that steers clear of the online issue should really do the same for the mobile issue. Furthermore, optimization is necessary for mobile-compliant contents and format-compliant websites. The offer for mobile services

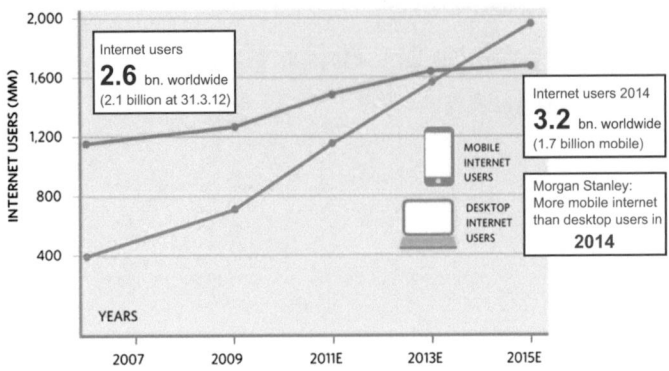

Fig. 4.1 Mobile Internet users worldwide (Source: Own illustration based on ExamOne 2013)

and applications, or killer applications, should also be expanded. Situational and lifestyle-compliant adjustment of offers to the individual shopping habits of customers is certainly a master class in mobile commerce. That is the only way to leverage the synergies that result from social, local and mobile networking. Such synergies include customizable virtual shelves and the use of augmented reality in all conceivable facets. Mobile 2.0, i.e. mobile-oriented implementation of social media instruments with networking to Facebook, Twitter and the like is standard. Twitter accounts do not only function as a service tool to answer customer questions here, but can also sustainably fuel other sales channels. A high level of mobile navigation and mobile usability is also ensured to a much greater extent in mobile commerce than in the online shop. Much greater attention should be paid to the highest level of mobile navigation and mobile usability in mobile commerce than the online shop. Flexible formatting also helps in this regard, which allows for the use of different types of devices, including tablet PCs. Page loading speed and accessibility should also be implemented as optimally as possible, particularly with regard to transmission problems. Content-heavy websites with loading times lasting minutes scare customers away and drive them to competitors, which are only a click away.

Mobile commerce, combined with dynamic smartphone penetration, is currently undergoing a radical change of generations as disruptive technology and is suited to transforming all commercial sectors in the long-term, as already apparent in the USA. Given that establishing a presentable, considerably-sized online shop is a key factor in the success of mobile commerce, the mobile shop can also be regarded as an "extended arm of e-commerce". This includes a far-reaching side effect, since the strong growth in online commerce is also fueled by the mobile boom.

4.1.1.1 Mobile Commerce as an Extended Arm of E-Commerce

The question of the specific meaning of mobile commerce, m-commerce or m-shopping is often unclarified. The term "mobile" or "M" illustrates that this form of shopping is not tied to a fixed location. Shopping becomes mobile through the use of devices designed for mobile use (cf. Turowski and Pousttchi 2004, p. 2). They can be carried and used in everyday life and are capable of displaying the mobile Internet (cf. Bernauer 2008, p. 26). Mobile devices include traditional mobile phones (cellphones) in the wider sense, "personal digital assistants" (PDA) or smartphones (cf. Wiecker 2002, p. 405). However, in order to distinguish it from conventional online commerce, the notebook is excluded as an m-shopping option, since it is too similar to the stationary PC in terms of capabilities (e.g. with regard to display size, input options, etc.). In respect of the PDA, it can be stated that the sale of such devices is in decline. They are increasingly being replaced by the smartphone – a combination of cellphone and PDA – (cf. BITKOM and Goldmedia 2008, p. 13; Wiecker 2002, p. 417). The smartphone is viewed as a mobile phone, which can be used synonymously with the term "cellphone". By means of transmission technologies such as UMTS, this facilitates access to the Internet, which, in such a combination, then constitutes the mobile Internet. The m-shop is therefore differentiated from online commerce through the use of a mobile device instead of a stationary PC. Otherwise, it has the same features as "classic" online commerce and thus distance retailing (cf. Thelen 2009, p. 4). M-shopping is a sub-segment of mobile commerce (m-commerce). The focus here is on the exchange of goods and services, but information and communications processes, such as the location-based services outlined above, also form part of m-commerce (cf. Scheer et al. 2002, p. 100; Lehner 2002, p. 8; Turowski and Pousttchi 2004, p. 2). M-commerce and e-commerce are primarily distinguished from one another in terms of the devices used. E-commerce generally involves stationary devices, by means of which commerce is predominantly carried out at fixed locations, whereas m-shopping is not tied to one location (cf. Turowski and Pousttchi 2004, p. 1).

Over the next few years, mobile commerce will sustainably shape e-commerce and shift online commerce into a new stage of evolution. A series of simple concepts were launched in the initial phase from 1993 to 1999, and investments made in traffic, and this learning phase was followed by the age of shopping comparisons, in which many price comparison sites were established, and these are now experiencing a second boom in mobile commerce. The shop optimization phase, in which websites are perfected, has continued since 2005, and represents a very important basis for the success of mobile commerce. Moreover, the era of socialization of e-commerce, in which shopping clubs were established and most Web 2.0 functions installed, has been ongoing since 2008 (cf. BV Capital 2011). Online commerce is currently largely marked by explosive use of the mobile Internet. Mobile commerce can now be assumed to represent the highest stage of evolution in e-commerce (cf. Heinemann 2012a, p. 19).

4.1.1.2 Development and Status of Mobile Commerce

Surfing the Internet by mobile phone has been possible since the introduction of the "Wireless Application Protocol" (WAP standard) in 1997 (cf. Turowski and Pousttchi 2004, p. 89; Alby 2008, p. 22). However, slow connections, shortage of supply and high costs initially resulted in unsatisfactory usage of WAP. In the meantime, new prospects have been generated for mobile Internet as a result of technical development in the area of transmission technologies and mobile devices (cf. Bernauer 2008, p. 4). As shown by the "Mobile Web Watch" study conducted by Accenture in 2010, 17 % of all German Internet users already used mobile Internet in 2009 (cf. Accenture 2010b). This was equivalent to 7.7 million people in Germany, but with a sharply increasing trend. Mobile devices with user-friendly operating systems and in particular the iPhone play a key role in this development (cf. Accenture 2010b, p. 4). Touch-sensitive displays create a new form of interaction. Modern applications therefore simplify administration of the mobile Internet, enable access, and adjust contents transmitted on the World Wide Web to fit the smartphone's small display (cf. Otto Group and Google Inc. 2012, p. 18). In contrast to the "stationary web", mobile shopping has the advantage that almost every consumer now carries a mobile device as a constant companion. In combination with improving transmission technology, this inevitably leads to heavier Internet usage. The market penetration of the mobile phone today is already considerably higher than that of the PC. In statistical terms, one in five Germans owns more than one cellphone. The threshold of 100 million mobile phone subscribers in Germany was exceeded back in April 2008 (cf. Gruner + Jahr 2008, p. 6). As at 2012, around 20 million such subscribers in Germany are smartphone owners, more than half of whom surf the Internet in mobile form every day. This figure could even double by the end of 2013 (cf. AGOF 2013). An essential reason for the increased use of smartphones is the improved interface with user-friendly touchscreens. Mobile devices, such as the Apple iPhone, are becoming increasingly user-friendly and displays are getting larger and easier to read (cf. Otto Group and Google Inc. 2012, p. 5; Negele 2011, pp. 1 et seqq.). However, the "Universal Mobile Telecommunications System" (UMTS) mobile technology should be regarded as a significant obstacle. It was originally viewed as a motor of growth for mobile Internet, but can no longer cope with the increased data volume in mobile communications and is now considered to be outdated (cf. Kowalewski 2010, p. A7; Spehr and Jörn 2010, p. T1). The explosive increase in data traffic by mobile phone is promoted by the strong decline in network technology prices, which increasingly allow for lower-priced offers for mobile surfing. With regard to current data volume, UMTS has proved to be a failure in hindsight. In this respect, the new mobile frequencies auctioned in 2010 point the way forward: "Long Term Evolution (LTE) is a paradigm shift, representing the fourth mobile generation, which is intended to make everything better – greater capacity, higher bandwidths, better coverage – and at lower cost" (cf. Spehr and Jörn 2010, p. T1). This will also inspire mobile Internet usage again, even if the number of mobile search queries is growing enormously. As shown by Fig. 4.2, mobile search queries increased by 80 % in Germany just in 2012 alone (cf. Focus 2013b).

With the additional, dynamic spread of smartphones, the digital retailing revolution has taken its course. The speed and power of the mobile web eclipses everything else that had previously been observed in terms of dynamic retailing: through mobile devices, the "wheel of retailing" is almost becoming a turbocharger,

4.1 Development and Future Prospects for Mobile Commerce

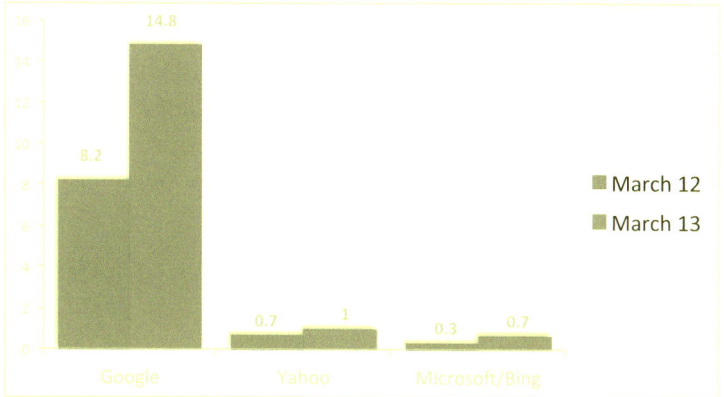

Fig. 4.2 Mobile searches in Germany (Source: Focus 2013b)

taking online purchase from the desk to the sofa and the street and thereby enabling new applications. The appeal of using a smartphone with an integrated operating system is the constant availability of information on the net. Users quickly get accustomed to this, since it can make everyday life easier and offer added value (cf. Otto Group and Google Inc. 2012, p. 12; Negele 2011, pp. 1 et seqq.). Customers want to be able to use the mobile Internet and its applications in mobile shopping without barriers if possible. The operating system of the mobile device plays a decisive role in the choice of smartphone, since it allows for simple and rapid operation (cf. Negele 2011, pp. 1 et seqq.). Depending on the origin of an operating system, the technical configuration of the hardware, and the market region, mobile devices may differ from one another in terms of functions and options. In general, manufacturers are under enormous pressure with regard to innovation, since the lifecycle of a mobile device on the market is exactly 8 months before it is theoretically replaceable by a new development (cf. Klopfleisch 2009, p. 56). The range of differing operating systems and smartphones is very large. Most hardware manufacturers use one and the same operating system for their end products. Users do not only have to choose a specific operating system, but also the executing hardware.

Competition on the market for mobile operating systems is more intense than ever. Not all that long ago, it was still not easy to opt for a multifaceted smartphone with an operating system. The first Apple iPhone only went on sale in Germany in November 2007 and brought about a revolution in mobile devices, operating in a previously unknown way. The wide variety of applications for mobile devices was also driven upwards by the app store and operating system capabilities. However, the competition quickly caught up. The Google operating system Android managed to replace the iPhone OS in first place within just 1 year. In 2011, Android is already quite far ahead, with a market share of 38.9 %, and will even manage to expand this lead in the next few years (cf. Gartner 2011).

4.1.2 Popular Applications in Mobile Commerce

The mobile Internet opens up new prospects for retailers and provides room for new business models. In this regard, innovations such as GPS geo-location using apps can be very helpful. However, the mobile Internet may also simply be transferred to an existing stationary website and support it through mobile access (cf. manager magazin new media 2010). An initial overview here will identify the benefits that various applications can provide to the customer in mobile shopping, and will be dealt with in greater detail in later chapters (cf. Negele 2011):

4.1.2.1 Mobile Shopping Website
A developed mobile website is not specifically designed for a certain operating system and in theory operates on all operating systems used in mobile devices. The customer's selection is not limited by the choice of operating system on the available websites. Every mobile shopping operating system has an Internet browser, which can be used to search for mobile websites on the net. This does not necessarily require the installation of an app (application). In addition, companies are responsible for maintaining their mobile websites, which proves to be a positive factor for customers in mobile shopping, since the user himself must perform updates for native apps (cf. Alby 2008, pp. 103 et seqq.). The mobile Internet user is sometimes redirected to the specialized mobile website version, since he or she is automatically identified in the browser. On the other hand, each company can also install a link to the mobile website on the standard website if the customer is not automatically identified (cf. Negele 2011). Access to the mobile Internet can provide customers with information on prices and product comparisons in mobile shopping. As a result, with the aid of the browser, it is often preferred by smartphone users and used for applications (cf. ibid.).

4.1.2.2 Mobile Shopping Apps
An app or application must always be specially designed for the specific operating system of a mobile device and becomes practicable for the customer through the internal operating system code. As a result, the same option is not always provided to customers, depending on the operating system. But this is not necessarily a disadvantage if it is ensured that all functions can operate on the mobile device without restriction. In contrast to the mobile website, applications can access specific functions of the smartphone and thereby allow for personalized use. In contrast to the mobile website, apps can often be used more quickly, since they usually concentrate on a specific task or function (cf. Rio mobile 2010, p. 11; Alby 2008, pp. 103 et seqq.). This could be one reason why most users of the mobile Internet now use applications (cf. Google 2012, Google and Ipsos OTX MediaCT

2012). Implementation of mobile shopping applications has particular high potential for success in conjunction with brick-and-mortar online retailing if they are directly connected to the available online shop. Both can provide reciprocal support and thereby contribute to mutual growth in sales and turnover (cf. Rio mobile 2010, p. 13; Negele 2011).

4.1.2.3 Mobile Shopping Services in Brick-and-Mortar Retailing

Mobile applications can also provide opportunities to brick-and-mortar retailing and do not automatically signify a loss for offline channels (cf. Klopfleisch 2009, pp. 21 et seq.). As described in the previous chapter, it even becomes possible to attract customers to stores through mobile services or location-based services. In this regard, there are various service functions which retailers can provide to their customers in the form of mobile shopping apps. The store locator function has now almost become a basic application of any app, since it is very useful in attracting customers to the store in the simplest possible way.

The customer's location can be defined most accurately through the position of his smartphone via GPS geo-location and reconciled with available information from his environment on the Internet. Using graphs, a retailer can provide information on the nearest store (cf. Rio mobile 2010, p. 14). H&M and ZARA already make use of this option around the world in their mobile channel. Both companies make the store locator available to customers via an app, which makes it possible to automatically locate the nearest store, regardless of the user's current location. However, one disadvantage of this service function is that it only addresses customers who intend to search for a specific store from the outset. As a result, it represents an advantage if a service application automatically provides information and offers as soon as a customer is near the store. This is possible on the basis of geo-targeting. Location-based services (LBS) can target customers, who are near the store and have consented to the service, by SMS (text message) or email and deliver information on the latest offers. Figure 4.3 presents a summary of which mobile commerce applications are already used by smartphone users and to what extent.

4.1.3 Tablet Shopping and Future Prospects for Mobile Commerce

When examining mobile sales revenues for large e-commerce providers, mobile commerce evidently has huge potential for retailers. For example, eBay had turnover of more than 20 billion US dollars commercial volume with mobile commerce in the 2013 financial year. The exact level of mobile commerce turnover potential in Germany is difficult to estimate. With estimated turnover of around 2.0 billion euros in 2012, its share in online commerce is fluctuating at around 7 %, which is equivalent to growth of 141 %. In addition, app and service turnover amounts to 2.5 billion euros, which does not relate to retailing. Turnover forecasts rely on the assumption that more than one third of online turnover of products will be transacted on mobile devices by 2020, without considering the enormous feeder

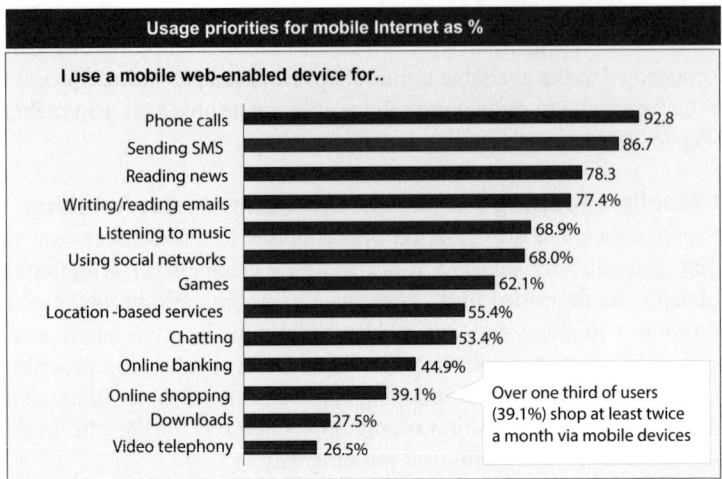

Fig. 4.3 Smartphone usage (Source: Own illustration with data source from AGOF 2013)

function that such devices have for other forms of commerce. This makes it all the more astonishing that not even half of all online shops are mobile-optimized in Germany. The current trend among consumers towards greater mobility and ubiquity also proves that m-shopping will become considerably more important in the future. An increasing number of people are using mobile communications. There were 64.8 million mobile users in Germany in 2004 (cf. Zander 2011, p. 9; Küllenberg and Quente 2006, p. 33), and the same figure today is around 80 million.

"The cellphone is not a replacement for the home PC. It's a replacement for chewing gum and cigarettes" (Küllenberg and Quente 2006, p. 169). At the same time, the mobile device in the form of a smartphone is becoming increasingly prevalent in the population at large. As the latest ARD-ZDF online study from 2012 shows, mobile Internet usage is growing dynamically, in particular among younger target groups aged between 14 and 29 (cf. ARD-ZDF 2012). The trend is increasingly towards the cellphone becoming a multifunctional device, which, in addition to IP telephony, also integrates useful features, such as clock, camera, MP3 player, navigation and Internet functions, in one device. Figure 4.4 shows the trend towards smartphones. Sales of 28 million smartphones are therefore expected in Germany for 2013, which is equivalent to a 29 % increase on the previous year.

The importance of mobile Internet for brick-and-mortar stores will continue to grow in future. The role of the mobile Internet in general preparations for purchase is constantly growing and has a sustainable effect on in-store purchases, as already discussed in the previous chapter.

4.1.3.1 Tablet Shopping as a New Form of Mobile Commerce

The market for tablets is growing faster than any other technology market. The tablet PC share increased from 4 % to 14 % in 2011, although potential is still far from being exhausted (cf. FAZ 2011f, No. 177, p. 17). Tablets are in line with the

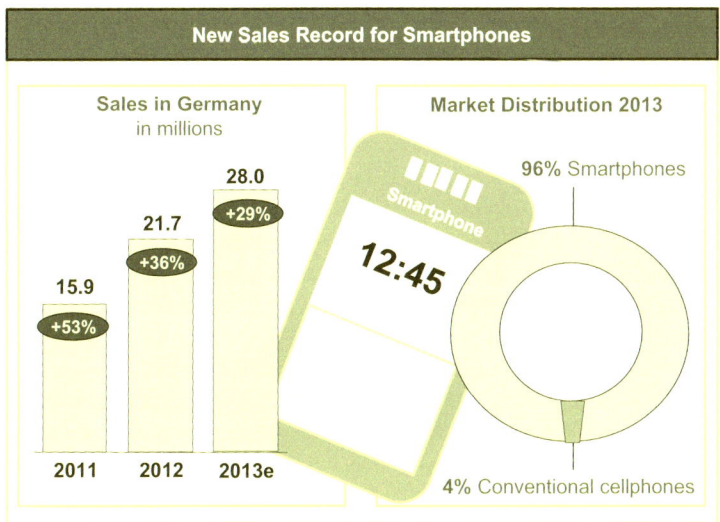

Fig. 4.4 Smartphone sales in Germany (Source: Own illustration based on Bitkom 2013 with data source from EITO, IDC)

trend: whether at the Consumer Electronics Show in Las Vegas, CeBIT in Hanover or the Internationale Funkausstellung global trade show for consumer electronics and home appliances in Berlin, exhibitors are presently outdoing one another at the latest entertainment electronics trade fairs, in particular with alternatives to Apple's iPad. A flood of new tablet models are being released by Motorola, Dell, Asus, Acer, HTC, etc. Although only Dell and Samsung have so far supplied tab products which come close to Apple, with the smaller – compared to the iPad – tablet models Streak and Galaxy, a massive expansion is anticipated in the range of offers (cf. FAZ 2011a, No. 2, p. 15). Use of a tablet PC is not applicable to mobile commerce, based on current definitions. The notebook has so far been excluded as an m-shopping option, as distinguished from classic online commerce, since it is too similar to the stationary PC in terms of its capabilities (e.g. in respect of display size, input options, etc.). However, given that the tablet PC constitutes more of a hybrid between smartphone and notebook, and allows for a telephone option through additional devices, the previous exclusion in respect of mobile commerce can no longer be upheld. Smartphones and tablet PCs are frequently used in a dual role and with a dual twin card for on the move. The tablet computer allows for improved reading options through the larger display and also fuels the trend towards e-books and newspaper and magazine apps. The smaller format (9.25 × 12.4 in.) and fast OTA ("over the air") delivery addresses younger readers in particular. As one of the first publishers, British newspaper The Independent managed to increase circulation on the British newspaper market by 20 % in tablet format. However, reformatting requires different page breaks and therefore higher production costs in the case of a simultaneous release of different formats.

Both the digital bookshelf and digital kiosk are already "app reality" on the iPhone and iPad. For the first time, Amazon sold more e-books than printed books back in April 2011. The 10 % market share threshold for e-books is expected to be exceeded in the USA in 2012 (cf. Die Welt, June 4, 2011e, p. 12; Die Welt, August 12, 2011f, p. 12). Even if the German book trade fails to achieve a 5 % turnover with electronic books in 2012, experts in Germany still expect an e-book market share of over 10 % by the end of 2015 (cf. ibid.). The e-books are not only read with e-readers, such as Amazon's Kindle or the Nook from Barnes & Nobles. IT giant Apple in particular, which also supplies a reading app on the iPad and distributes e-books through its own iTunes online shop, is one of the top three e-book providers in the USA. In Germany, it is primarily Amazon and Apple which deal in e-books. The Kindle and iPad not only accept all book formats, but also show simple PDF or text files without any problem. In the future Amazon will also increasingly rely on mobile commerce for e-book sales. The latest Amazon app also works in iPad's Safari browser and thereby intensifies the competition with Apple (cf. Die Welt, August 12, 2011f, p. 12). Nevertheless, Apple's position in tablet PCs is (still) dominant. With the iPad, Apple currently controls around three quarters of the fast-growing tablet market. However, of the 280 million sales of tablet computers forecast for 2015, "only" 120 million will likely be attributed to Apple (cf. Fig. 4.5), while the second-largest provider Samsung will in particular catch up strongly (cf. Die Welt, August 27, 2011h, p. 13).

The driver of the trend towards the tablet computer is the shift of computer output from stationary to mobile devices. According to one study, more than 40 % of Germans already surf the mobile Internet (cf. kaufDA 2013). Emails, weather information, directions, news and searches for travel connections are cited as the most common mobile applications (cf. ibid.). But the games industry is also affected by the digital mobilization trend. Over ten million Germans already play online (cf. BITKOM 2009). Around 1.86 billion euros were spent on computer and video games software in Germany in 2010 (cf. Die Welt, April 27, 2011h, p. 14). According to one recent market analysis, social games are making above-average

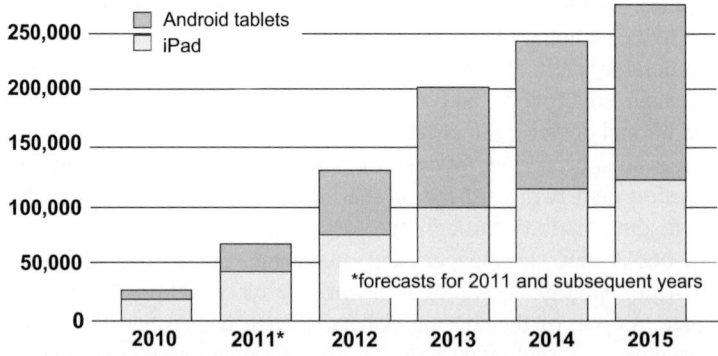

Fig. 4.5 Global distribution of tablet PCs in thousands (Source: Own illustration based on Die Welt (2011h), p. 13)

progress, in combination with Facebook, and already represent a global market of four billion US dollars (cf. Mücke Sturm 2011). Digitalization also accommodates the desire for "immediate gratification", i.e. immediate availability and delivery of mobile services (cf. BV Capitals 2011).

4.1.4 Mobile Commerce Added Value

Mobile commerce offers advantages to the customer in the form of mobile added value, including mobility, accessibility, context sensitivity and identification (cf. Pichlmeier 2010, pp. 27–29).

- **Mobility:** The user of a mobile technology is not tied to any specific location or specific time. Physical presence is optional provided that the mobile power supply is in place, which may only be a secondary condition. The omnipresence of information systems can also be characterized by the concept of ubiquity, which is given additional "added value" through ad-hoc access in mobile commerce.
- **Accessibility:** The mobile user is accessible anywhere and anytime, provided that the mobile power supply is in place. This allows for proactive services – such as recommendations for the sale or purchase of shares – or synchronized communication between users. The dynamic spread of SMS (text messaging) as compared to WAP technology can no doubt be attributed to the accessibility of subscribers and also the horrendous prices per minute for online time in case of WAP usage.
- **Context sensitivity:** Services relevant to the user can be localized and actively provided by recording and evaluating his or her environment. A tourist in a foreign city will require different information than a business traveler. Preferences could also change depending on the time of day, which may be based on opening times or occasions (e.g. concert visits or theater). Mobile technologies allow any type of context to be dealt with. Location-based services refer to the local context, whereas up-to-date times or hourly offers relate to the time context. The personal context takes preferences and personal attributes into account. Context sensitivity allows for the use of LBS (location-based services) in particular.
- **Identification:** The identification function for users also represents mobile added value. As a result of user classifications of devices, ownership of a device is sufficient identification for many applications. This does not exclude additional authentications, e.g. for authorization of payments by inputting a PIN. Additional security requirements can be fulfilled through the use of mobile signatures.

4.2 Technological Principles of Mobile Commerce

Given that the spread of mobile commerce or m-shopping is significantly influenced by the development of faster transmission technologies, more user-friendly mobile devices in relation to mobile operating systems, as well as current technological trends, these aspects should be recognized in particular (cf. BITKOM and Goldmedia 2008, p. 11).

4.2.1 Mobile Transmission Technologies

Mobile networks founded on the "Global System for Mobile Communications" (GSM standard) since the start of the 1990s form part of the second generation (2G) of mobile communication systems. As a result of slow data transmission rates for GSM (9.6 kbit/s), bridging technologies were developed at the end of the 1990s, described as 2.5G. The "General Packet Radio Service" (GPRS) is probably the best known and most widely-used technology and was introduced in Germany in 2001. This technology is an upgrade of the GSM standard, which allows for faster data transmission (115 kbit/s) (cf. Bernauer 2008, p. 22). The third mobile generation (3G) is constituted by UMTS ("Universal Mobile Telecommunications System"), which has been available in Germany since 2004 (cf. Thelen 2009, pp. 6 et seq.). However, in contrast to the upgrade of the GSM standard through GPRS, simple updating is no longer possible for UMTS. It requires the construction of an internal network, and as a result UMTS coverage is not yet comparable with the almost nationwide GSM network. Due to the downward compatibility of the UMTS network, a switch is automatically made to the relatively widespread GSM/GPRS network, wherever UMTS is not yet presently available. While telephone customers do not receive any benefit from this, the change is suboptimal for Internet users (cf. Alby 2008, p. 24), since the GSM/GPRS network is slower. However, UMTS cannot compete with the speeds of a DSL connection on the stationary Internet. Yet UMTS has long been regarded as the system of the future, which has driven forward the spread of the mobile Internet and is largely founded on future technologies (cf. Alby 2008, p. 26). Such technologies include already-developed UMTS upgrades, e.g. "High Speed Downlink Packet Access" (HSDPA) or "High Speed Packed Access Plus" (HSPA+). They are termed 3.5G and can be compared with the upgrade of GSM through GPRS.

Data transmission speed has increased quite significantly as a result (cf. Alby 2008, pp. 26 et seqq.). There are different views on the question of which technologies will prevail as the fourth generation (4G) mobile communication system: for some people "Long Term Evolution" (LTE) is seen as the "mobile supernet", while others view technologies such as "Worldwide Interoperability for Microwave Access" (WiMAX) or "IP Multimedia Subsystem" (IMS) in the lead role (cf. Alby 2008, pp. 30 et seq.; Bernauer 2008, pp. 24 and 26 et seqq.). Different transmission speeds up to 3.5G, i.e. without LTE, are summarized by way of comparison in Fig. 4.6. Regardless of which of these options prevails, it should

4.2 Technological Principles of Mobile Commerce

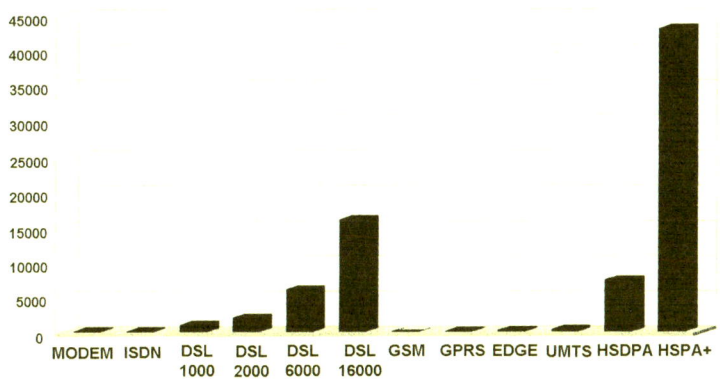

Fig. 4.6 Transmission speeds without LTE, comparison (in kbit/s) (Source: Alby 2008, p. 27)

be clear that in each case such transmission technologies will supply necessary capacities for m-shopping in the near future. The new "Next Generation Mobile Networks" (NGMN) project of mobile communication companies and mobile communication suppliers deals involves the further development of LTE, which is also based on UMTS infrastructure technologies. The fourth mobile communication generation represents a faster and more value-for-money upgrade of the existing third-generation mobile networks and decisively increases the comfort and convenience for m-shopping users. An additional benefit is produced through the faster download rate of 100 megabits per second, which is considerably higher than for UMTS. Devices with LTE should also have a permanent connection with the Internet. Users could thereby operate video telephony with an instant messenger anywhere and anytime online, depending on the mobile provider. This would mean that the fourth generation would enable constant mobile communication through location-independent, wireless broadband Internet access at almost any location, "anytime, anywhere" (cf. Zander 2011, p. 15). LTE uses channel bandwidths of 1.4–20 MHz for a cross-border function. Given that LTE is based on the third generation, existing infrastructures can be used. As a result, the existing radio masts only have to be upgraded by fourth-generation technical components for the conversion of mobile communication networks from the third to the fourth generation (cf. ibid.). Transmission speeds for LTE, by comparison with previous mobile technologies, are depicted in Fig. 4.7. WiMAX is regarded as a synonym for mobile systems based on IEEE standard 802.16 (Institute of Electrical and Electronics Engineers). This was initially designed as a broadband mobile transmission system for stationary devices, e.g. for the personal computer.

WiMAX has now been developed into the fourth generation and is viewed as a competitor to LTE. Under WiMAX, devices and network components are given 802.16 specification and certified. WiMAX mobile networks are presently being constructed in various different countries (cf. Zander 2011, p. 15). The goal of the "IP Multimedia Subsystem" (IMS) is to gain automated access to services from the various different networks. Technical specification TS 23.228 forms the basis here,

Mobile comm. technology	GSM		UMTS			LTE	
	GPRS	EDGE	UMTS	HSPA HSUPA	HSPA+	LTE	LTE advanced
Downlink	53.6 kBit/s	236.8 kBit/s	384 kBit/s	1.8 MBit/s 3.6 MBit/s (7.2 MBit/s) (14.4 MBit/s)	up to 42 MBit/s	up to 75 MBit/s	up to 1 GBit/s
Uplink	13.4 kBit/s (26.8 kBit/s)	118.4 kBit/s (236.8 kBit/s)	128 kBit/s (384 kBit/s)	1.8 MBit/s (3.6 MBit/s) (5.8 MBit/s)	up to 11 MBit/s		up to 500 MBit/s
Latency	500 ms or more	300 - 400 ms	170 - 200 ms	60 - 70 ms			
Provider (planned or in progress)	T-Mobile Vodafone E-Plus O2	T-Mobile Vodafone (E-Plus) (O2)	T-Mobile Vodafone E-Plus O2	T-Mobile Vodafone (E-Plus) (O2)		(T-Mobile) (Vodafone) (O2)	

Fig. 4.7 Transmission speeds for LTE, comparison (in kbit/s) (Source: Own illustration based on Alby 2008 and Zander 2011)

which is available free of charge on the third Generation Partnership Project website. Communication is based on an all-IP network for IP. IMS supports existing networks, such as the GSM network. "Pre-4G technologies" are currently already being used. Such preliminary stages to the fourth communication generation include, for example, UMTS Release 8, a development of the UMTS network, including Release 5 HSDPA ("High Speed Downlink Packet Access") and Release 6 HSUPA ("High Speed Uplink Packet Access") upgrades. Such pre-4G technology guarantees a cost reduction with increased accessibility, higher speeds on the Internet and increased security (cf. ibid.).

4.2.2 Mobile Devices

Mobile devices are the key to the mobile Internet and thereby to mobile shopping. The constant development of new devices raises the question of exactly what is meant by the term "mobile device" (cf. Negele 2011, p. 3). Figure 4.8 below classifies the different device types and defines a mobile device (cf. Scholz 2010) if voice and data communication are regarded as the most important basic functions of mobile devices in mobile shopping. Data communication only allows for access to the Internet and thus connects the provider with the customer. The three

4.2 Technological Principles of Mobile Commerce

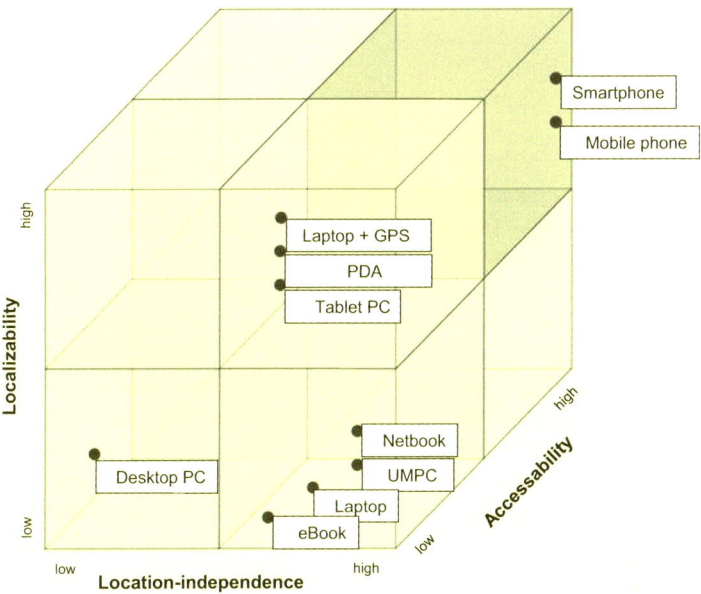

Fig. 4.8 Classification of mobile devices (Source: Scholz 2010)

significant characteristics below are the basic features which a mobile communication-enabled device must provide, and form the three axes of the matrix (cf. ibid.; Scholz 2010):

- Localizability
- Accessibility
- Location-independence

Depending on the nature of the device, it may be transferred into the matrix. Those devices that have the most distinctive basic features are classified as mobile devices. The mobile phone and smartphone can therefore be defined as mobile devices (cf. ibid.; Scholz 2010).

Display size and limited input options on the conventional cellphone keyboard impede use of the mobile Internet. An essential prerequisite for surfing the mobile Internet is a web-enabled device. A "fast" connection to the mobile network via UMTS is only possible with a special, UMTS-compliant device. In this regard, mobile phones/cellphones available on the market today are – almost without exception – UMTS-compliant (cf. Bernauer 2008, pp. 26 et seqq.). Cellphones primarily differ from smartphones in their smaller size. Smartphones are a combination of mobile phone and PDA, which, taken by themselves, do not really have a telephone function. They usually have a larger display than mobile phones and may display a greater number of colors (cf. Bernauer 2008, pp. 27 and 28 et seqq.). Input options also differ from those of cellphones through smaller, retractable or extendable keyboards (QWERTZ keyboards) or touchscreens, and can usually be operated with a finger or stylus pen. As compared with the mobile phone, the display size and input options of the smartphone allow for simpler and more convenient use of the mobile Internet. Given that sales of such devices are increasing, they are clearly gaining ground (cf. Bernauer 2008, p. 28). With perhaps the most prominent representative of the smartphone, the Apple iPhone, the "pocket-size Internet" has finally made a breakthrough. But competitors have now caught up on a broader front.

Despite growing capacity and increasing performance, device prices are continually falling. This makes web-enabled smartphones more attractive to customers (cf. Otto Group and Google Inc. 2012, p. 5). It is therefore reasonable for many customers to turn to smartphones with integrated operating systems, which in addition to the Internet function also offer additional added value, like the "personal information manager" (cf. Negele 2011). The reasons for greater use of smartphones are the improved interface with user-friendly touchscreens and ever-improving transmission capacities (cf. Otto Group and Google Inc. 2012, p. 5). "Usage loses its virtuality through tactile navigability within content and applications. The Internet is becoming a touchable experience" (cf. ibid., p. 19). The combination of touch-sensitive touchscreens, voice and text input, cameras or motion sensors opens up a broad spectrum for input and interaction (cf. Rio mobile 2010, p. 11).

Use of a smartphone with an integrated operating system has the attraction of constant availability of information on the net. The user quickly gets accustomed to the smartphone, since it can make everyday life easier and offer added value (cf. Otto Group and Google Inc. 2012, p. 12). Haak, Finger and Smolinski demonstrate that the stock of smartphones and above all tablets will increase significantly by 2015. Both devices will be winners and stifle PC growth (cf. Fig. 4.9).

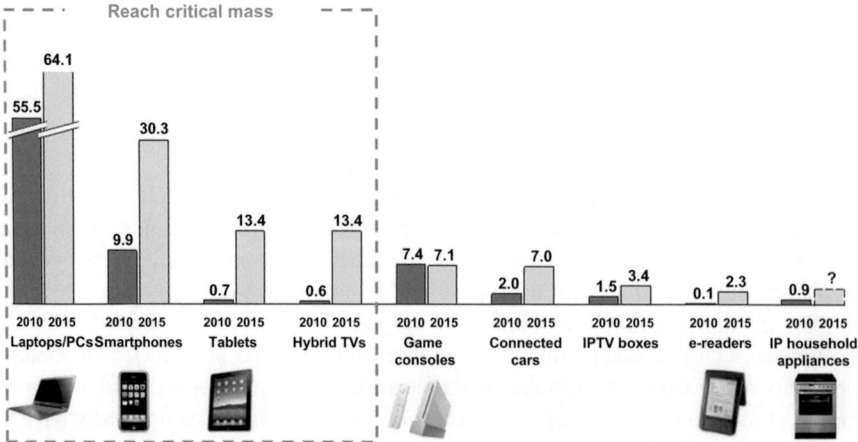

Fig. 4.9 Stock of end devices from 2010 to 2015, in millions (Source: Haak et al. 2013)

4.2 Technological Principles of Mobile Commerce

In comparison with the desktop, a very small display is characteristic of mobile devices. However, the trend is increasingly towards larger displays, since small cellphone displays only enable unsatisfactory product depiction. Misconceptions about the product, which arise due to the use of a display that is too small, often result in consumers being disappointed. Such disappointments are particularly powerful if the consumer ultimately acquires the product and it fails to comply with expectations, and thus has to be returned. Larger cellphone displays are required in order to avoid such negative shopping experiences for the consumer, where possible (cf. Zander 2011, p. 17). The same applies to the 14–29 age group, who represent the majority of smartphone users (cf. Negele 2011, p. 9; BITKOM 2010).

4.2.3 Mobile Operating Systems

Smartphones are equipped with software – the operating system – which enables the complex operation of the device. Operating systems play a central role in the use of the mobile Internet. As on the desktop, user-friendliness allows an Internet browser to be used and standard websites accessed (cf. Accenture 2010b, p. 12). The latest mobile phones often also have an Internet browser or Internet application, which enable surfing on the mobile net. Yet due to their small display size and in some cases lack of touchscreens or QWERTZ keyboards, the mobile phone is still associated with restrictions for mobile Internet, as far as some users are concerned (cf. Negele 2011; Bernauer 2008, p. 27). Another reason for the sometimes conditional usage of the mobile Internet on the mobile phone depends on the type of contract with the network provider. In conventional mobile phone contracts, or with prepaid rates for mobile network operators, usage of mobile Internet is largely charged based on minutes or data volume. Concern about inflating the monthly bill has so far inhibited use of the mobile Internet and thereby mobile shopping with the smartphone (cf. kaufDA 2013; ECC 2010). However, it is expected that the current obstructions will largely be eliminated in the foreseeable future through changed data rates and enlarged displays. The answer to the question of which operating systems are currently available to the customer in mobile shopping requires an initial survey of the most popular operating systems. Seven different operating systems from different sources are highlighted. The following seven operating systems have been identified and selected, and are first described in greater detail (cf. Negele 2011, pp. 23 et seqq.):

- **iPhone OS/Apple:** Following lengthy speculation, Apple first published information on the iPhone on September 9, 2007. Just 6 months later the first Apple iPhone went on sale (cf. Alby 2008, p. 110). The iPhone OS operating system was designed by Apple in a targeted manner. It is worth noting that Apple has so far only placed four similar-looking smartphones on the market, which are almost identical in terms of concept. The iPhone OS is based on the Mac OSX computer operating system, which originates from the Unix operating system

(cf. Eckstein and Theiss 2010, p. 9). The latest Apple version is the iOS 7, which has been available for download since September 18, 2013.
- **Android/Google:** The Android OS operating system was jointly developed by several leading companies in the Open Handset Alliance (OHA). The OHA was created on November 5, 2007, under the leadership of Google and 33 other companies from the mobile operator (T-Mobile, Telefónica), semiconductor (Intel Corporation), handset manufacturer (LG Electronics, Samsung Electronics), software (eBay) and commercialization (Wind Rivers System) sectors. The newly founded OHA publicized the official launch of Android OS at the same time (cf. Mosemann and Kose 2009, pp. 1 et seqq.). Google then took over the Android company, along with Vice President for Development, Andrew Rubin, to whom the current success can largely be attributed (cf. Eckstein et al. 2010, p. 9). The OHA currently has 79 members. The Android OS operating system is founded on the Linux operating system. Device manufacturers can use Android OS free of charge, in order to design a mobile device. License fees are not charged. This has a positive impact on the market development of lower-priced smartphones. Most of the Android OS operating system is opened by the open-source license for application developers, meaning that Android OS supports active projects for mobile devices and applications in the open-source community. Users of Android OS are not tied to apps available on the smartphone, since the operating system also allows for third-party applications. The Android OS is consistently based on touchscreen technology. The first mobile device with the Android OS operating system was the HTC Dream, marketed under the name T-Mobile G1, which was first placed on the US market in October 2008. The launch in Germany followed on February 2, 2009 (cf. Mosemann and Kose 2009, pp. 1 et seqq.).
- **Windows Phone OS:** The first Microsoft operating system for mobile devices was presented in 1996. However, the name Windows CE turned out to have less advertising appeal. The decision was therefore made to rename the operating system Pocket PC. Depending on the device, the same operating system was given other names, such as Pocket PC Phone Edition, Microsoft Smartphone and Handheld PC 2000. With the launch of Windows Mobile 5, the name was finally systemized, pursuant to which all mobile devices are designated as Windows Mobile. Similar to Windows, there were different versions of Mobile 5 and 6 operating systems. Available as Professional, Classic and Standard versions, these were clearly understandable to customers and developers (cf. Immler and Kaiser 2010, p. 9). Windows Mobile was re-launched at the end of 2010, since it could no longer keep pace with the touchscreen capabilities of other operating systems (cf. ibid.). With the launch of the latest Mobile Phone 7 operating system, the systemized designation was also upgraded. All mobile devices – whether with or without touchscreen – are therefore referred to as the Mobile Phone (cf. Immler and Kaiser 2010, p. 9). With the latest operating system, Microsoft merely provides the software. The hardware is undertaken by companies such as LG, HTC, and Samsung. The latest Windows Phone 7 version does not have much in common with Windows Mobile. The reason for this is

that Windows Mobile was designed for smartphones in which the user's input was entered using a stylus, and not a touchscreen (cf. Eckstein et al. 2010, p. 15). The extent to which the new alliance with Nokia will result in changes to Mobile Phone 7 remains to be seen.

- **Symbian/Nokia:** The origin of the Symbian OS dates back to 1981, when physicist David Potter established Psion. In June 1998, the independent company Symbian was founded by Psion, Motorola, Nokia, Ericsson and Panasonic (cf. Gerlicher and Rupp 2004, pp. 4 et seqq.). The foundation of the company required several developments of mobile devices and operating systems. The primary goal was to close the gap between mobile phones and personal digital assistants. Exactly 10 years after Symbian was founded, Nokia bought all of its partners' shares and set up the Symbian Foundation. By October 2010, this included 50 members, with companies such as Samsung, AOL, MySpace, VISA, Ericsson, SanDisk Corporation, T-Mobile and Vodafone. The Symbian Foundation has supported the principle of the open-source system since 2010, given that it holds the promise of strong developments in innovation. Symbian OS is continuously furnished with a special user interface, meaning the optimized Symbian^3 version must be used for touchscreens (cf. Eckstein and Theiss 2010, p. 9; Alby 2008, p. 109).
- **RIM/Blackberry OS:** The Blackberry product line represents Canadian company Research in Motion, which has its head office in Waterloo, Ontario. It was founded by Mike Lazaridis in 1984 and independently designs hardware and software. The first Blackberry smartphone was placed on the market in 1999 (cf. Eckstein and Theiss 2010, p. 9; Research in Motion Limited 2010). However, the Blackberry, as used with today's functions, has only been on the market since 2002. Blackberry achieved a high level of recognition through the push email function (cf. Alby 2008, p. 108). Emails no longer have to be manually picked up, but are "pushed" onto the device via mobile networks, thereby exceeding all other available PDA functions in terms of their popularity (cf. Alby 2008, p. 108). Continual adjustments of the operating systems to user requirements gave rise to the OS 6 version. In contrast to the Windows Phone 7 operating system, Research in Motion never completely overhauled the operating system, but constantly upgraded the available versions within the context of evolutionary development (cf. Eckstein et al. 2010). The new version supports a touchscreen-compliant smartphone for the first time in the history of Research in Motion.
- **WebOS/HP:** The predecessor to the HP Palm WebOS is the Palm OS operating system. Palm OS was certainly one of the most popular platforms in the 1990s. It has been available on mobile devices since 1996, initially without a phone function. In 2003, Palm developed its first personal digital assistant with a phone function, the smartphone (cf. Alby 2008, pp. 106 et seqq.). In July 2009 an alliance was formed between HP Palm and Telefónica to distribute the first smartphone Palm Pre (cf. Kaliudis 2010; Negele 2011). This operating system was specially designed for use of the Internet and is the official successor to the Palm OS.

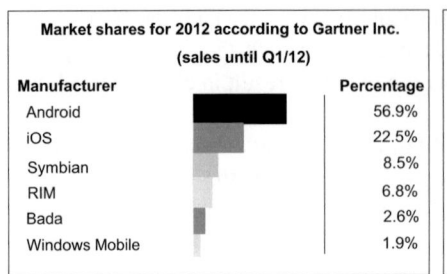 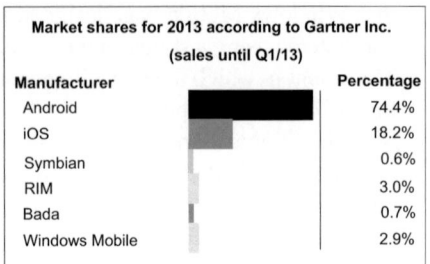

Fig. 4.10 Global market shares for operating systems 2012–2013 (Source: Own illustration based on source from ZDNet and Gartner 2013)

- **bada OS/Samsung:** In May 2010, Samsung Electronics Co. Ltd. announced that the Samsung Wave was available with immediate effect, with the most recent of all operating systems. This applied – among others – to Germany, Great Britain and France. Samsung Bada SDK is open to all application developers, thereby guaranteeing constant innovation on the applications market (cf. Samsung Electronics 2010b). With its low-cost smartphones, Bada OS aims to serve the lower price category and thereby address the general public, rather than compete with existing operating systems on the market (cf. Samsung Electronics 2010a).

The global market shares of operating systems for 2013 are compared with those for 2012 in Fig. 4.10. This impressively demonstrates the triumphal march of Android. In Q1 2013, the Google operating system, with a market share of 74.4 %, is the clear market leader ahead of Apple iOS, which has a market share of just 18.2 %. They are followed by RIM in 3rd place (3.0 %), Windows Mobile in 4th place (2.9 %) and Symbian in 6th place, with a market share of only 0.6 %.

4.2.4 Mobile-Relevant Trends

Mobile commerce (m-commerce) represents an amalgamation of Internet and mobile communications. Whereas devices are getting ever closer to PCs and represent a kind of "miniature PC with telephony" in this respect, the transmission routes are different. A mobile communication standard has so far been provided in Europe by the UMTS (Universal Mobile Telecommunication System), which has progressively become closer to broadband transmission in terms of performance. In this regard, reference is also made to the third mobile generation (G3), which should now be replaced by the next generation, LTE (Long Term Evolution) technology.

Whether for fixed or mobile communication, there are no limits on further technological development. However, the slogan "mobile first" defines the latest technological trends on the subject of mobile commerce (cf. Heinemann et al. 2013):

4.2 Technological Principles of Mobile Commerce

- **Trend 1 – Mobile devices hybrid:** Whether larger smartphones or smaller tablet PC, the crossovers between smartphones, tablets and laptops will continue to disappear. Smartphones and tablets cause difficulties for other product categories because they are very versatile, thereby significantly enlarging their scope of operation (cf. FAZ 2013a, No. 6, p. 16). For example, this includes digital music games, video game consoles, navigational devices and above all cameras. Accordingly, devices are used less often for telephony and sending emails, but increasingly serve as a control center for a wide variety of everyday tasks. Whether as household appliances, medical devices or measuring instruments, there is a broad range of usage options (cf. FAZ 2013a, No. 6, p. 16). Experts are already talking about the "post-smartphone era" and devices as a "remote control for life" or "digital Swiss knife" (cf. Go-Smart study 2012; FAZ 2013a, No. 6, p. 16)
- **Trend 2 – Secondary tablets and budget tablets:** The iPad mini paved the way and other providers followed, such as Google with the Nexus 7 or Microsoft with its own tablet based on the new operating system Windows 8. In addition, there is a flood of new tablet models, including from Motorola, Dell, Asus, Acer and HTC. Another massive expansion of offers should be expected (cf. FAZ 2011a, No. 2, p. 15). Primarily low-budget devices will inundate the market. Amazon led the way with the Kindle Fire and Kindle Fire HD at competitive prices. Acer is also making its mark with a tablet PC at a competitive price of 119 euros (cf. FAZ 2013b, No. 9, p. 17). Smaller tablets are better suited for shopping on the move and supplement larger devices, which are preferred "on the sofa", alongside the TV. A trend towards a secondary tablet and budget tablet is being established.
- **Trend 3 – Data glasses or SmartGlass:** Google has already sent the first glasses with a display to developers, in order to design apps for them. Google glasses should be available starting in 2014 and resemble a headset with a display mounted on a clamp (cf. Welt am Sonntag (WAMS) 2013, No. 5, p. 50). Vuzix is likely to launch its M100 Smart Glasses, which have an integrated GPS module and run on the Android operating system, in the near future. The same applies to the Oculus Rift. Application options are varied and a good fit for the "post-smartphone era": a glance out of the window can automatically indicate how warm or cold it is outside and what the weather is like, or a map shown in the display gives directions to a destination. If the user falls down, he or she is automatically asked whether he/she wants to look for a hospital. Furthermore, all other functions which a modern smartphone of the fourth generation has to offer are possible. However, it is still unclear exactly how data glasses should be used. Voice control or keyboards projected onto body parts are being tested. In each case, usage with a smartphone should be no problem.
- **Trend 4 – Web-enabled consumer goods:** An increasing number of familiar devices from everyday life will sooner or later become web-enabled. Cameras led the way and 13 megapixels and eight core processors are no longer a rarity. In

addition to web-enabled TV devices, which allow for access to TV and Internet, smartwatches are also being tested. These are wristwatches, which supplement the smartphone or will even replace them at some stage. Google and Apple are also working on such watches. Toshiba has already introduced a prototype with the Graphic Watch (cf. Welt am Sonntag (WAMS) 2013, No. 5, p. 50). One problem, however, is the small screen and thus its unwieldiness, but researchers already have larger screens in mind, e.g. car windows or special window glass as an interactive display. In this way, consumer goods are turning into computers and a new type of medium.

- **Trend 5 – Supernets:** Mobile supernetworks ("supernets") with an LTE standard are currently being constructed. The expectation is that domestic use of the mobile network will become more affordable through the extension of flat-rate offers. Use of the Internet abroad is also set to be less expensive from 2012, as ensured by a new EU Commission regulation. Customers should then only have to pay one fifth of the current rate (cf. RP 2011b dated May 20, p. B3). Nevertheless, many of the conceivable Internet applications will not be feasible, even with mobile supernets. Intelligent power supplies, high-resolution 3D films, telemedicine, remote control at home and objects which can communicate with one another require gigabit speeds of at least 1,000 megabits. This is only achievable if data are transmitted via optical fibers and requires a completely new network. Germany now lags behind other EU countries in optical fiber penetration, with a 3 % penetration rate. The EU average could be considerably above 10 % (cf. Die Welt 2011b, dated March 1, 2011, p. 3; FAZ 2011d, No. 53, p. 19).
- **Trend 6 – Cloud computing and direct browser editing:** The combination of smartphones and fast data networks represents a breeding ground for the giant data center, called the "cloud" (cf. FAZ 2011b, No. 21, p. 16). In this respect, the new browsers for Microsoft (Explorer 9), Google (Chrome 10) and Mozilla (Firefox 4 – beta) can be regarded as new windows in the cloud, since they can display much more than websites. If an increasing number of applications for computer users are relocated from hard disks to the Internet (cloud), the browser becomes more important, since text editing, spreadsheet analysis, presentations, email and videos are then processed directly in the browser, regardless of the location of the relevant servers. What is important here is to ensure that users can access their applications without any problem.
- **Trend 7 – Lean apps and browser books:** Cloud computing enables the technical outsourcing of server functions, so that computers can dispense with hard drives in the future and thereby become cheaper and faster. The first such netbook – the Chromebook based on the Samsung series 5 model – displays a list of the most important apps just a few seconds after start-up and can therefore be used immediately. This is made possible by eliminating Bluetooth, digital video output and hard drives. Instead, there is a flash player with 16 gigabytes and a main memory limited to 2 gigabytes. Essentially, only the Chrome browser has to be started up, and the user then moves around in its windows – instead of in the

desktop background as was previously the case. Apps are the most important tools when working with Chromebook, but it only works if users are online, which requires a mobile supernet (cf. Welt am Sonntag (WAMS) 2011, No. 26, p. 63).

The trends outlined above go hand in hand with the expansion of network infrastructure. However, one current issue is the lack of availability of faster DSL connections. Nevertheless, technological trends are inseparably associated with expansion of the mobile network infrastructure. Mobile providers are currently building their LTE networks with the primary focus on rural regions. This is implemented based on long-wave frequencies, which were formerly used by radio transmitters. The advantage is that radio transmitters no longer require the frequencies due to conversion to digital technologies and fewer radio stations must be constructed when building such networks. Telekom, for example, planned to build around 2,500 LTE base stations by the end of 2011. The speed should be doubled to 42 megabits per second in Germany, which has evidently not yet been fully achieved. UMTS successor technology is officially called 4G in Germany, in contrast to 3G for UMTS technology HSPA+. However, based on the official definition of the International Telecommunication Union, LTE does not currently comply with 4G standards and should therefore be regarded as 3G. But no doubt it is only a matter of time before these standards are fulfilled (cf. Die Welt dated February 16, 2011a, p. 12).

Technological developments allow for a digital revolution in retailing and the rapid penetration of smartphones. This in turn promotes the mobilization of customers and provides the network fundamentals for new-generation mobile commerce.

4.3 Business Models in Mobile Commerce

Mobile commerce began in the early 1990s. The first commercial GSM mobile communication networks (Global System for Mobile Communication) started in Germany back in 1992, at roughly the same time as the provider CompuServe began using the Internet for commercial use (cf. Pichlmeier 2010, p. 30). As a result of the enormous growth and associated increase in mobile providers and subscribers, this initial phase ended with the auctioning of the first UMTS licenses in 2000. Around the turn of the millennium, the dotcom bubble burst and had a sustainable impact on the development of e-business and subsequently m-commerce. This essentially heralded the transactional era of m-commerce in Germany, with real product and service packages. The technological quantum leap was initially used by established companies to consistently drive forward the expansion of data services, such as MMS (Multimedia Messaging Service), email and mobile Internet (cf. ibid., p. 37). Demand for smart terminals rose incessantly, as a result of which the power structures have also increasingly shifted among device manufacturers and mobile communication providers. In essence, this phase culminated in the auctioning of further UMTS frequencies by the German Federal Network Agency in April 2010 (cf. ibid.).

The various phases of m-commerce are frequently presented and discussed from different perspectives, which are not comparable. At the start of the mobile revolution, mobile operators dominated the m-commerce supply. This was initially founded on general technological conditions at the time and was very strongly related to data transmission and performance of devices. Device manufacturers also played an increasingly large role in this phase and sometimes provided their own m-commerce services. However, the dominance of mobile communication providers and device manufacturers, which initially held the customer master data and variable data, continually declined due to changes in marketing models. Cooperating partners increasingly conducted customer data surveys for data collection and held information which was critical to success, allowing them to implement a "branded resell" in which the partner also operates as a distributor of mobile devices and can influence device software and configuration of the SIM card (e.g. for access to portals and value-added services). Existing m-commerce technologies (IVR – Interactive Voice Response – and SMS – Short Message Service) were supplemented by MMS and WAP ("Wireless Application Protocol") technology and apps. WAP technology, which feature simple drop-down menus and text input, allowed for Internet-based transactions and thereby online commerce. Apps represent the provision of additional services and are based on the employed operating system.

In order to correctly understand the phases and various opportunities and potential of m-commerce, different mobile commerce perspectives should be clarified based on the value chain (cf. Pichlmeier 2010, p. 44).

4.3.1 Prospects and Value Chains in Mobile Commerce

For the sake of simplification, value-added sectors in mobile commerce can be subdivided into infrastructure, operation, content, applications and portals. They are represented by players, such as mobile pure players, Internet companies, old economy players, mobile network operators and device manufacturers (cf. Logara 2008, p. 19). A map of mobile business is shown in Fig. 4.11:

- **Infrastructure** includes everything required for the operation of applications on mobile devices, including the mobile communications network, software platforms and the devices themselves.
- **Operation** represents the interface to the customer. This does not involve end customers, but rather providers of subsidized mobile phones or smartphones with a contract on the market.
- **Applications/apps** include business models which are geared to customer benefit and are currently revolutionizing total commerce, for example through their disruptive nature. Applications are much more than WAP pages, but differ

4.3 Business Models in Mobile Commerce

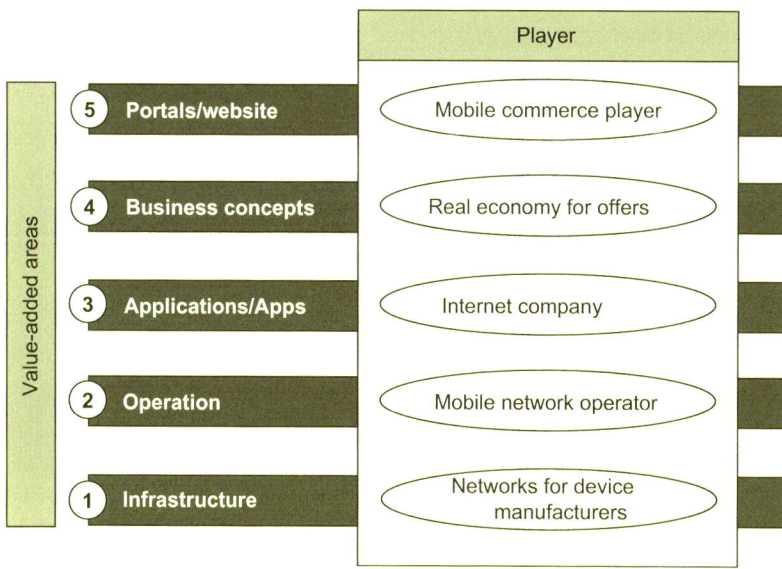

Fig. 4.11 Map of mobile business (Source: Based on Zobel 2001, p. 4; Logara 2008, p. 22)

greatly depending on the underlying business concept. Applications are now offered for all kinds of services and products in the form of apps.
- **Business concept** has long been regarded as content, i.e. what is provided as information for access via a radio telephone network (e.g. German Bundesliga results for those interested in soccer). However, today's technology also allows for supplying all products and services with a transactional nature. Depending on the nature of the transaction, a fundamental differentiation is required between B2C and B2B offers, whereby this book exclusively refers to B2C.
- **Portals** are frequently identical to Internet portals and usually attempt to integrate providers of content and applications, in order to gain direct access to the user.

With regard to players, device manufacturers which are generally very well-known, e.g. Nokia, Sony, Ericsson, Motorola and Samsung, should be dealt with first. On the other hand, mobile operators are oligopolies which have been promoted by high infrastructure costs and high investments for new entrants. Therefore, they also hold a relatively strong position among players. The real economy is now extensively involved in mobile business. A differentiation needs to be made here between B2B and B2C companies and business concepts. The unlimited potential of the old economy is unlocked through innovative applications, similar to the Internet hype before the turn of the millennium. In this respect, Internet companies now play a leading role in the value chain, since cellphones are increasingly well connected with the Internet outside of WAP (cf. Logara 2008, p. 21). Until a few years ago, websites had to be customized for WAP. However, the newly integrated

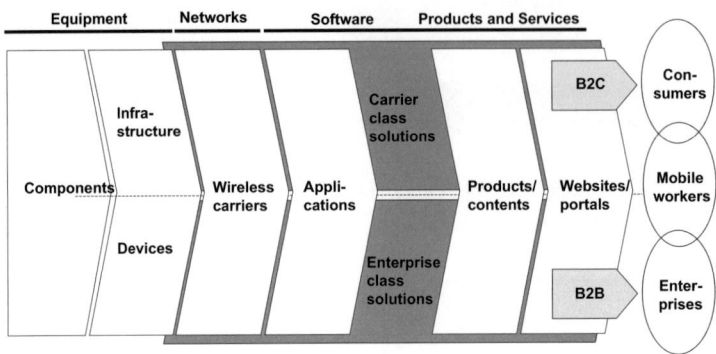

Fig. 4.12 Value chain in mobile commerce (Source: Based on Spielberg 2001, p. 291)

WWW browsers, in combination with fast data connections, allow for problem-free surfing on the Internet via mobile phones and smartphones. Mobile pure players can also successively expand their range of offers for devices here. For example, this includes companies which design applications with the advantage of a localization option. Mobile games should also be mentioned here, which now enjoy greater popularity in mobile commerce.

4.3.1.1 Value Chain in Mobile Commerce

It has only become possible to offer services and products in mobile commerce by establishing the entire value chain. The value chain sensibly merges all value-added sectors in a smooth process. One such value chain is depicted in Fig. 4.12, which differentiates between B2B and B2C alignment based on business concepts.

However, the exclusive focus of this book is on B2C (cf. Spielberg 2001, p. 291). The entire value chain can be controlled by a service provider, or merged based on specialization. Figure 4.12 represents a largely self-controlled value chain, forming the basis for relevant software solutions. This begins with the merger of periphery components, which are either introduced by providers themselves or selected as a standard solution.

Mobile data transmission is generally assured through network operators. Different core competencies may exist within the value chain, including in the development and operation of applications, which requires a high level of technical, operational and marketing expertise. However, offers may include specific services, i.e. products, services or contents, which are then marketed on websites or portals and differentiated based on B2C or B2B. In addition to core competencies, all other business activities within the value chain should be supportive in character. Which type of service is provided and how revenues are generated in mobile commerce result from the underlying business concept.

4.3.2 Business Concepts in Mobile Business

M-commerce services go beyond voice telephony, but are sold via mobile devices and mobile communication networks. The innovation rate is very high for business concepts and new business ideas are constantly emerging. In relation to SoLoMo, the "Business-to-Consumer" (B2C) business model and thereby retailing is primarily taken into consideration. The "million dollar question" in this context is: "How can sales and turnover be generated?" (Kollmann 2007, pp. 49 et seqq.).

In order to respond, it is necessary to present and explain the fundamental options for electronic business concepts. They describe the replacement of a service provided within the scope of mobile business with respect to content and the resultant remuneration. Through mobile content, mobile commerce, mobile context and mobile connection, four ideal types of business concept options can essentially be differentiated (cf. ibid.). Figure 4.13 provides an overview of the described mobile business concepts.

	Mobile content	Mobile commerce	Mobile context	Mobile connection
Definition	Collection, selection, systemization, compilation and provision of contents on the Internet	Initiation, negotiation and/or completion of business transactions on the Internet	Classification, systemization and consolidation of available information on the Internet	Creating the opportunity for exchanging information on the Internet
Goal	Provision of consumer-oriented, personalized contents on the Internet	Supplement or substitution of traditional transaction phases on the Internet	Reduction in complexity and provision of navigational aids and matching functions on the Internet	Establishing technological, commercial or purely communication connections on the Internet
Revenue model	Direct (premium content) and indirect revenue models (advertising)	Transaction-dependent direct and indirect revenue models	Direct (content inclusion) and indirect revenue models (advertising)	Direct (object inclusion/ connection fee) and indirect revenue model (advertising)
Platforms	e-shop, e-community, e-company	e-shop, e-procurement, e-marketplace	e-community, e-marketplace	e-marketplace, e-company e-community
Example	genios.de, sueddeutsche.de, manager-magazin.de guenstiger.de	hutshopping.de, amazon.com, buch.de gourmondo.de	google.de yahoo.de msn.de Chiao.com	immoscout24.de travelchannel.de t-online.de web.de
Added value	Overview, selection, cooperation, execution	Overview, selection, execution	Overview, selection, brokering, exchange	Overview, selection, brokering, execution, exchange

Fig. 4.13 Business concepts in mobile commerce (Source: Based on Kollmann 2007, p. 138)

- The **"Mobile Content"** business concept refers to the marketing of content on an internal platform within a network. This is primarily a matter of presenting and handling content for users in a manner that is simple, convenient, visually appealing and accessible online. Content can be informative, entertaining or educational, while in this concept, revenues can be generated directly (e.g. sale of content) or indirectly (e.g. advertising in content presentation). The provider LZ-net.de, from which specialized items can only be bought in return for user fees, earns direct revenues for example, whereas all news on t-online.de is free of charge and income is generated indirectly through advertising (e.g. via banners). The entertainment, audio and video clips, gambling and interactive games sector is also increasingly involved here. But search and information services should also be classified as content, which includes news, stock exchange, weather, company, product and consumer information.
- "Real" online commerce is included in the **"Mobile Commerce"** business concept, since this involves the initiation, negotiation and completion of business transactions via networks. Transaction phases do not substantially differ from those of "traditional providers" and are usually electronically supported, supplemented or substituted in individual phases. The goal of this concept is to simplify buying and business processes, or to implement them more conveniently and quickly. Revenues are predominantly generated directly here (real sale of products and services). But indirect income may also be earned, e.g. through advertising or advertising subsidies. Typical representatives of this business concept include buch.de, Amazon and travel company expedia.de. Both buy products and/or services, in order to sell them onto their customers with a markup. Mobile commerce encompasses the purchase, reservation or booking of goods and services (cf. Pichlmeier 2010, p. 26), including digital goods, e.g. downloads, the purchase of physical goods, such as a book or dress, as well as reservation of hotel rooms, ticket purchases, and participation in auctions.
- With respect to the **"Mobile Context"** business concept, the priority is on the classification, systemization and combination of available information and services in networks. The focus is on improving market transparency for the customer and making searches easier and more effective. Revenues are generated here directly through fees (for inclusion and/or placement of content) or indirectly (e.g. through advertising, statistics, content, etc.). Search engine providers, such as Google and Yahoo, practice this business concept, through which network contents are searched and catalogued. Web catalogs which conduct quality evaluations of websites can also be cited as an example. Search and information services are particularly relevant in mobile business, which relate to the relevant location. This concerns geo-location or positioning services for example. Location-dependent information services can also be used for events, special offers, or navigation and search services for cash machines, restaurants or stores (cf. Pichlmeier 2010, p. 26). Geo-location and localization refer to the identification of a location for the positioning of an object or person. Pull and push services can be differentiated here. Whereas pull services require

an explicit request, push services are directly delivered to recipients on the basis of their basic consent or subscription, without a direct request (cf. ibid.). "Mobile context" business concepts now go beyond the approaches outlined here. Location-based services in particular allow for innovative business concepts in combination with social networks, which can also be allocated to location-based services (LBS). These include the new area of near-field communication, which is discussed again within the scope of mobile commerce tools.
- The fourth business concept, **"Mobile Connection"**, organizes the interaction of players in data networks, which can be done not only on a commercial level, but on a communicative or technological level as well. Revenues are generated directly (e.g. with object receipt/linking or connection fees). However, indirect revenues are also common, e.g. via advertising, statistics or cross-selling. This type of "technological merger" is utilized at t-online, for example, since general access to the Internet is provided for a connection fee. One example of a commercial merger is the Scout24 marketplaces, e.g. ImmobilienScout24.de, which bring real estate agents onto an e-marketplace with a database connection for the purpose of selling houses. Communities and email service providers (e.g. gmx.de) are examples of communicative mergers. Social software with instant messaging and social networks, e.g. Facebook and Xing, are also included in the "mobile connection" segment.

Business concepts in mobile business now go beyond the four conventional concepts outlined above and business concepts that generally form the basis for e-business. Business concepts are increasingly combined, which is often also associated with verticalization. This will be discussed again at a later point.

4.3.3 Telematics and Cross-technology Platforms in Mobile Commerce

The relatively new field of telematics has emerged with the amalgamation of telecommunication and information technology, and involves the applied information technology of distributed systems, as is the case in interlinked IT systems. These include PCs, smartphones, mobile phones, PDAs, servers, satellites and other systems (cf. Negele 2011; Logara 2008, pp. 22–23). The added value of the overall system results from communication between individual elements. Global networking and its continuous improvement led to a massive increase in telematics applications and their fields of application. Wireless communication in the telematics sector is usually implemented though mobile communication. The field of telematics is still in the starting phase, but a trend towards amalgamation of technologies can be more strongly discerned. In addition to telecommunication and information technology, this concerns the area of multimedia as well (cf. ibid., p. 24). Telematics systems are also deployed as toll systems and used to manage vehicle fleets.

The latest generation of smartphones and tablets reveal the extent to which technologies are already interlinked and affected by telematics. They allow everyday life to be permeated with multimedia contents and have storage capacity up to 32GB or more. In addition – at least in the case of iPads – a QWERTZ keyboard can be connected, allowing for conversion to a laptop. Communications options range from UMTS, HSDPA, EDGE and GSM up to WLAN. Moreover, mobile Internet Explorer is installed on devices, enabling access to the WWW just as conveniently as at home on the PC. Furthermore, devices have several high-megapixel cameras, email push services, MP3 players and GPS models. It is only a question of time until a second camera on the front, for video telephony purposes, becomes a standard feature on devices, thereby enabling mobile video telephony on the move, based on standardized communication with other devices. Such a networking of systems will result in devices, e.g. digital camera, MP3 player, navigation system, telephone and computer, increasingly being combined with one another in future. This development in mobile commerce also complies with the trend towards a cross-technology platform, which has made the use of location-based services and mobile payment possible.

4.3.4 Websites Versus Applications/Apps

When entering the world of mobile commerce, the first question to be answered is whether an app should be developed or mobile shops should work on their own websites. Whereas the app can only be specifically designed for one operating system and requires different codes for different platforms, websites usually run on different mobile phones or operating systems. However, a combination of both approaches is also an option in the form of "native applications", which load data from the Internet and upload data from the mobile device onto the Internet. Specific functions of the mobile device can be accessed with native applications, which web applications are unable to access (cf. Alby 2008, p. 103). In the event of a decision in favor of apps, the app should at least be operable on the two market leaders – iPhone OS and Android. Whereas the Apple App Store has registered the most downloads so far and iTunes has global turnover of around eight billion US dollars, the Android market is catching up strongly. Although many companies generally want to start with an iPhone app, in almost all cases an Android app is also considered (cf. Mobile Internet 2011, p. 4). The ideal solution here includes two native apps, which are tailored to operating systems and are superior to hybrid HTML5 approaches. On the other hand, the development and marketing of a mobile website is much more advantageous.

Considerable costs may arise in particular when it comes to marketing apps. With more than one million apps provided on different operating systems, a new app can only make it to the top with sophisticated marketing. Roughly the same budget should therefore be set aside for publicizing an app as for development, meaning that budgets of up to six figures may be involved (cf. ibid., p. 5). The most

	Mobile website	**App**
Pros	Found by search engines Reviewed surf result Comparably cost-efficient Can link as usual	Offers natives outstanding usability Very popular among users Telephone functions easy to integrate Many functions also usable offline
Cons	Slightly restricted usability Low range Requires streamlining Regarded as less high-quality	Only compatible with one operating system Optimization depends on user update Must be downloaded Not selectable via link Comparatively expensive

Fig. 4.14 Pros and cons of website versus app (Source: Based on Mobile Internet 2011)

important advantages and disadvantages for making a decision between a mobile website and app are depicted in Fig. 4.14.

4.4 Special Characteristics of Mobile Marketing

With the emergence of online commerce, a fundamental paradigm shift has already been included in marketing, and carried forward into mobile marketing. The goal of mobile marketing is to provide the right product range and services for attractive customers and support existing offline activities. New CRM systems, customer databases and intelligent 1:1 marketing are required, unless already covered by existing online activities. Information technologies are primarily deployed with the goal of enhancing customer value. All marketing tools are aligned to this goal. The basic principles of new marketing primarily relate to specific marketing applications along with CRM and customer retention management in mobile commerce, but also directly influence near-field communication and viral marketing.

4.4.1 Specific Applications in the Mobile Marketing Mix

Apart from the general principles and special characteristics which pertain to the marketing mix and are also relevant to mobile marketing (cf. Heinemann 2012a, p. 35), online marketing is primarily characterized by additional Web 2.0 applications or social media aspects. However, the term Web 2.0 is frequently used imprecisely and not without overlaps (cf. Möhlenbruch et al. 2008, p. 228). Based on the original approach by O'Reilly, the following ideal requirements should be fulfilled (cf. ibid.):

- Network-based applications, which only require a web browser.
- Dynamically-generated contents, which change depending on user inputs.

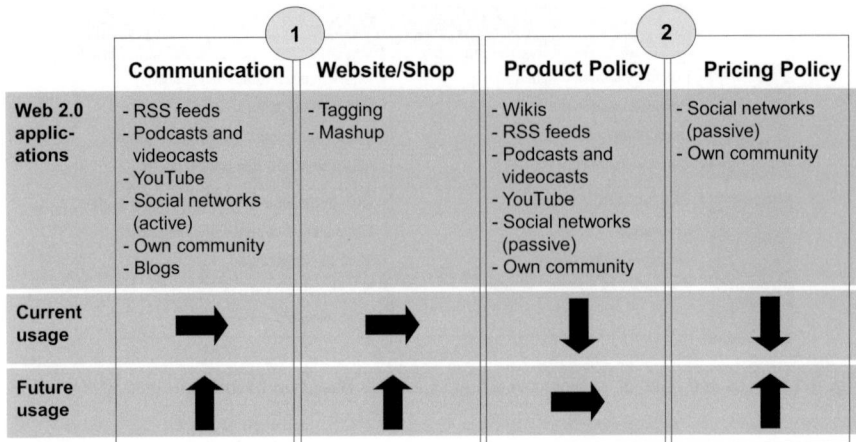

Fig. 4.15 Web 2.0 applications for mobile commerce marketing tools (Source: Based on Möhlenbruch et al. 2008, p. 228)

- Users can also create contents themselves.
- Differentiation is possible with respect to who is able to review and edit contents for which individuals.
- Users can edit their own data and personalize contents and layouts.
- The contributions of others can be commented on, and mutual communication is possible.
- A sense of togetherness exists among users (community concept).

The resultant usage options for Web 2.0, based on application priorities, can be attributed to different mobile commerce marketing tools. Such a classification is depicted in Fig. 4.15.

In addition to applications, estimates are also shown with regard to current usage and future potential (cf. Möhlenbruch et al. 2008, p. 228). Social media applications, which cannot be directly attributed to a marketing tool, are not assessed. For example, this concerns Web 2.0 applications, such as social news, social bookmarking and Internet-based desktop applications (cf. ibid.).

The marketing tools are subdivided into two groups, i.e. communication and website (front-end) and product and pricing policy. Trend arrows in Fig. 4.16 illustrate the present and future direction of the performance of Web 2.0 applications. In general, it can be stated that current utilization of future options and potential is lagging considerably behind (cf. ibid.).

4.4.1.1 Communications Policy in Mobile Commerce

Web 2.0 applications are already extensively used in communications today. Subscription services (RSS feeds) frequently support permission marketing and represent a targeted form of SMS subscriptions. As unidirectional applications, feeds are well-suited for building individual and innovative push channels for the

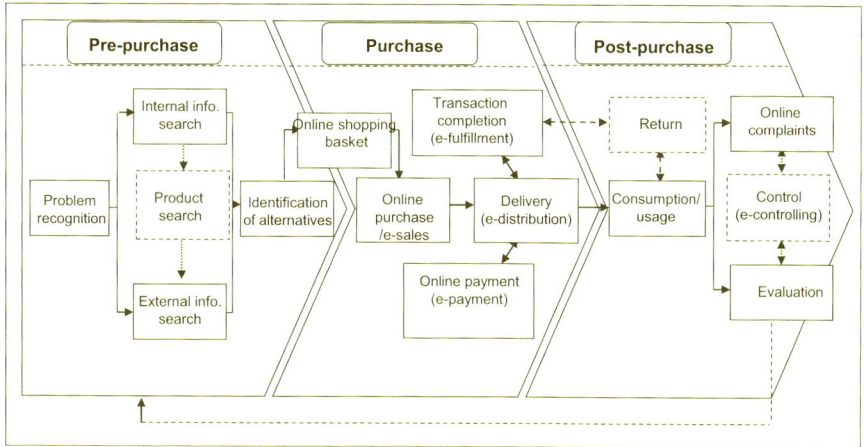

Fig. 4.16 Process areas in front end of mobile commerce (Source: Based on Kollmann 2007)

customer. Given that mobile devices are usually constantly connected to the network, news can be delivered with precise timing. The user accepts receipt of the news and promptly processes the delivered information. This allows for the creation of customized profiles on the basis of SIM identifications, meaning that customized information on product preferences can be collected and used for individual offers (cf. Möhlenbruch et al. 2008, p. 230).

Customer-oriented applications can also be realized through podcasts and videocasts, and made available to mobile users through subscription services in the form of audio or video files. Such files are then made available on a web server and regularly updated or supplemented. They can be displayed regardless of time and location and enable mobile commerce providers – in conjunction with the RSS feed push channel – to constantly provide customized information. This largely complies with the principle of one-to-one marketing (cf. ibid.; Heinemann 2012a, pp. 138 et seqq.). YouTube represents a special opportunity in the form of interactive videos, which can easily be used for campaign purposes.

The issue of social networks and community incorporates the integration of private online presence on the World Wide Web. Even for small and medium-sized mobile commerce providers, a private virtual Internet community also makes sense with regard to an offer, product, service or related issue, for example in the form of a "bulletin board" or guestbook. Furthermore, participation in established forums and virtual communities is also an option, in order to present and call attention to a company's own professional expertise (cf. HMWVL 2007, p. 13). In addition to setting up a private Internet community, i.e. a community or social group, in which customers share a consumer experience, the focus is increasingly on the use of external Internet communities for advertising purposes and customer acquisition. Highly interactive communications environments in Web 2.0 offer customers completely new opportunities to coordinate their interests. Tapping into and leveraging customer potential in such environments, recently described as "societing" (cf. Bolz 2008, p. 255), is increasingly emerging as a key issue. The Internet and the networking of millions of people all over the world mean there are now concrete experiences for every situation – every location has already been visited, every product purchased by someone, every positive or negative service has been experienced by somebody (the "global brain"). Advertising claims no longer have any credibility in this world. "Only call it good if it is good"– this should be every company's strategy: with the help of the customer, to offer good products and services with added value and motivate customers to report credibly on them through customer recommendations and/or product ratings (cf. Haug and Küper 2010, p. 117).

The assumption can be made that the potential of social networks and communities will grow strongly with the constant technological improvements to smartphones. Blogs – which can be described as a diary or journal that is updated and publicly accessible on the website – are already being used. The blog represents a medium which is easy to manage and is used, for example, to present aspects of personal lives, opinions on issues, or shopping experiences within a community. It resembles an Internet forum and serves as a platform for sharing information and experiences (cf. Wikipedia 2008). One specific form is the microblog. Logged-on users can send limited text messages (e.g. 140 characters on Twitter) and receive messages from other users. Other users' messages can be subscribed to as "followers". Messages can be entered on the Twitter start page and messages from people followed can be sorted chronologically. The sender decides whether to restrict messages or allow access to a group of friends (cf. ibid.). Great future potential is ascribed to such microblogs in the context of smartphone technology.

4.4.1.2 Shop and Front-end in Mobile Commerce

The mobile shop represents the front-end. Customer-oriented process areas can essentially be subdivided by pre-purchase, purchase and post-purchase phases in the front-end (cf. Fig. 4.16). The pre-purchase phase involves attracting potential customers and confronting them with the product range. A key role in this phase is attributed to the product search (e-search process), in which an offer matching the need is searched for and possibly found by the customer. Through product selection and placement in the shopping cart, the transition is made to the purchase phase, which is started by clicking on an order button. This phase (e-sales process) involves a business agreement between suppliers and buyers, and completion of the transaction (e-fulfillment), which includes online payment (e-payment) and product delivery (e-distribution). Once the purchase and full transaction is complete, the post-purchase phase begins, which involves support and service offers, as well as customer reviews. This phase includes handling returns and online complaints, as well as controlling (e-controlling) for the purpose of optimizing the process structure and reviewing all sales-relevant business activities (cf. Kollmann 2007, pp. 148 et seqq.).

Apart from communication policy activities, Web 2.0 applications can also be used in the front-end. Tagging, for example, makes it easy for users to describe contents individually. When storing data in files, a tag describes meta-information or additional information (e.g. keywords in the form of tabs) that is attached to a file in order to find such data on another website at any time, merely by clicking, and access it directly. In addition to data to be stored, additional information is filed, e.g. about its source or intended use (cf. Wikipedia 2008). The ID3 tag therefore provides information, for example in music files, on the name, genre, artist, etc. The "Tagged Image File Format" (TIFF) is popular for image data. Moreover, the "Exchangeable Image File" (EXIF) can also be used for tagging. Companies may use tagging technology as an analytical tool in particular, in order to analyze trends and preferences.

Web-based services that can be used in the front-end also include "information remixes", or "mashups", from other website operators (cf. Möhlenbruch et al. 2008, p. 232). Mashups use the concept of open interfaces and generate added value for the user through a combination of contents and data from different providers. Relevant services for new offers are often combined. Even if mashups are still relatively unusual in mobile marketing due to technological restrictions, this could change in the future in the course of technological advancements in devices.

4.4.1.3 Product and Range Policy in Mobile Commerce

The product range also constitutes "the heart" of the store in mobile commerce. In comparison to brick-and-mortar and mail-order retailing, online commerce and mobile commerce feature an "unlimited" product assortment, resulting from the elimination of time and space restrictions. In the conventional business approach (brick-and-mortar or mail-order store), the "$100,000 \times 100,000$ combinations" problem cannot be resolved due to the physical limitation (cf. Ahlert et al. 2002, pp. 22 et seqq.). This is where digital category management comes in, which allows for the customized configuration of categories if products can be digitally displayed. Spatial restrictions and time limits, or combination problems and display difficulties, do not play any role in the virtual world.

Even if Web-2.0 applications have only been used sporadically so far in the area of product and range policy, promising applications can be expected in mobile commerce in the future (cf. Möhlenbruch et al. 2008, p. 232). Social networks and communities are very well-suited for generating consumer ideas (consumer-generated content), for example. Users are increasingly turning from consumers into "prosumers", i.e. customers involved in the creative process. Through Internet shopping and in particular product configuration, consumers voluntarily disclose information about their preferences, which form the basis for creating the actual product. The boundary between consumer and producer is becoming blurred. Accordingly, user-generated content is handled as an elementary product on the web, as demonstrated impressively by YouTube, Flickr, and Facebook. Most of the more than seven billion online videos viewed each month evidently have user-generated content (cf. Unterberg 2008, p. 205). Online retailers can no longer avoid interactive discussions on consumer experiences. Consumers have become emancipated through the Internet and are increasingly making decisions on when, where and how media are used and advertising thus "consumed". The passive recipient consumer is increasingly becoming a thing of the past. It is becoming more and more important for advertisers to participate in consumer discussions or even organize such discussions. The associated activation of customers forms part of consumer-generated advertising (CGA). This term describes all contents generated by the consumer that are promotional in character. If a company initiates the generation of advertising content for consumers, this represents a consumer-generated advertising campaign, which, as experience shows, is perceived by other consumers as more honest and credible. Participants in CGA campaigns are also frequently opinion leaders in their consumer worlds or even the first users of the advertised product (cf. Unterberg 2008, pp. 208 et seqq.).

RSS feeds also offer starting points for optimizing the product range. Providers are able to generate information about individual tastes and use this within the framework of product policy. Such information may also be used to reduce inventory stocks and for cross-selling activities.

Wikis can also be used as a Web 2.0 application. They describe software solutions or collections of websites, which can be read by users and even directly changed online. They enable various authors to work together on texts and thereby collaboratively record the authors' experience and knowledge (cf. Wikipedia 2008). Wiki applications are still not used to a sufficient extent in mobile marketing, in particular due to inadequate display sizes. However, they have great potential, since user-generated contents can easily be used to develop value-added services.

4.4.1.4 Pricing Policy in Mobile Commerce

Mobile commerce is affected to a large extent by dynamic pricing, as already shown in the previous chapter, taking local relevance into consideration. The prices of various providers can be quickly and easily compared on the mobile web, supported by price comparison sites. Price comparison thus also plays a prominent role here. This has not only contributed to an increase in price transparency, but also has a decisive impact on customer buying behavior. In the course of mobile shopping, Internet users emphasize low prices, and thus are increasingly utilizing price agents or price search engines (e.g. guenstiger.de, preisvergleich.de, geizhals.at, and preissuchmaschine.de). Online power shopping and group selling, in which buyers join forces, are also heading in this direction, in order to effect price pressure through the resultant greater sales volumes. This also promotes the price war in mobile commerce and increases the buyers' power (cf. Heinemann 2012a, p. 39). As a result of increasing market transparency and the associated competitive pressure from the mobile Internet, the customer expects suppliers' price margins to allow for discounts. Customers have learned that price calculations in the new channels are often lower than in other channels. This is also promoted by the fact that customers are themselves taking over some of the tasks in the buying process (e.g. self-service, order processing, etc.). Experience shows that the price level for comparable items in the mobile channel is lower than in brick-and-mortar stores. But on the downside, the customer does not receive any personal advice about the item and often has to pay shipping costs, which cannot be disregarded as a price component (cf. Die Welt dated May 9, 2011d, p. 17).

As a result of great price transparency on the mobile Internet, the latent risk of a price squeeze arises for providers, which they are only able to withstand by customizing and personalizing their offers. Moreover, the reliability of providers on the net is playing an ever greater role and could have an impact on users' willingness to pay (cf. ibid.). Furthermore, offering private brands on the web is recommended. A retail company can also put together package offers or price bundles for assembled products, in order to hinder comparability with competitors. Essentially however, the price calculation in electronic sales is based on the same principles and methods as in non-electronic commerce. However, dynamic price strategies based on the online request principle or online auction principle constitute an exception here. A distinguishing feature of the online request principle is the aggregated recording of demand in respect of buyer requests and target prices, which are passed onto an agent (e.g. marketplace operator). The agent checks the data in anonymized form (including a credit assessment) and forwards them to relevant transaction partners on the supplier side (request for proposal). They then decide whether to make an offer appropriate to demand. Such an online request principle is applied, for example, at travel marketplace operator askerus.de (cf. Kollmann 2007, p. 124).

Through the online auction principle, mobile Internet providers try to quantify the buyer's individual benefit and personal willingness to pay by employing different forms of auction. An open price mechanism comes into play, during which the purchase price of a product emerges, based on the provider's starting price, through higher bids from different buyers for the same offered product (unilateral dynamic pricing). The auction is usually time-limited (cf. Kollmann 2007, p. 127). The online auction principle is used, for example, by electronic marketplace eBay, via which even Deutsche Bahn AG has already offered tickets.

Many Web 2.0 applications can also be used for pricing policy. Passive participation in social network activities allows companies to make observations about willingness to pay. But great importance is also attached to price comparison sites, since they enable a quick and easy online comparison of various providers' prices. Price comparison is playing a prominent role in mobile commerce in this respect and is reflected in relevant apps (e.g. woabi.de). This also has a huge impact on brick-and-mortar stores of multi-channel retailers when customers are online in-store using their smartphones to compare prices. Above all, mobile shopping promotes price-oriented business models, such as "daily deals" and "collective buying" (cf. Heinemann 2012a, p. 75). With Groupon, for example, local retailers can sell coupons containing large discounts and thereby acquire new customers. On the subject of couponing, real purchasing is linked to online sales (cf. FAZ 2011c, No. 26, p. 17). Groupon offers coupons to its several million users, more than three million of whom are in Germany. Groupon has not made any commitment to group buying with predefined minimum or maximum quantities. The subject of coupon services – whether Groupon.de, Dailydeal.de or mobile coupons from Coupies.de and Mymobai.com – is currently a hot topic at all the professional conferences (cf. Internet World Business 2011e, No. 12, p. 26). Groupon's major competitor is LivingSocial, which has just been taken over by Amazon and subsequently posted the largest group sales of all time with more than one million coupons. Google (Google Offers) and Facebook (Facebook Deals) are also entering this business, which is primarily well-suited for customer acquisition ("laser beam focus acquisition").

But social shopping is also relevant to pricing policy in mobile commerce. This category includes social commerce providers, like Etsy and Dawanda, open-innovation platforms, such as Threadless and Spreadshirt, shopping exchanges like Ginahhot, and shopping clubs with club sales. Vente Privée is regarded as a pioneer in club sales. The online retailer launched this new sales concept in 2002, which has been copied very successfully in Germany by the BuyVip and Brands4Friends shopping clubs. Both German club shops were founded in 2007 and now generate turnover in three-digit millions. Customers can only buy at club sales if they have registered in advance, but can only register if they have been invited by a friend beforehand. Exclusivity is thus at the forefront, while the focus of the offer – under the principles of "closed shop, customer loyalty, shortage" – is on brand, fashion and lifestyle products (e.g. Diesel, Swatch, Dolce & Gabbana, Armani or Converse). Five promotional actions a week, which club members are notified about by email, are common and usually run for 1 or 2 days (cf. Heinemann 2012a, p. 75). One sustainable field of application could be regional price differentiations in conjunction with location-based services (LBS).

Allocating Web 2.0 applications to marketing mix tools delivers a systemized approach, which will be discussed again in the next chapter on CRM and customer retention management.

4.4.2 mCRM: Customer Relationship Management in Mobile Commerce

As a result of the interactivity of the Internet medium, mobile commerce and customer relationship management (CRM) are also inseparably interrelated, as reflected by the term mCRM (cf. Silberer and Schulz 2008, pp. 150 et seqq.; Schneider 2001, pp. 31 et seqq.). Customer acquisition, shaping of customer relationships, and the targeted alignment of all processes to customer requirements are extremely important for mobile commerce. Establishing direct and loyal customer relationships is directly relevant to success in mobile commerce – with the goal of increasing the individual customer's value to the company, thus boosting profits and company value. CRM involves a radical realignment of marketing policy in mobile commerce. In contrast to mass marketing, which is widely used in brick-and-mortar retailing and primarily entails marketing as many standardized mass-produced products as possible in order to increase market shares, CRM relies on the long-term building of loyal customer relationships. The major objectives of CRM in online commerce are therefore (cf. ibid.):

- Acquiring and retaining individual customers
- Maintaining long-term customer relationships
- Constantly increasing customer satisfaction and customer value

Close customer relationships and high customer loyalty are important prerequisites for success, in particular for interactive sales channels, and have a direct impact on the operating result in this regard. It is important here that customer retention measures are aligned to the potential of respective customers in mobile commerce, which requires detailed knowledge about each individual customer. Loyal customers and long-term business relations are therefore irrevocably associated with cost reductions, turnover increase and growth. In addition, a high share of regular customers gives the provider better planning reliability and lower error rates with regard to scheduling products and services for follow-up periods.

Classification of individual customers in a typical lifecycle may be useful. Thus, for example, age and marital status play an important role for marketing activities in furniture retailing, since the needs of single people, retired persons, and families differ strikingly in this respect. A customer becomes more valuable to the online retailer with each year of the business relationship. The annual profit which can be achieved with loyal customers after several years often reaches a multiple of the basic profit in the first year. The strategic potential of customer retention can primarily be seen on markets in which first-time buyer potential is almost exhausted, as is currently the case in the mobile communication sector, for example. In light of the increasing substitutability of products and services, the significance of customer retention as a factor in success is increasing. The correlations outlined demonstrate that it is becoming more important for online providers to increase customer retention and keep the "churn rate" or migration as low as possible. This includes identifying customers at risk of migration in good time. Online retailers should also analyze the circumstances, in conjunction with migrated customers, which ultimately led to the migration. Information on customers who are willing to migrate or have already migrated, and the findings obtained about the reasons for migration may be used to prevent the migration of further customers in the future through the implementation of appropriate measures (cf. Schrödter 2003, pp. 14–15). From an economic perspective, customer retention activities can consequently be regarded as strategic and worthwhile investments (cf. Möhlenbruch et al. 2008, p. 223). This essentially comes about through satisfaction and trust, when they are assessed on a voluntary basis.

The customer retention functional chain is shown in Fig. 4.17. The first phase comprises satisfaction, which comes about through a positive target/actual comparison. The comparison of targeted expectations with actually performed services (confirmation/disconfirmation paradigm) results in a confidence level. This leads to customer loyalty in the second phase, based on trust and acceptance. Moreover, it may build enthusiasm and ultimately leads to customer retention in the third phase. This is partly expressed in repurchases, cross-buying, recommendations and in a decrease in price sensitivities (cf. ibid., p. 224).

Information is the focus in the customer satisfaction phase, essentially supported by wikis, RSS feeds, and podcasts and videocasts. RSS feeds deliver customized

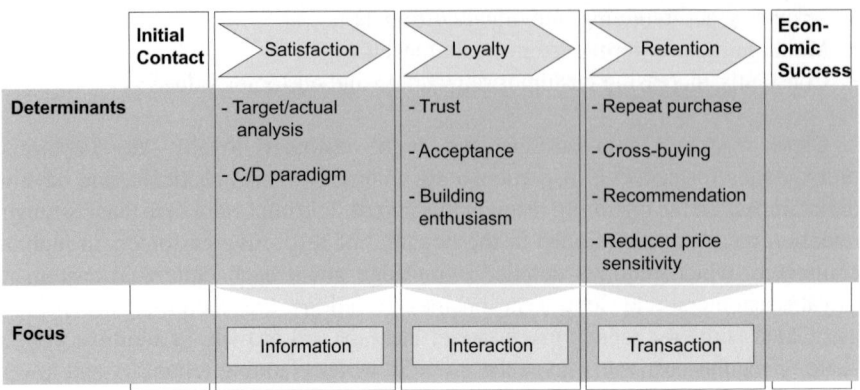

Fig. 4.17 Functional chain for customer retention in mobile commerce (Source: Möhlenbruch et al. 2008, p. 228)

contents upon request, and also document individual preferences. Within the scope of promotional activities, they also promote an increase in customer satisfaction, since they are often used for targeted push communication. The same applies to videocasts and podcasts. Wikis also have the potential to generate user-controlled information, which can have a positive impact on customer attitudes towards the company. However, the complexity of the data input for mobile devices has to be reduced, in order to cope with the increased quantity of provided contents. Within the front-end policy of mobile marketing, tagging is another application focused on information; it enables a customer-oriented information search and also increases company-specific transparency (cf. Möhlenbruch et al. 2008, p. 234).

As a second functional chain, customer loyalty places the emphasis on interaction. Social networks can be regarded as interaction-based applications, which have a positive impact on customer loyalty (cf. Heinemann 2012a, p. 75). Precise information obtained from passive monitoring helps to improve trust and customer acceptance. Moreover, it allows for a targeted influence on the community, in order to have a positive impact on the product and company image. However, this requires authenticity, otherwise the risk of failure will increase. Social shopping may be used through user interaction, in particular for price setting, since direct information on the (customers') willingness to pay can be obtained (cf. ibid.; BV Capitals 2011). The integration of interactive opportunities offered by web blogs allows for active communication, which can also have a positive effect on customer loyalty. The same applies to mashups, which represent a combination of different services and can increase user acceptance of websites (cf. Möhlenbruch et al. 2008, p. 235).

With regard to customer retention, social shopping may contribute to a positive impact on transactions (cf. Heinemann 2012a, p. 75; BV Capitals 2011). Cooperative buying experiences can help increase repurchase rates and cross-buying. Moreover, trust in communities is higher, in particular with respect to purchase recommendations. The same applies to mashups in relation to value-added services (cf. Möhlenbruch et al. 2008, p. 235). All in all, the innovative applications of Web

4.4 Special Characteristics of Mobile Marketing

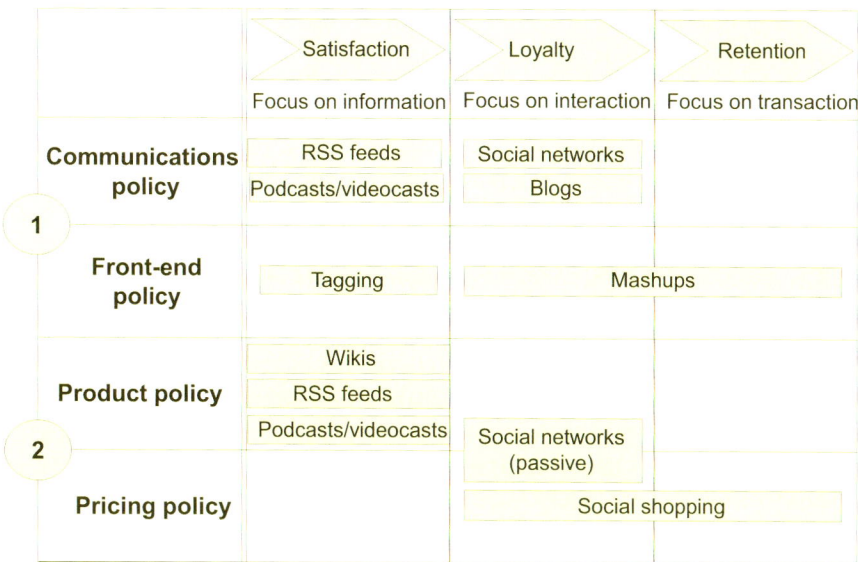

Fig. 4.18 Application of Web-2.0 customer retention management (Source: Möhlenbruch et al. 2008, p. 22)

2.0 functions – due to the opportunities they provide to influence customer satisfaction and customer loyalty – offer starting points for customer retention management, which are summarized in Fig. 4.18. An integrated view is very important, since support has a positive impact on customer retention in all phases of the functional chain.

4.4.3 NFC: Near Field Communication in Mobile Commerce

NFC is among the leaders in the annual "Gartner Hype Cycle" of the latest technology trends. The focus is on "NFC payments", whereby smartphone owners will, in the future, be able to pay their bills almost in passing (cf. FAZ 2011g, No. 189, p. 17).

NFC (Near Field Communication) is a wireless technique or technology, with which data can be exchanged in a non-contact manner (cf. Alby 2008, p. 204). NFC is employed in the user-friendly networking of mobile devices. Cellphones, PDAs or smartphones may be interconnected or connected to fixed units such as customer or EC terminals (cf. Wiedmann et al. 2008, p. 306). NFC will likely be intensively used by device manufacturers, network operators and service providers in the future to provide innovative services to mobile customers, which may emphasize the benefits of mobile commerce more strongly. Relatively few NFC-compliant devices are currently in use, but several field trials are already taking place (cf. Alby 2008, p. 204). In addition to the increase in user-friendliness through technical progress, in particular the question of how mobile commerce can offer genuine benefits from the customer's perspective should be examined. In addition to easy access, this concerns the ever-present availability of information, entertainment, service and product offers. NFC represents a significant pioneer here. It should be possible for users to get connected with other mobile phones, small electronic appliances, customer terminals or cash machines simply by touching the cellphone, and to start integrated services immediately (cf. Wiedmann et al. 2008, pp. 306–307).

The goal of the NFC research project in 2002 was to create a standard communications protocol, which was intended to combine the previously competing smart card standards of Philips and Sony. Smart cards are storable credit, store or access cards. Information and personal data are stored on such cards for electronic authentication and authorization, whereby the Philips MiFare card is the most widespread system in Europe. The maximum NFC signal range is 20 cm, which has a security advantage, since it means infringements of data integrity or manipulation of data transmission are hardly possible (cf. ibid.).

4.4.3.1 Conditions for Use of NFC in Mobile Commerce

Mobile services offer the user the advantage of being available anywhere and anytime, and thereby create the prerequisite for payment services and contents. Given that mobile marketing frequently serves the cross-advertising financing of other mobile services, NFC should be positioned precisely at the interface between electronic and mobile commerce. The transition to other fee-based mobile services can therefore be alleviated. Opportunities for using NFC in mobile commerce are shown in Fig. 4.19. Specific NFC usage options can be mentioned for each marketing tool (cf. Wiedmann et al. 2008, pp. 310–311).

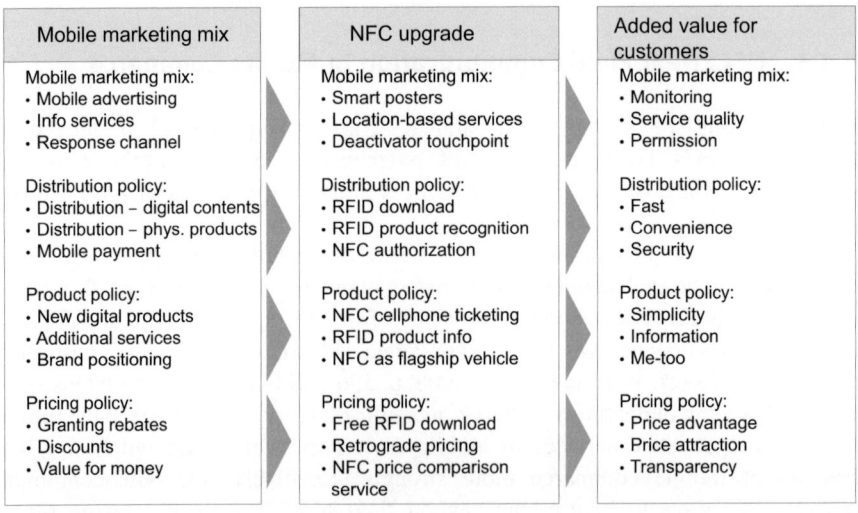

Fig. 4.19 NFC use in mobile commerce (Source: Wiedmann et al. 2008, p. 311)

4.4 Special Characteristics of Mobile Marketing

In accordance with the large contact range and minimal spread, mobile marketing primarily features a high level of customization and thereby personalization (cf. Heinemann 2012a, p. 137), which is also made possible by the specific feature of cellphones being able to display content based on location, time and context. In turn, the high contact range is the result of location and time-independent, ubiquitous availability (cf. Pichlmeier 2010, pp. 27–29).

Another special characteristic of mobile marketing is classification in push and pull services. Whereas push services are sent – unrequested – for sales promotion purposes, pull services are only forwarded based on direct request, and the risk of reactance is therefore lower. NFC represents an unambiguous pull service and is thereby useful in reducing the problems of excessive permission marketing, which refers to the forwarding of advertising and information messages based on the user's express and revocable permission. In this respect, the frequently pejorative "accessibility dilemma" should not be exploited. An NFC-supported opt-out method would be advisable here, which enables simple recall of subscribed services by contacting a "deactivator touchpoint". This could also help to allay concerns about "obscure technological processes" (cf. Wiedmann et al. 2008, p. 311).

The opportunities for NFC applications are really limitless. No limits are placed on applications associated with emulation of smart cards. Above all, applications in the area of advertising and communication could become disproportionately important. This includes the Smart Poster, which integrates the already mentioned RFID (Radio Frequency Identification System) tag in a print advert or advertising poster (cf. Heinemann 2012a, pp. 89–90). Whenever someone holds a cellphone at a site or touchpoint marked with the NFC logo, the mobile device automatically recognizes the RFID tag and conducts a data query and peering. The context menu loaded onto the cellphone allows visual or audio advertising units to be played. Internet addresses can also be transferred into the web browser for the device and accessed, which makes it much easier to use. Additional downloads of software, apps, MP3 demo songs or advertising videos can also be provided or downloaded at no added cost from the RFID tag. Given that the user who is being actively and deliberately targeted by advertising is identifiable through his or her mobile phone SIM card, additional offers and links may be implemented in accordance with the location and customer profile (cf. Wiedmann et al. 2008, p. 311). NFC can also be used for creative and image-promoting advertising campaigns – through possible downloading of large data quantities from Smart Poster – which go far beyond the options afforded by SMS.

NFC also allows for mobile payment and mobile ticketing and primarily changes the method of access (cf. Internet World Business 2011f, No. 13 p. 12). With NFC, it is sufficient to hold the cellphone to the cash terminal touchpoint for internal authentication and authorization of the payment process. Supplementary add-on services can also be used as acquisitive measures or for customer retention activities, e.g. customized discount and bonus systems. The short range not only enables the clear allocation of application and user, but also ensures inherent protection against operating errors or manipulation.

4.4.3.2 Current Example of NFC Usage

Deutsche Bahn already tested NFC under the name "Touch & Travel" on November 1, 2011, and then equipped all main-line stations with this technology. Passengers could log on with their smartphone when boarding the train and log off again at the destination, whereby the system then calculated the number of kilometers traveled and deducted the ticket price from the specified account using the direct debit procedure (cf. FAZ 2011g, No. 189, p. 17). Interested parties had to register with the rail company and store their account details, which required a credit check. Touch & Travel could only be used on the mobile networks of Deutsche Telekom and Vodafone. Moreover, apps were only available for smartphones with the Apple and Google (Android) operating systems, but the system should be open to other providers. It was relatively customer-friendly, since the control of chip cards was not required. Moreover, there was a large – at least theoretical – benefit to customers in that they could change means of transport without cumbersome batches of tickets, but this presumed the integration of public transport companies in cities. This was certainly a great challenge, since only the Berlin-Brandenburg transport authority joined the system in the pilot phase. Another 70 transport systems were supposed to take part. Results of the test have not yet been communicated, at least not publicly. Therefore, it should be assumed that the Deutsche Bahn railway company will not be able to help mobile payment systems make a breakthrough with NFC usage (cf. FAZ 2011g, No. 189, p. 17).

4.4.4 Mobile Viral Marketing

Viral marketing traditionally refers to a marketing tool for the targeted acquisition of customers in e-commerce. It may be regarded as the modern form of word-of-mouth advertising and is viewed as an efficient and effective marketing tool in online commerce. Internet users should be encouraged, in a targeted way, to distribute communication messages free of charge, similar to the principle of word-of-mouth advertising. However, the networking effects of the Internet are used to realize free distribution of information as quickly and efficiently as possible. Viral marketing uses various carrier instruments, such as search engines (e.g. yahoo.de, google.de) and link sites (e.g. ec-net.de). Additional free services may be publicized on special link sites (e.g. umsonst.de). Furthermore, virtual communication space, such as subject-related forums or chats, special communication media, e.g. Hotmail, or recommendations for content sites (e.g. spiegel.de) can be used to spread information. Lastly, contests are also an effective tool to draw attention to service offers (cf. Heinemann 2012a, p. 58; Schwarz 2007, p. 37; Kollmann 2009, p. 304).

4.4.4.1 Application of Viral Marketing in Mobile Commerce

As on the stationary Internet, a reference to viruses is also used in mobile commerce to describe the exponential diffusion of contents. Users receiving mobile content send recommendations to other users, who are then "infected". In mobile viral

Characteristic	Distinctive characteristics of features					
Stakeholders	Initiator	Connection point	First contact	Communicator		Recipient
Motive of communicator	Intrinsic			Extrinsic		
Role of communicator	Standardized			Differentiated		
Added value for recipients	Information	Entertainment		Contest	Monetary added value	
Type of content	Mobile application	Video	Audio		Image	Text
Type of content generation	User-generated content			Company-generated content		
Valence	Positive			Negative		
Level of network effect	High			Low		
Costs	Premium rate		Volume fees	None		
Recommendation type	Pull			Push		
Implementation technology	Higher programming language	Mobile tagging	WAP/ i-mode	Mobile email	MMS	SMS	IVR
Mobile communications technology	Mobile telephony	Wireless LAN	Bluetooth		Infrared	RFID/ NFC

Fig. 4.20 Features of mobile viral marketing (Source: Pousttchi et al. 2008, p. 295)

marketing, consumers are motivated to send mobile viral content – using mobile technology – to other potential customers from their personal network, who are then encouraged to make a further recommendation. Mobile content generally relates to mobile services and advertising messages, which are typically shared between persons with the same interests and thereby allow for target group-specific and personalized promotional activities. Moreover, this type of advertising is seen as very efficient due to lower wastage (cf. Pousttchi et al. 2008, p. 293). Typical features of mobile viral marketing are described in Fig. 4.20 (cf. ibid.). A difference can be made between user-generated content and company-generated content in terms of types of content generation. Contributions on mobile communities may be regarded as an example of user-generated content, in which private individuals act as initiators.

Only a few selected characteristics and not all features will be addressed in the following. The valence indicates whether mobile viral marketing has a supportive or damaging nature. There are hardly any examples of negative effects, but opinion platforms show potential threats.

In contrast, the level of the network effect influences the diffusion curve of products. Starting from a specific critical mass of users, it is expected that the acquisition of additional customers will develop by itself. For example the more users utilize the instant messaging service, the greater the benefit that a user can achieve, since the number of communication relationships increases as a result.

There are low network effects for SMS coupons, for example, given that neither the communicator nor the recipient benefit from high distribution. Monetary costs, on the other hand, represent a potential obstacle to participation in viral marketing campaigns. No costs generally arise with the use of Bluetooth or NFC (cf. Alby 2008, p. 56). However, volume fees are frequently incurred when sending an SMS or downloading data through a mobile communications device But premium rate fees are also conceivable for services provided, e.g. in the case of premium SMS. The push principle in mobile marketing is seen as a trigger for a campaign, which comes about through external simulation, with the use of an advertising medium. In contrast, the pull principle describes the unrequested sending of a mobile advertising message. Both push and pull are interpreted as a type of recommendation in mobile viral marketing (cf. Pousttchi et al. 2008, p. 293).

4.4.4.2 Preferences and Classifications of Mobile Marketing Strategies

Empirical studies on consumer behavior in mobile viral marketing show that ad-financed free SMS services for websites, video clips and mobile coupons are used most. The same applies to location-based friend-finder or instant messaging services. Figure 4.21 shows the corresponding preferences for different mobile viral marketing strategies. Classifications of mobile marketing usage can be derived from the various preferences. The mobile viral marketing classification developed by Pousttchi and Wiedemann on the basis of Subramani and Rajogopalan indicates typical patterns, which relate to the two dimensions of "role of communicator" and "level of network effect". The classification is depicted in Fig. 4.22 and shows four standard types, i.e. motivated evangelism, signaling use/group membership, targeted recommendation and awareness creation/benefit signaling (cf. Subramani and Rajagopalan 2003, pp. 300 et seqq.; Pousttchi et al. 2008, p. 298):

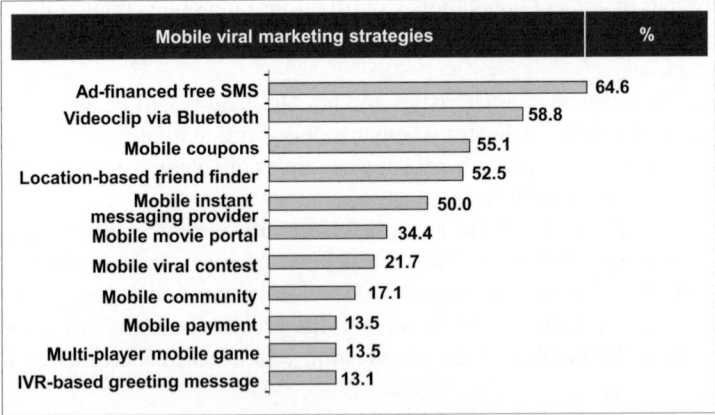

Fig. 4.21 Preferences for mobile viral marketing strategies (Source: Pousttchi et al. 2008, p. 298)

4.4 Special Characteristics of Mobile Marketing

Fig. 4.22 Mobile viral marketing standard types (Source: Pousttchi et al. 2008, p. 299)

- The **Motivated Evangelism** type features high network effects and an active role of the communicator. In this type, both the communicator and recipient have to use the relevant service to obtain added value, thereby motivating communicators to actively convince other users to utilize these services. Examples of such services are special mobile communications services, e.g. Zlango, mobile instant messaging services, e.g. Bing, mobile communities (e.g. Peperonity) or location-based friend-finders, e.g. Qiro (cf. ibid.).
- The standard **Signaling Use/Group Membership** type arises from a combination of high network effects and a passive role for the communicator. Mobile payment method Paybox can be cited as one of the few examples of this type. A Paybox user instructs a non-registered user to make payment. The non-registered user is notified and receives information about the required registration. The payment can only be received following registration (cf. ibid.).
- The **Targeted Recommendation** type features the absence of network effects and an active role for the communicator. A typical example is the send-to-a-friend application. The communicator sends viral content, e.g. mobile coupons or mobile short films and videos. Bluetooth is used for transmission due to the usually high data volume. This type includes contests requiring the participation of others (cf. ibid., p. 300).
- The fourth type, **Awareness Creation/Benefits Signaling**, can be identified by the absence of network effects and a passive role for the communicator. Recognition of a service is only increased through its usage. Mobile greeting cards can be cited as an example, which use Interactive Voice Response (IVR) and are connected to a subsequent SMS. This provides information about the communicator and the transmission mechanism.

In summary, with regard to mobile viral marketing it can be stated that it is an innovative marketing tool, which has not yet been sufficiently investigated, but will increasingly gain importance in the future as part of rapid mobile phone penetration.

4.5 Forms of Mobile Commerce

There are now various common forms of mobile commerce. The leading players here are certainly the pure online retailers, almost all of which have an operational mobile shop. With parallel operation from classic online commerce and mobile commerce, they form "hybrid mobile commerce", a widespread type of mobile commerce. This can be differentiated from pure mobile commerce. "Pure mobile commerce" providers often offer information and entertainment services and focus on the digital product. But mobile commerce cooperations can also increasingly be observed on portals, forming "cooperative mobile commerce". Search engine providers, such as Google, which are now offering e-books as retailers and forcing the pace towards open marketplaces, can also be classified in this category. Another form of mobile commerce is multi-channel mobile commerce. This identifies a combination of brick-and-mortar and electronic sales channels, including mobile commerce, with no-line commerce representing a special form of such multi-channel mobile commerce. However, mobile communication companies and device manufacturers are increasingly using the mobile channel to distribute products and services. This form of mobile selling to end customers is called "verticalized mobile commerce". The different forms of mobile commerce are depicted in Fig. 4.23 and described in detail in the following chapters.

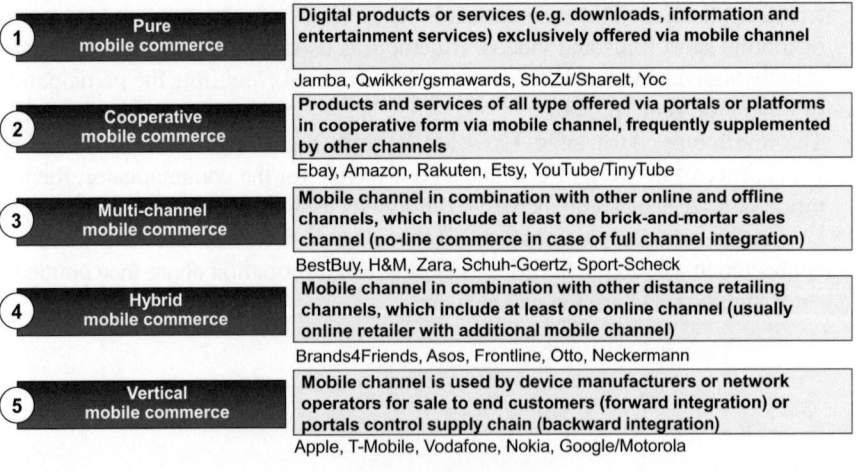

Fig. 4.23 Forms of mobile commerce (Source: Internal research)

4.5.1 Pure Mobile Commerce

If the mobile channel is used as the only distribution channel for products or services, this represents a "mobile commerce pure player", which applies to providers of ringtones, or apps and tickets, for example. Jamba can be regarded as a typical representative of pure mobile commerce and is considered to be a leading provider of mobile content (cf. Richter 2009, pp. 32 et seqq. – AP WIGE Leipzig). As a mobile music representative, Jamba can also be classified as pure mobile commerce. Jamba is seen as a well-known portal for downloading music titles onto cellphones, and in conjunction with Debitel, actively targets mobile customers for advertising, when concluding contracts with additional services. Yoc AG can be mentioned as another representative of pure mobile commerce. Yoc provides mobile content in the area of mobile B2C services, which involves digital products, e.g. ringtones, images, logos or animations. Such services are sometimes self-developed, but may also be purchased from service providers. End consumers can buy such services by subscription or individual order. Promotional campaigns are also run on classic communications media, such as TV and newspapers, but also via the Internet and cellphone. However, sales are exclusively transacted on the mobile channel. In addition, mobile contents are provided to registered users of their own community. Yoc AG also offers its customers design and development services for mobile portals, which are available from the customer's cellphone.

4.5.2 Cooperative Mobile Commerce

Use of a mobile shop on auction house eBay or as a partner of Amazon is also possible now. This is relatively uncomplicated and can be implemented at reasonable expense. Using external tools, an eBay shop can be developed relatively easily and quickly into a full e-commerce system. Common eBay services, such as PayPal, Inkasso (cash collection) and Treuhandkonto (escrow account) support transactions. Moreover, it lets users benefit from the potential trust, recognition, and promotional campaigns of these two popular commercial platforms. Amazon, for example, is dynamically linked to a large number of external websites. The "Amazon Payments" cash collection service can also be utilized. Cooperative mobile commerce, which includes mobile auctions, clearly has great potential, as evidenced by the business figures for Amazon and eBay. Amazon already made turnover of one billion US dollars via its mobile website in the 2009/2010 financial year, while eBay even achieved turnover of over two billion US dollars with mobile commerce in the 2010 financial year. Jesta Digital also implements cooperative mobile commerce and, in addition to mobile services, offers the design and development of mobile portals, which are accessible from the customer's cellphone (cf. Richter 2009, pp. 32 et seqq. – AP WIGE Leipzig). Representatives of mobile TV can also be allocated to cooperative mobile commerce. Alongside an increasing number of live-streaming TV broadcasters, there are also some specially designed channels, e.g. a comedy channel that offers the most popular comedies from various private broadcasters. Television on cellphone or mobile devices through "Digital Video Broadcasting" (DVB-H, DVB-T) and "Digital Multimedia Broadcasting" (DMB) are classified as mobile TV. Data are not transmitted via the Internet Protocol (IP), but via satellite. The video portal YouTube is also represented in mobile commerce by a portal for mobile devices. This is implemented under the name TinyTube.net, which shows films for the 3GP format standardized for cellphones.

4.5.3 Multi-channel Mobile Commerce

As part of online diffusion and evolution, an increasing number of retail companies from the brick-and-mortar sector include the Internet in their sales portfolio and also utilize mobile commerce as a new sales channel. The mobile channel is also frequently used as an information medium for the brick-and-mortar channel. Moreover, the brick-and-mortar store has certainly retained its exceptional importance, but can no longer be viewed in isolation, given that most customers of brick-and-mortar stores are also online and want various means of access. In up to 50 % of purchases, searching and browsing on the net is now seen as the starting point of a buying process. Only after researching on the retailer's website is a decision made – depending on the situation and timing during the day – whether to purchase online or visit the store, regardless of the intended delivery destination of the product. And retailers which do not offer a buying option on their website are already losing out, although many of their regular customers already search there every day and thereby generate a lot of "natural" frequency. "ROPO" – research online purchase offline – i.e. most purchases in-store are now preceded by a search for information on the Internet, is demonstrably shifting to the smartphone (cf. Heinemann 2011a, p. 19; cf. Bruce 2011, pp. 50 et seqq). Customers therefore demand multi-channel hopping, including the mobile channel, and pay a fee enabling them to switch freely between the mobile shop and store. This switching between channels takes account of their changed buying behavior, and is demonstrably rewarded by higher purchase amounts (cf. Heinemann 2011, pp. 1 et seqq.). This applies in particular to products which can be digitalized, e.g. e-books or videos. Publishing houses, which increasingly offer their newspaper and magazine contents online or in the form of apps, can also be regarded as representatives of multi-channel mobile commerce. At Springer, around one quarter of the group's turnover originates from digital business. In addition to investments, publisher Axel-Springer relies on new "paywalls" on the net. In contrast, Burda's online strategy is more comparable to that of a financial investor. In addition to journalistic websites, Burda also buys online platforms which have nothing to do with journalism. Gruner + Jahr is lagging slightly behind, since the digital magazine kiosk is dormant.

4.5.4 Hybrid Mobile Commerce

Online retailers which use m-commerce in addition to the online channel deal in "hybrid mobile commerce". Together, they use the same sales channel and – with an additional mobile shop – cater to the mobilization trend of customers. With a few exceptions, well-known online retailers do not also conduct mobile commerce. Mail-order retailers that operate an online shop and are also involved in mobile commerce can also be regarded as representatives of hybrid mobile commerce. Altogether, they use the same distance retailing channel and are now very important in terms of sales and turnover in mobile commerce. The mobile success of mail-order retailers is no coincidence. In many cases, the natural strengths of distance selling can be used in the Internet channel. This relates to logistics and enterprise resource planning, the catalog as a good basis for mobile adaptation, and CRM capabilities in relation to individual customer optimization. With regard to mail-order, the focus is initially on the customer-oriented maximization of turnover. It is imperative to take the greatest possible advantage of the available customer addresses, which also requires involvement in mobile commerce as part of the general mobilization trend. Whether this relates to new turnover or substitution in the mobile channel is irrelevant here. Every traditional retailer is affected if a significant share of sales is achieved in its segment via mobile Internet and such sales revenues are lost because the online shopping option is not being provided to customers. A virtual video rental store which distributes its videos in parallel through the online and mobile shop can also be regarded as representatives of hybrid mobile commerce. One leading example of this is the best practice company Netflix. US online retailer Netflix offers rentals of movie DVDs and Blu-rays by postal mail and via video-on-demand streams, as well as corresponding technical devices and equipment. This essentially constitutes a combination of virtual video rental store and electronic retailer, which represents an ideal platform for further growth via hybrid mobile commerce with digitalized products (cf. Heinemann 2012a, p. 193).

4.5.5 Vertical Mobile Commerce

Mobile communications companies and device manufacturers, such as Apple and T-Mobile, are increasingly using the mobile channel to distribute products and services. This form of mobile selling to end customers constitutes "verticalized mobile commerce". As a typical device manufacturer, Nokia has included the mobile Internet in its business strategy in recent years and thus verticalized in mobile commerce. Nokia was not only one of the protagonists in the creation of . mobi-TLD, but with Ovi, has also launched a portal for users, which provides Nokia Internet services. The range of offers includes, for example, a map service, a Nokia music store, sharing services and an interface to the N-gage platform. Social network "mosh" was launched by Nokia back in 2007, on which users can upload and download media and applications. With Nokia's "Comes with Music" program, buyers who purchase a Nokia device are given free music downloads for 1 year. Furthermore, Nokia provides a location-tracking service on Plazes (cf. Alby 2008, pp. 89–90). Unlike Nokia, device manufacturer Apple relies on the mobile channel. Apple uses the virtual Apple Store as a sales channel for its own devices and the iTunes Apple Store to sell a wide variety of apps. In addition to device manufacturers, such as Nokia and Apple, various network operators also conduct verticalized mobile commerce. Along with T-Mobile, which uses the T-Online platform for mobile commerce of any type, Vodafone should be noted here, which is number three on the mobile download market. Vodafone offers mobile music, for example, and markets the song title on posters by placing a photo of the barcode on the poster and only the transaction has to be confirmed. Vodafone provides over 600,000 music titles for download and has even been given a platinum award for 2,000,000 sales of a Nelly Furtado song (cf. Logara 2008, p. 84). Whereas the previously described forms of verticalization show forward integration of network operators and device manufacturers towards the mobile shop, there is also an example of backward integration at present (cf. Fig. 4.24). Google is mutating into more of a mobile commerce provider and has already launched the "Google eBooks" book platform in the USA. At the same time, Google is developing its own payment systems ("One Pass") and like Amazon ("Simple Pay") is now competing with eBay subsidiary PayPal. On the other hand, Google is turning into a device manufacturer, through the acquisition of Motorola, and thereby into a backward-integrated mobile commerce company (cf. Die Welt 2011e dated August 16, 2011, p. 11).

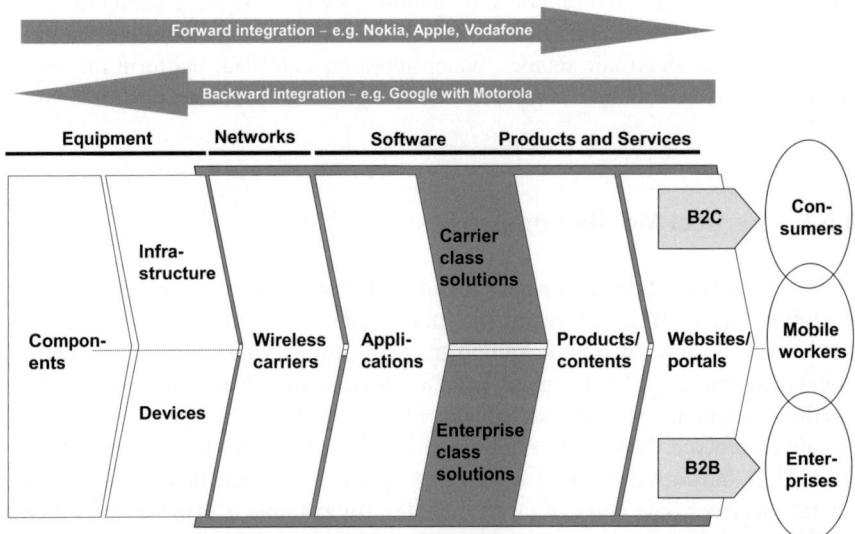

Fig. 4.24 Forms of verticalization in mobile commerce (Source: Based on Spielberg 2001, p. 291)

4.6 Relevant Success Factors for Mobile Commerce

Mobile commerce, in conjunction with rapid smartphone penetration, is currently undergoing a radical generation change as a disruptive technology and is involved in sustainably transforming all retail sectors. Such a change is already apparent in the USA. The question of how "new generation mobile commerce" can best be used as a disruptive technology identifies seven key success factors ("7 B-success factors") (cf. Heinemann 2012a):

1. **Success factor no. 1 – existing and already successful online shop:** A fundamental prerequisite is the existence of a successful online shop. First of all, a presentable significantly-sized online shop should have been established, which is certainly no bed of roses and will not function without substantial investments, because the mobile shop is almost its "extended arm with an additional function". Any retailer that steers clear of the online issue should really do the same with the mobile issue. The same effective regulations apply to mobile online commerce as online commerce, but in intensified form. Furthermore, optimization is necessary for mobile-compliant contents and format-compliant websites. The range of offers has to be expanded with mobile services and applications.
2. **Success factor no. 2 – importance for situational and real life environment:** The situational and lifestyle-related adjustment of offers to the individual shopping habits of customers is the master class of mobile commerce. That is the only way to leverage the "SoLoMo synergies" that result from social, local and mobile networking. Such synergies include customizable virtual shelves and the use of augmented reality in all conceivable facets. Mobile 2.0, i.e. the mobile-oriented implementation of social media tools with networking to Facebook, Twitter and the like, is standard. Twitter accounts do not only function as a service tool to respond to customer questions, as practiced at BestBuy with Twelpforce. They can also sustainably fuel other sales channels, as demonstrated by Whole Foods Market (WFM).
3. **Success factor no. 3 – best price and bargaining:** The mobile shopper is seen as a smart shopper on the search for smart information and bargains. Couponing, SMS coupons and virtual bonus cards are suitable for feeding other channels to such customers. Localization, i.e. "local pricing", plays a key role here. However, best price guarantees must be coordinated with other distribution channels, which require a cautious approach in view of the lack of valid studies or findings on multi-channel pricing.
4. **Success factor no. 4 – broadcasting and blogging:** The sending of content and interaction with the customer is aligned with the trend towards crowdsourcing and leads to the assessment that the "Internet (is turning into) the Outernet". A completely new language is spoken, which many retailers still have to learn: whether "pay with a Tweet", "pay with Facebook credits" or "sellaround with widgets", new-economy terms are becoming standard language. "Group deals" and "shopping together" are also buzzwords for mobile commerce, which also provide for the use of virtual games ("gamification").

5. **Success factor no. 5 – user-friendliness and block reduction:** An upper limit on mobile navigation and mobile usability should be ensured to a much greater extent in mobile commerce than in the online shop. A flexible format design, enabling the use of different device forms through to tablet PCs, is also useful here. Quick page loading speeds and accessibility have to be implemented in the best possible way, particularly with regard to conceivable transmission problems. Content-heavy websites with loading times lasting minutes scare customers away and drive them to competitors, which are only a click away.
6. **Success factor no. 6 – operating system and browser technology:** The (still) wide range of operating systems cannot hide the fact that – apart from Apple's iPhone OS – no operating system is capable of implementing the necessary commercial options, not even in a rudimentary manner. This can be linked to the largely inadequate number of mobile shopping apps. Even Android has so far only allowed for Amazon and eBay applications, but is set to catch up radically in this area in the near future. The choice of appropriate operating systems and browser technologies, in combination with the right device configurations, plays an absolutely critical role in success here. The network coverage and availabilities of different providers should also be included in the calculation, in order to give the customer accurate recommendations with regard to selection of the best-possible network provider for an operating system.
7. **Success factor no. 7 – back-end security and user risk reduction:** Growing awareness and sensitivity with regard to data protection requires precise wording of security goals and limitation of contact points. The use of WLAN still poses major security risks, which are extensively reduced in GSM through temporary subscriber identity. Bluetooth also achieves a certain level of security against interception through encryption, but only at a relatively short range. In any case, the existing risks should be openly presented to users and alternative risk options provided.

Combined with the success factors outlined above, mobile commerce, in conjunction with rapid smartphone penetration, is not only undergoing a radical generation change, but is also enjoying a new lease of life, following its foundation around 20 years ago. After initial euphoria in the 1990s and languishing for a while in the first decade of the new millennium, mobile commerce is now growing almost exponentially. This trend includes a wide-ranging "side effect", since strongly-growing online commerce is also fueled by the mobile boom. Sales through the online channel will continue to boom in Germany in the next few years, whereas brick-and-mortar retailing has been treading water for years. Another rise in the online shares of retail sales revenues is evidently assured for the next few years.

Study: Status and Potential of Location-based services

5.1 Concept and Objectives of the Study

5.1.1 Initial Situation and Reason for Study

An extreme dynamic rarely seen in any other sector can currently be observed in retailing, resulting in enormous changes to commercial structures. In particular, the digitalization of commerce and the development of mobile Internet are drivers of this trend. In this regard, it becomes clear that smartphone usage and location-based services (LBS) present great opportunities for brick-and-mortar retailing.

5.1.2 kaufDA as an LBS Provider

Start-up company kaufDA is an app-based platform with location-based services for brick-and-mortar retailing. Such services offer retailers access to consumers with local relevance, as the kaufDA mobile network provides consumers with convenient and up-to-date information about local shopping. This works on all established operating systems. Users of kaufDA can browse and compare circulars, offers and opening times online, from their immediate environment.

5.1.2.1 Services and Importance of kaufDA and Bonial International Group

kaufDA is part of the Bonial International Group with local brands in nine countries, over 300 staff members and offices in Chicago, Berlin, Paris, Barcelona, Sao Paulo, Moscow and Munich. The company belongs to Axel Springer SE. Since its foundation, consumers have so far accessed more than five billion digital pages at kaufDA. In Germany alone, information is constantly updated for around 227,000 retail stores. The group works with more than 600 leading retailers on a global scale.

The kaufDA mobile website is already ranked 16th among mobile Internet sites in Germany (AGOF mobile facts 2011).

5.1.3 Initial Position and Core Issues

The commercial sector is clearly in transition as a result of the change in usage and buying behavior, particularly of younger consumers described as digital natives, and due to the changed infrastructure of the Internet. Long-established retail companies are putting their business models to the test, leapfrogging parts of the established value chain through the use of digital media, and are sometimes overtaken by newly-founded Internet pure players. In order to be able to change and adapt retail formats, knowledge is required of the factors which influence the commercial sector today, and will do so in future. Moreover, knowledge of new interests and requirements, and of consumers' usage patterns in relation to mobile Internet via smartphones and tablet PCs is indispensable. Within the scope of this study, the fundamental thesis "Mobile Internet promotes the rediscovery of brick-and-mortar retailing" will be reviewed. Furthermore, the study intends to examine the awareness, knowledge and readiness of consumers with regard to the subject of location-based services (LBS).

The following core issues are in the focus of the study:

1. How does mobile Internet usage affect information-seeking and buying behavior?
2. How will commercial formats have to change and adapt?
3. Which factors affect future commerce?
4. What will future commerce look like?

5.1.4 Study Design and Socio-Demographics

In cooperation with Niederrhein University of Applied Sciences and the Edelman GmbH agency, and with the support of kaufDA, a representative consumer survey was conducted on the subject of location-based services (LBS). Within the study, the fundamental thesis "Mobile Internet promotes the rediscovery of brick-and-mortar retailing" was analyzed.

5.1.4.1 Type of Survey
The survey was conducted in two stages, in two survey rounds, with support from INNOFACT AG:

- **1st survey round: CATI survey** (Computer-Assisted Telephone Interviewing). A representative random sample of consumers were called from the INNOFACT telephone studio and interviewed. Only experienced interviewers were employed, who had been specifically trained in the project and were subject to

constant monitoring and instruction from INNOFACT project managers. n = 2,000
- **2nd survey round: online survey.** Test subjects were recruited from the INNOFACT AG consumer panel. A random sample was invited by email and took part in an online questionnaire. Each participant could only access the online survey via an individual transaction number, thereby excluding multiple participations. n = 1,017.

5.1.4.2 Study Design

In the first round, 2,000 persons aged 14 and above were surveyed in telephone interviews, during the period from July 23, 2013 to August 1, 2013, in a structure representative of the overall population in respect of gender, age and employment. The second survey round was also conducted with persons aged 14 and above. The random sampling of 1,017 respondents, who are smartphone or tablet PC users, was conducted after the first survey round, from July 30, 2013 to August 1, 2013 (source of predefined quotas: AWA 2013 (Allensbacher Markt- und Werbeträgeranalyse). This was followed by weighting of the online random sample based on distribution of the CATI survey of smartphone or tablet PC users with regard to gender, age and employment. The random sample description for the first CATI survey round is depicted in Fig. 5.1. The same description for the second online survey round is depicted in Fig. 5.2.

5.2 Smartphone Ownership and Usage in Relation to LBS

The topic of smartphone ownership and usage in relation to LBS was examined in respect of four factors, which also formed the focus for the CATI survey. This first relates to the ownership and usage of smartphones, and to planned purchases of new ones. In addition, it concerns the use of smartphones and tablets and usage of information channels (Fig. 5.3).

5.2.1 Ownership and Usage of Smartphones

Almost half of all respondents (46 %) own a smartphone and/or tablet PC. Owners of such devices are primarily men, people aged under 50 and those with a high income.

Among respondents under the age of 30, around 80 % own a smartphone. The under 30s age group and the 31–50 age group own identical shares of tablet PCs, at around 20 % each.

Among respondents under the age of 50, the share of those who do not own any such electronic device is below 1 %. The share among the over 50s is 16 %.

The type of device usage is depicted in Fig. 5.2 and presents real representative values based on the CATI survey, since parts of the population who do not use the Internet and/or mobile technology are also shown in the telephone survey.

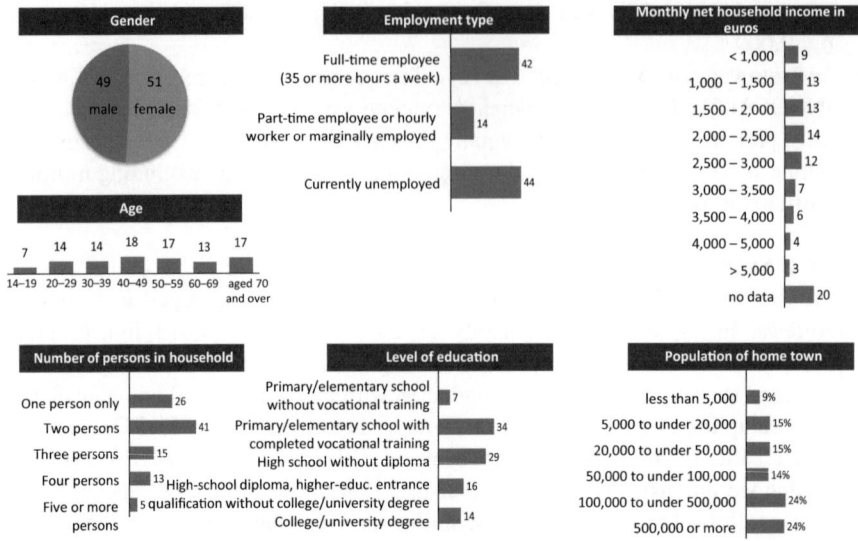

Fig. 5.1 Random sample description of first survey round, CATI (Source: Heinemann and kaufDA 2013, Basis: all respondents, n = 2,000; values as percentages)

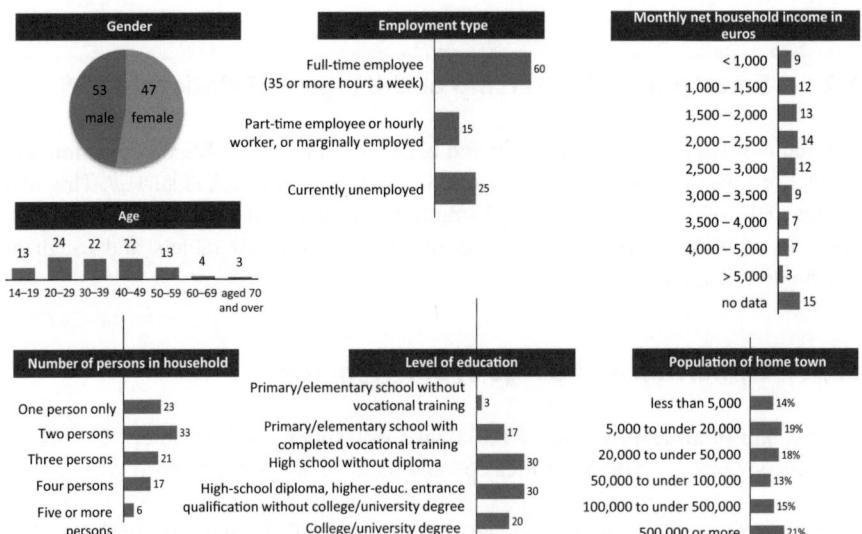

Fig. 5.2 Random sample description of second survey round, online survey (Source: Heinemann and kaufDA 2013, Basis: all respondents, n = 1,017; values as percentages)

5.2 Smartphone Ownership and Usage in Relation to LBS

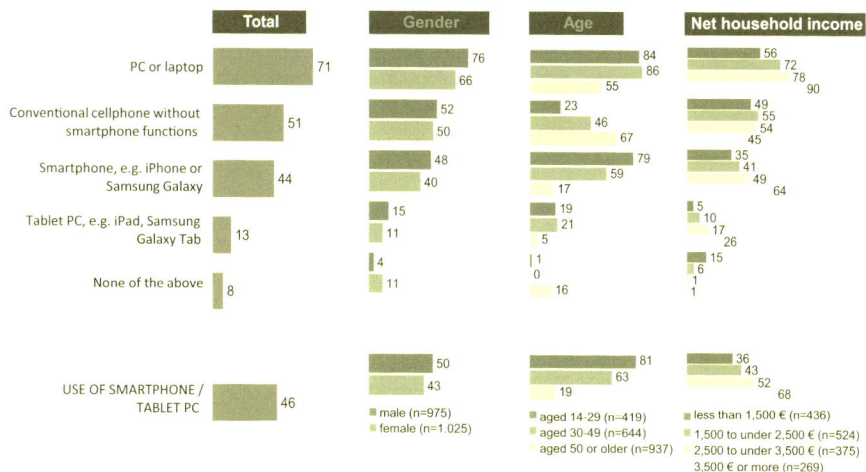

Question: "Do you personally use one or more of the following devices?"

Fig. 5.3 Device usage in the German population at the end of July 2013 (Source: Heinemann and kaufDA 2013; Basis: all respondents, n = 2,000; values as percentages)

5.2.2 Planned Purchase of New Devices

Approximately one quarter of respondents plan to buy at least one of the surveyed new devices in the next 6 months. 13 % intend to buy a new smartphone and only 2 % a conventional cellphone.

Respondents predominantly plan to purchase smartphones (13 %) and tablet PCs (9 %) in the next 6 months, and fewer laptops or PCs. A greater number of people under 50 are planning the acquisition of such a device than those over 50.

The planned purchase of new devices is depicted in Fig. 5.4.

5.2.3 Functions Used on Smartphones and Tablets

Apps that apply to the user's current location (e.g. weather apps and map services) are most commonly used by smartphone and tablet PC users, at 79 %. Half (50 %) of all users already use apps to display information on price and product offers from specific retailers or stores in the vicinity.

Fourty-six percent of smartphone and tablet owners use their device for online shopping functions, but only 9 % do so regularly. Given that the share of mobile commerce in online commerce is currently 10–20 %, the feeder role of smartphones for buying channels is also reflected in the acceptance level. Functions used on smartphones and tablets are depicted in Fig. 5.5.

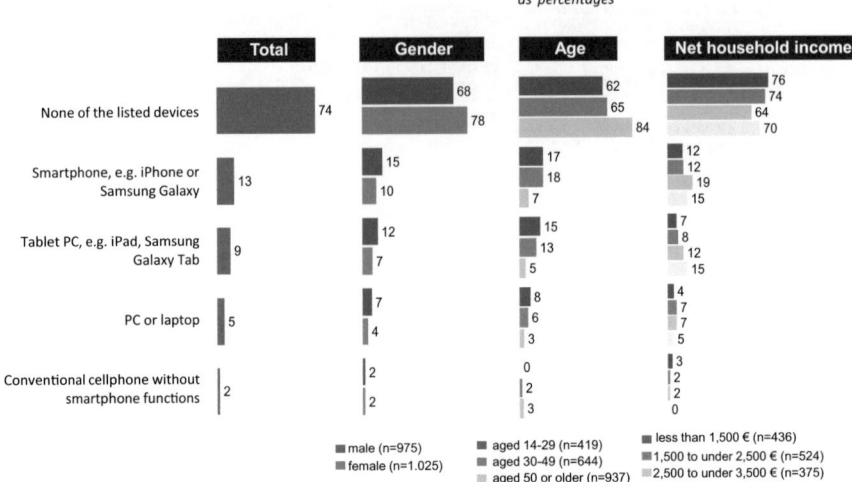

Question: "Do you plan to purchase one or more of the following devices for yourself in the next 6 months?"

Fig. 5.4 Planned purchase of new devices as at end of July 2013 (Source: Heinemann and kaufDA 2013)

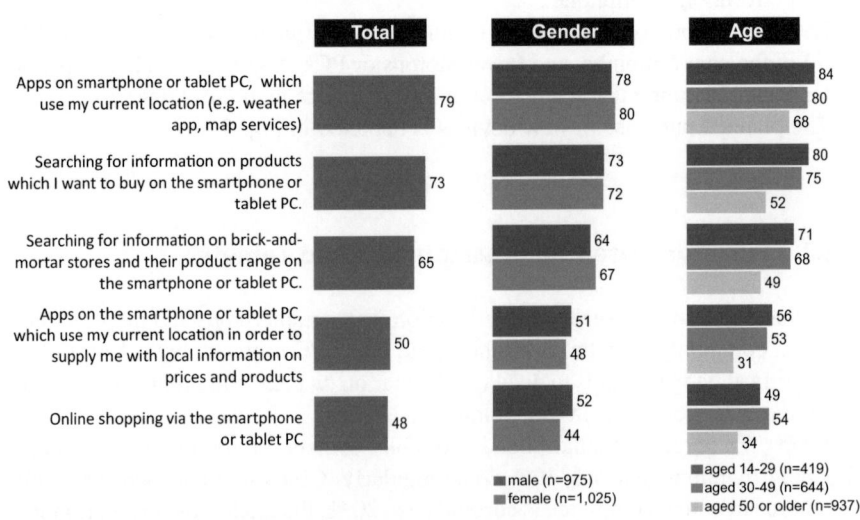

Question: "Smartphones and tablet PCs offer various options for use. What do you do with your smartphone or tablet-PC?"

Fig. 5.5 Functions used on smartphone or tablet PC as at the end of July 2013 (Source: Heinemann and kaufDA 2013)

5.2.4 Channels Used for Product Information Searches

In respect of the question concerning which channels are used to search for product information on mobile devices, search engines, such as Google (78 %), and large shopping platforms like eBay and Amazon (73 %) play an exceptionally important role, as expected. Price comparison sites (48 %) and retail shops (44 %) are also heavily used. Location-based services, such as kaufDA, are lagging relatively far behind at 12 %, but apps/applications come in at 32 %, which could primarily imply applications with local relevance, meaning that the two together add up to 44 %. Moreover, 22 % of respondents mention social networks. At first glance the social network seems to be relatively unimportant to consumers in the search for product information. However, in respect of the question about relevant aspects when searching for product information on mobile devices, "ratings of the product by other consumers", as a reference to social shopping, rank third (57 %). As regards the question about relevant contents of location-based services and expectations of location-based services, the opportunity to access product ratings from other customers also comes in third (71 %). This confirms the high importance of "local" and "social".

Overall, the survey results show a definite relevance to social shopping, but dependent on different social media on the Internet and rather unconsciously in terms of usage. In addition, the relevance of product ratings by other customers is emphasized.

Among respondents under the age of 30, the use of a portable web-enabled device is almost habitual. This provides the opportunity to use location-based services (LBS). However, the low level of awareness and recognition show that LBS are still in the introductory phase. This suggests that potential exists for brick-and-mortar retailers in particular.

Furthermore, usage of smartphones and tablet PCs shows in detail that they are primarily used to acquire information and less for buying products. Shares of usage of information with local relevance are indicated, but there is also further potential for retailers to make information available in accordance with user expectations here.

Channels used to search for product information and important pertinent factors are depicted in Fig. 5.6.

5.3 "So": Social and LBS-Relevant Buying Aspects

Social and LBS-relevant aspects of shopping form the starting point of the online survey, which focuses on the SoLoMo factor. This first concerns current and future information-seeking behavior and the impact of attractive offers on buying behavior. Moreover, it concerns locations of information usage and in particular the social media channel for local offers. The "bridge" is therefore built for the awareness, recognition and expectations of LBS from a social perspective.

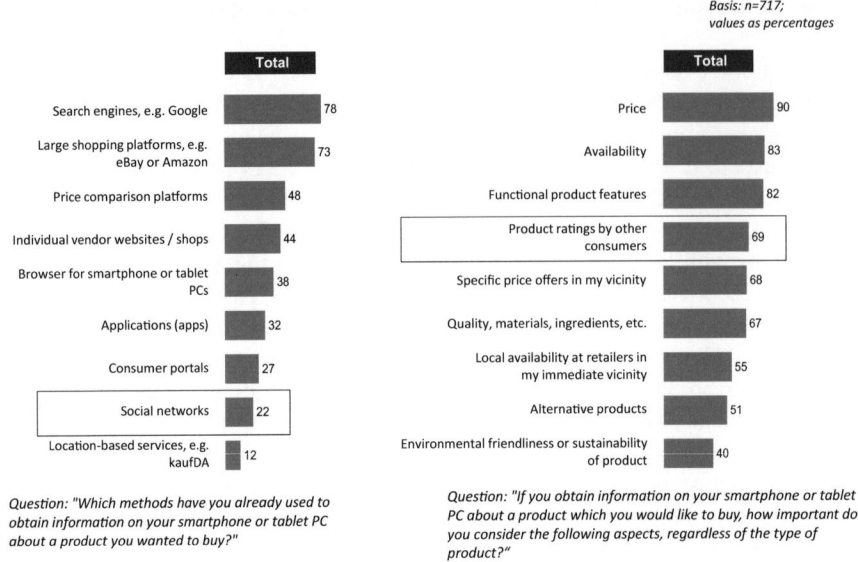

Fig. 5.6 Channels used to search for product information and important factors (Source: Heinemann and kaufDA 2013)

5.3.1 Current and Future Information-Seeking Behavior

In respect of the question about current information and buying behavior, most respondents (35 %) indicated a combination of searching for information on the laptop/PC and then making the purchase on the laptop/PC. In second place, at 20 %, was the combination of obtaining information offline and buying offline. The combination of searching for information on the laptop/PC and buying in a brick-and-mortar store came in third place, with 12 %. This is followed (at 10 %) by searching for information offline and making the purchase on a PC/laptop.

All other combinations relating to information searches and/or buying by smartphone and tablet PC fluctuate within a single-digit percentage range. Survey results therefore show that the "advice theft" frequently mentioned in the press is less common than the reverse combination of searching for information on the Internet and buying in a brick-and-mortar store. Information searches on the Internet thereby assume a feeder role for brick-and-mortar retailing. In addition, this feeder role and the still low usage of combinations including a smartphone or tablet PC as an information or buying medium shows that LBS has enormous potential as a feeder role for brick-and-mortar stores. Similarly, this is supported by the increasing willingness to use a smartphone or tablet PC to search for information and make purchases in the future. Current and future information-seeking and buying behavior is depicted in Fig. 5.7.

5.3 "So": Social and LBS-Relevant Buying Aspects

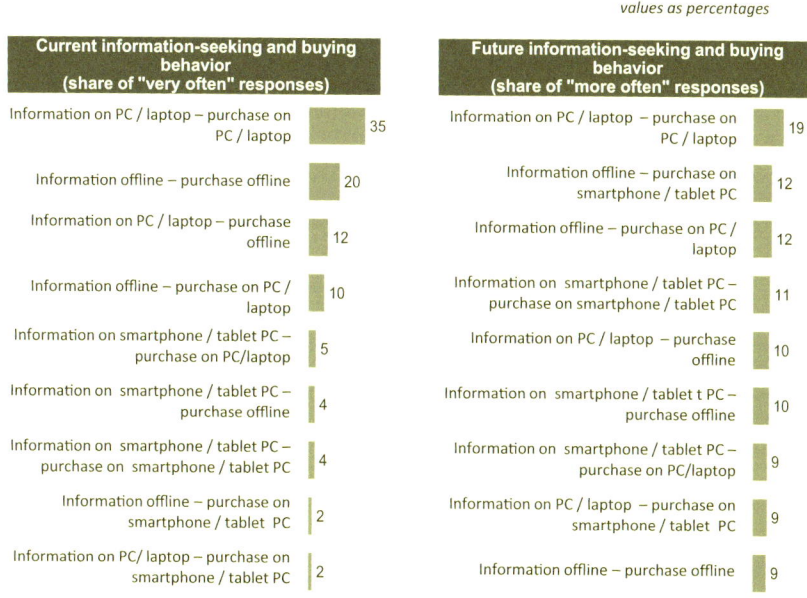

Fig. 5.7 Current and future information-seeking and buying behavior online/offline (Source: Heinemann and kaufDA 2013)

5.3.2 Impact of Attractive Offers on Buying Behavior

Interest in local retailers and product offers is indicated across all age groups. Around 85 % of respondents regularly obtain information on current offers with local relevance. With 92 % of respondents shopping at least occasionally in regular stores, and 70 % shopping with regular frequency and on certain days, buying behavior seems habitual. However, such behavior can clearly be influenced by particularly attractive offers: 93 % of respondents say they would not only go a greater distance for a particularly attractive offer, but would also visit a store other than "their" regular store. Likewise, a willingness to adjust shopping intervals to a particularly attractive offer is also indicated among respondents. Ninety-five percent indicate a willingness to adjust their shopping rhythm to an attractive offer. Another 96 % say they have already bought a particularly attractive offer after learning about it, without having planned to purchase the product in advance.

These survey results are indicative of greater potential for location-based services. Consumers are apparently receptive to attractive product offers in their vicinity and frequently react immediately upon learning about such offers. Longer distances and shopping at stores not previously used are also taken into account here. Moreover, location-based services gives rise to potential for spontaneous buys and cross-selling offers.

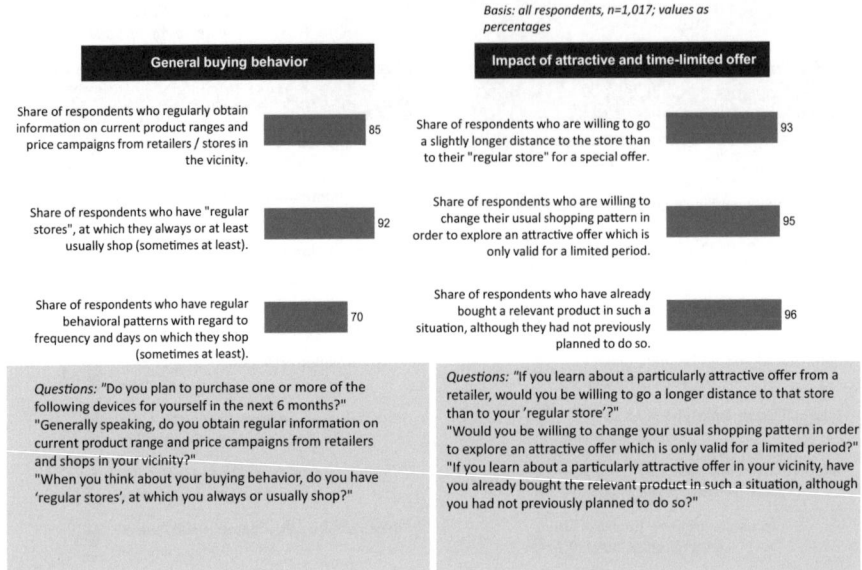

Fig. 5.8 Impact of attractive offers on buying behavior (Source: Heinemann and kaufDA 2013)

The impact of attractive offers on buying behavior is depicted in Fig. 5.8.

5.3.3 Usage Locations for Information Searches

In respect of the question about usage location for LBS services on mobile devices, the survey revealed that LBS is most frequently used at home on the couch (53 % tablet PCs; 55 % smartphones). Outside the home, LBS are used most on the move, "on the street". These survey results correspond to usage frequencies for LBS. "Searching for information on store opening times" and "Distance to brick-and-mortar retailers in the vicinity" were indicated most frequently here, at 33 %. Consumers therefore search for information about brick-and-mortar retailers in their vicinity while "on the move, on the street". This means that LBS has potential as a feeder role for consumers in brick-and-mortar stores.

Smartphones are predominantly used at the POS. The tablet PC is increasingly used at home. Fifty-four percent of respondents – the highest valuation – mentioned using the smartphone directly to acquire information on the product. In contrast, only 14 % use a tablet PC to directly obtain information about the product.

These survey results show that the use of smartphones at the POS is already part of everyday life. However, the smartphone is also used in many other situations outside the home. In respect of location-based services, it is important for web-enabled mobile devices to be available at the POS, as an essential prerequisite for using LBS.

Usage locations when searching for information are depicted in Fig. 5.9.

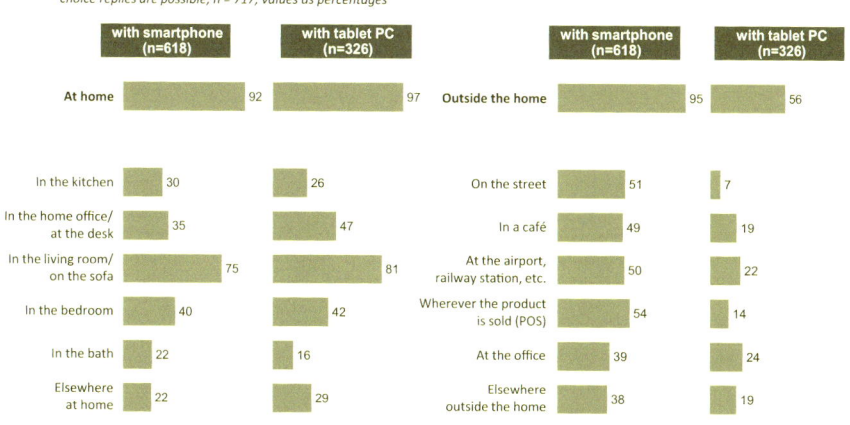

Fig. 5.9 Usage locations for product information searches on mobile devices (Source: Heinemann and kaufDA 2013)

5.3.4 Use of Social Media Channels for Local Offers

Forty-four percent of respondents are willing to share offers in a brick-and-mortar store with their own social network. From the users' perspective, extra-special offers and bargains (33 %) are in first place in terms of information worth communicating, with price and information on the price-performance ratio (value for the money) coming in second (23 %). They are followed, at some distance, by product reviews (7 %), interest from friends (6 %) and the provider's name (6 %).

The survey results show that a willingness to use social shopping exists, but is not regarded as elementary by the overwhelming share of consumers. It should be noted that customer reviews, included in the results at 7 % ("Review/quality of offer"), seem to be less relevant in the brick-and-mortar store. In contrast, sharing and communicating special offers is becoming more important to consumers.

Usage of social media channels for local offers is depicted in Fig. 5.10.

5.3.5 Awareness and Expectations of LBS from a Social Perspective

Around 70 % of respondents indicate that they have not yet heard of the term LBS. The level of awareness and recognition of location-based services via apps is also low, at 39 %. The under 50s are better informed than the over 50s in this respect.

Among LBS services recognized by respondents, kaufDA leads the ranking with around 15 %, followed by Google at 5 % and restaurant services/apps or barcodes, at 4 % each.

In this respect, it is apparent that LBS are still in the initial usage phase and not yet known under the term "LBS". Knowledge of the term itself will be less relevant

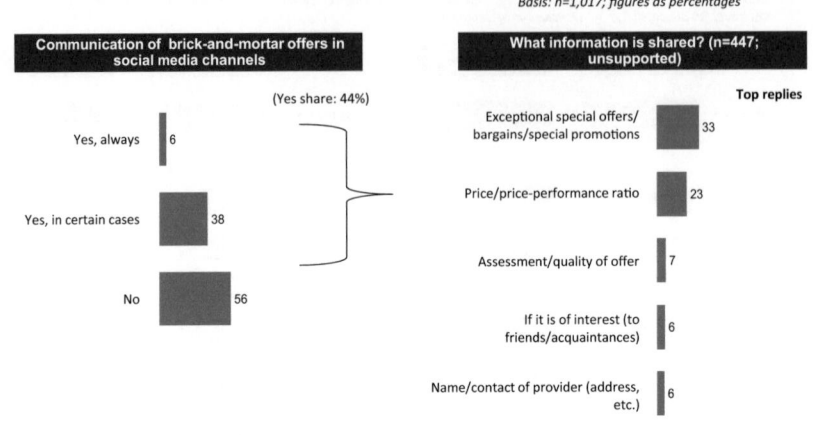

Fig. 5.10 Usage of social media channels for local offers (Source: Heinemann and kaufDA 2013)

to consumers than awareness of the offer from brick-and-mortar retailers to use LBS.

Only 10 % of respondents know precisely what is meant by the term "location-based services". In particular, this is mentioned much more frequently by persons under 50, men and people with a high household income.

The percentage of those who have never heard of this term is 72 %. It is relatively high among the over 50s, at 81 %.

Recognition of LBS from a social perspective is depicted in Fig. 5.11. In line with expectations, Internet users are aware of LBS to a much greater extent than the total population, including non-Internet users (cf. CATI). Recognition of LBS from the Internet user's perspective is depicted in Fig. 5.12 (cf. online survey).

In response to the question of which additional information they would especially like to receive about local offers, respondents mentioned "more detailed information on product features" as first place (78 %). "Information on availability in-store" is in second place (77 %), followed by "information on ratings from other customers" (71 %).

Expectations of LBS from a social perspective are depicted in Fig. 5.13. In respect of the question concerning the requirements of LBS for more frequent use, around one third mention greater security, larger range of offers and improved functions. At several points, the survey results indicate that consumers still have security concerns about the use of LBS. For brick-and-mortar retailers, this would mean that corporate communications should aim to build up trust with regard to these services. Other survey results show that LBS are still in the start phase and their potential has not yet been exhausted.

The requirements of LBS for more frequent use are depicted in Fig. 5.14.

5.3 "So": Social and LBS-Relevant Buying Aspects

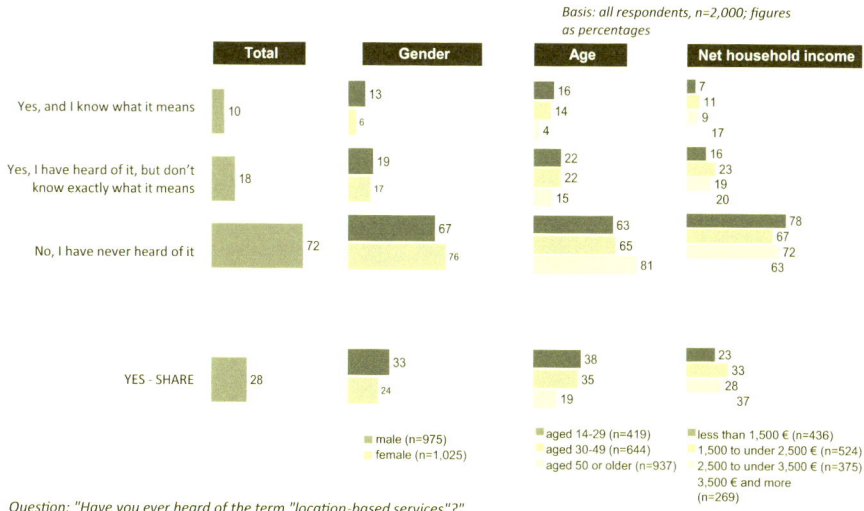

Fig. 5.11 Recognition of the term LBS from CATI survey (Source: Heinemann and kaufDA 2013)

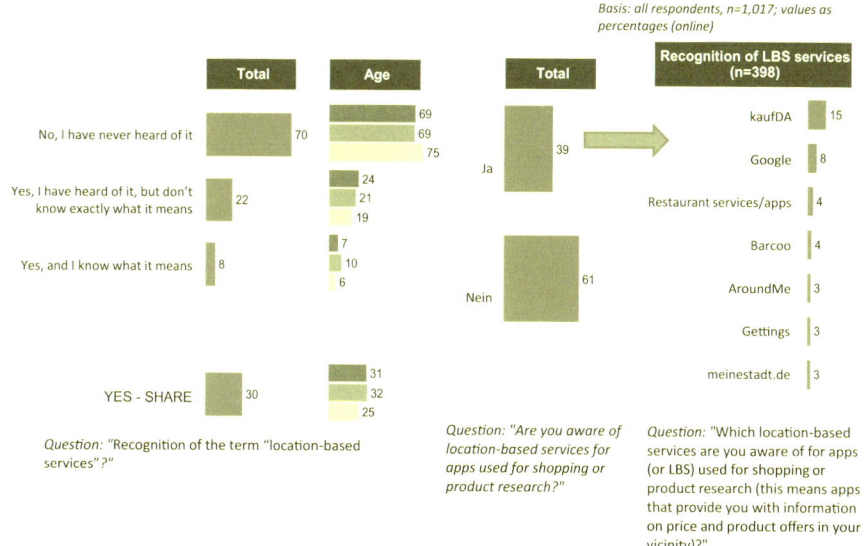

Fig. 5.12 Recognition of the term "location-based services" from online survey (Source: Heinemann and kaufDA 2013)

168   5 Study: Status and Potential of Location-based services

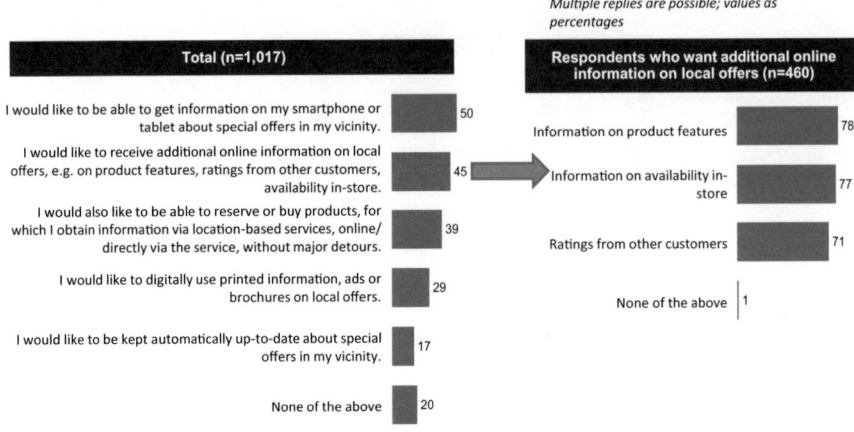

Fig. 5.13 Expectations of location-based services from a social perspective (Source: Heinemann and kaufDA 2013)

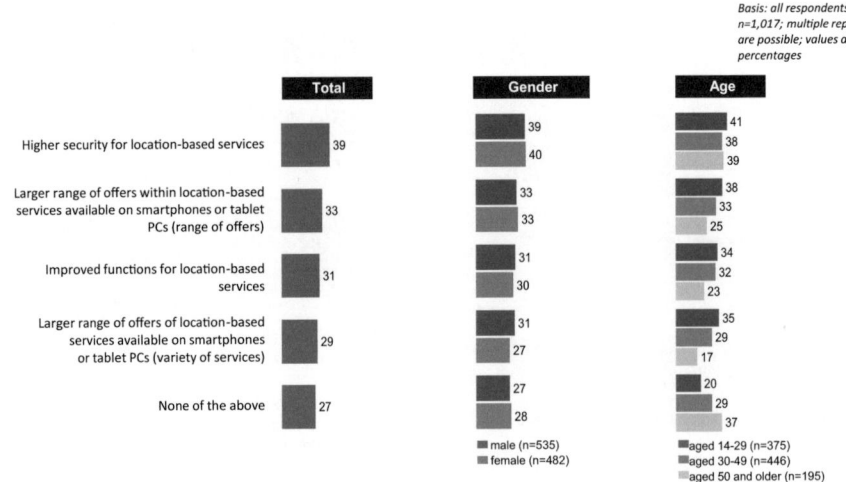

Fig. 5.14 Requirements for more frequent use of location-based services (Source: Heinemann and kaufDA 2013)

5.4 "Lo": Attraction and Usage of LBS at POS

The focus of this section is on local aspects, starting with the attraction of LBS. It continues with previous usage of LBS and usage frequency, followed by an examination of the reasons for the use or non-use of LBS. The chapter concludes with relevant LBS contents and interest in usage and purchase following LBS usage.

5.4.1 Attraction of Location-based services

LBS are attractive for around 52 % of respondents, regardless of whether or not they are already aware of them. Only around 5 % stated that LBS were completely unattractive. In this regard, distribution by gender is roughly equal. Distribution by age, however, reveals that LBS are more attractive to younger people than older people.

In these survey results, the high attraction of LBS also illustrates the great potential of LBS from the customer's perspective.

The attraction of LBS is depicted in Fig. 5.15.

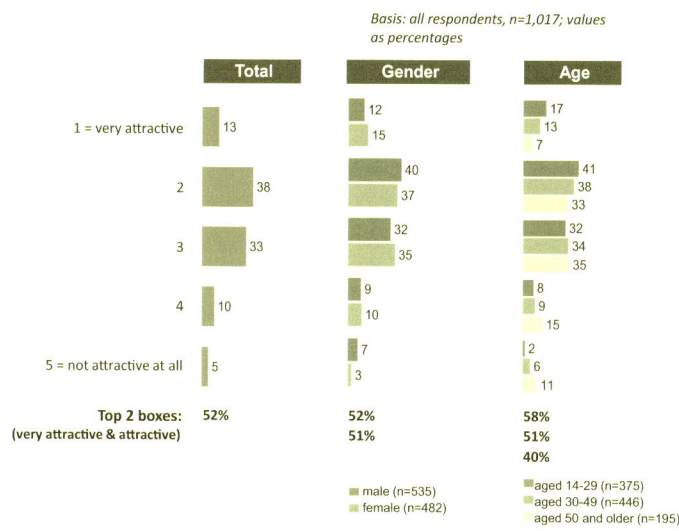

Question: "Regardless of whether you are already aware of location-based services, how attractive is this type of service to you?"

Fig. 5.15 Attraction of location-based services (Source: Heinemann and kaufDA 2013)

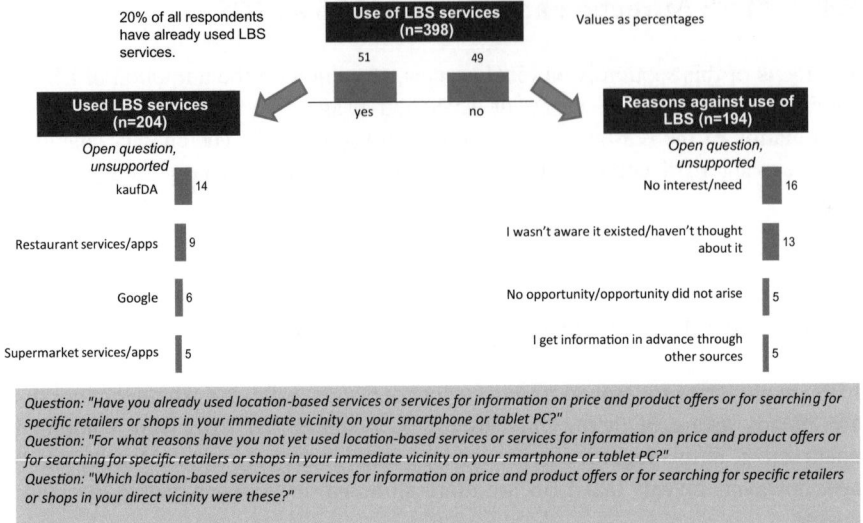

Fig. 5.16 Use of LBS and reasons for and against usage (Source: Heinemann and kaufDA 2013)

5.4.2 Previous Usage of LBS and Frequency of Use

A slight majority (51 %) say they have already used LBS. At 14 %, kaufDA is mentioned as the most-widely used LBS, followed by restaurant services/apps and Google. In respect of the question about the reasons for not using LBS, replies are divided roughly equally between "No interest/need" at 16 % and "I wasn't aware it existed" at 13 %. These two replies suggest a different attitude among respondents. No interest/need means that the respondent is aware of the service, but it does not satisfy any need and there is no potential for LBS here. However, those who replied "I wasn't aware it existed" show a definite potential for LBS usage. Use of LBS and reasons for and against such usage are depicted in Fig. 5.16.

In response to the question about frequency of use of different aspects of LBS, "Information on store opening hours" and "Distance from brick-and-mortar retailers in the vicinity" are most frequently mentioned, at 33 %. Special offers and promotional campaigns (29 %) and retailers in a specific category (28 %) are mentioned in almost equal shares, followed by information on availability and price (24 %).

These survey results suggest that awareness and recognition of LBS is not yet very high among consumers and on the other hand, consumers have not yet recognized the benefit of LBS for themselves. Publicizing LBS should therefore be prioritized, since a consumer can only use services that he or she is aware of.

The frequency of use of LBS is depicted in Fig. 5.17.

In respect of the question about the usage location for LBS services on mobile devices, it was made clear that LBS are most commonly used at home on the couch (53 % tablet PCs; 55 % smartphones). Outside the home, LBS are used most on the move, "on the street". These survey results fully coincide with those regarding the

5.4 "Lo": Attraction and Usage of LBS at POS

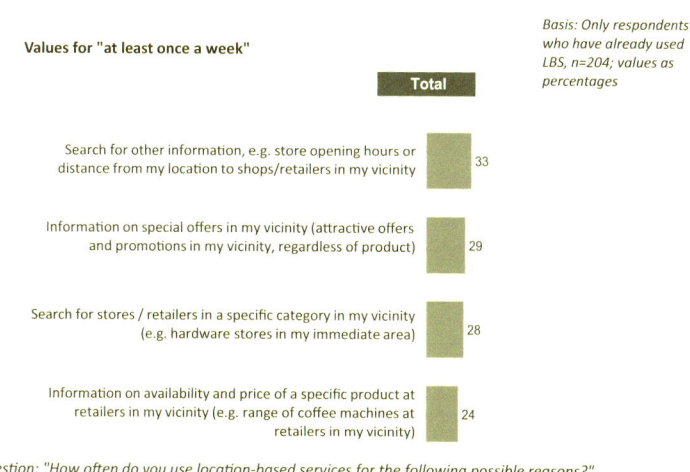

Fig. 5.17 Frequency of use of LBS aspects (Source: Heinemann and kaufDA 2013)

frequency of use of LBS. "Search for information on store opening times" and "Distance from brick-and-mortar retailers in the vicinity", at 33 %, were indicated most frequently here. Consumers also search "on the move, on the street" for information on brick-and-mortar retailers in their vicinity. This means that LBS have potential as a feeder role for consumers in brick-and-mortar stores.

Smartphones are predominantly used at the POS. The tablet PC is increasingly used at home. Fifty-four percent of respondents, and thereby the highest valuation, mentioned using the smartphone to directly acquire information on the product. In contrast, only 14 % use a tablet PC to directly obtain information about the product.

These survey results show that the use of smartphones at the POS is already part of everyday life. However, the smartphone is also used in many other situations outside the home. In respect of location-based services, it is important that web-enabled mobile devices are provided at the POS, as an essential prerequisite for using LBS.

Usage locations when searching for information are depicted in Fig. 5.18.

5.4.3 Reasons for Using and Not Using LBS

In response to questions about obstacles to more frequent usage of LBS, around half of all respondents mention a lack of knowledge and awareness of LBS as reasons, followed, at 37 %, by security concerns. In each case, one fifth mentioned a limited range of offers, not enough variety, or a too-narrow range of offers as other obstacles. Such responses again indicate that LBS have not yet made a full breakthrough and, from the consumer's perspective, really good offers do not yet exist or those which exist are not well enough known.

Obstacles to more frequent use of LBS are depicted in Fig. 5.19.

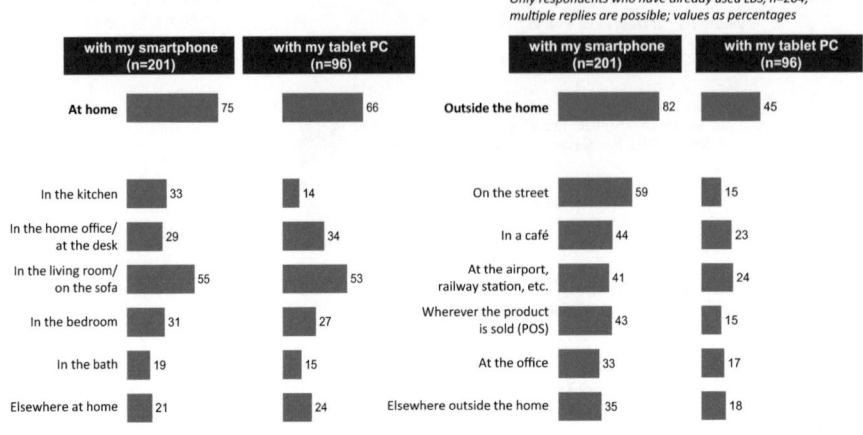

Fig. 5.18 Location where LBS is used on mobile devices (Source: Heinemann and kaufDA 2013)

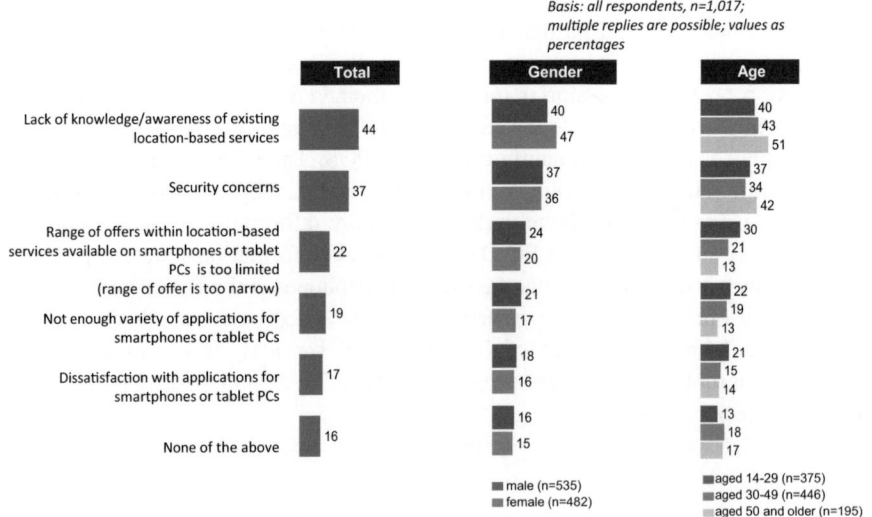

Fig. 5.19 Obstacles to more frequent use of LBS (Source: Heinemann and kaufDA 2013)

5.4.4 Relevant LBS Contents

Relevant contents of LBS for respondents are first price (90 %), followed by availability (73 %) in second place, ratings (57 %) in third, and product features (55 %) coming in fourth. These are trailed, at some distance, by quality and

5.4 "Lo": Attraction and Usage of LBS at POS

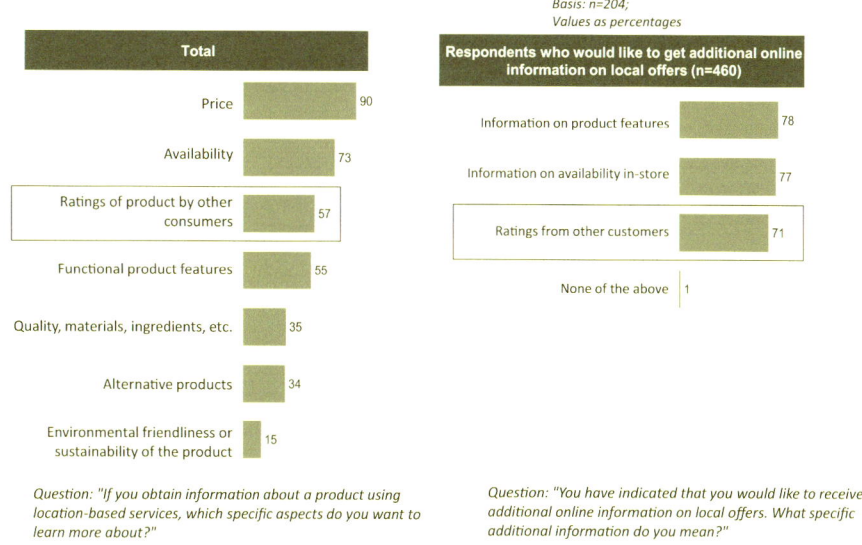

Fig. 5.20 Relevant contents of location-based services (Source: Heinemann and kaufDA 2013)

materials (35 %), alternative products (34 %) and information on sustainability (15 %).

Relevant contents of LBS are depicted in Fig. 5.20.

5.4.5 Interest and Buying Based on LBS Usage

Both "users and those who are aware" of LBS and "non-users and those who are aware" of LBS name similar aspects as very interesting information that can be accessed via LBS. These include store opening hours and locations of brick-and-mortar retailers in the vicinity. Nearby offers and information on availability and prices of products are also desired.

These survey results are indicative of consumers' expectations of LBS.

The interests in aspects of LBS usage are depicted in Fig. 5.21.

Fifty-six percent of respondents said they would also buy products that they have searched for and found via LBS in this way, if the opportunity arose.

This result for brick-and-mortar retailers indicates that LBS can also assume a feeder role in the brick-and-mortar store, but it also makes sense to offer a buying option via LBS or buying options on information channels where product information can be searched for and found.

Purchase intentions following LBS usage are depicted in Fig. 5.22.

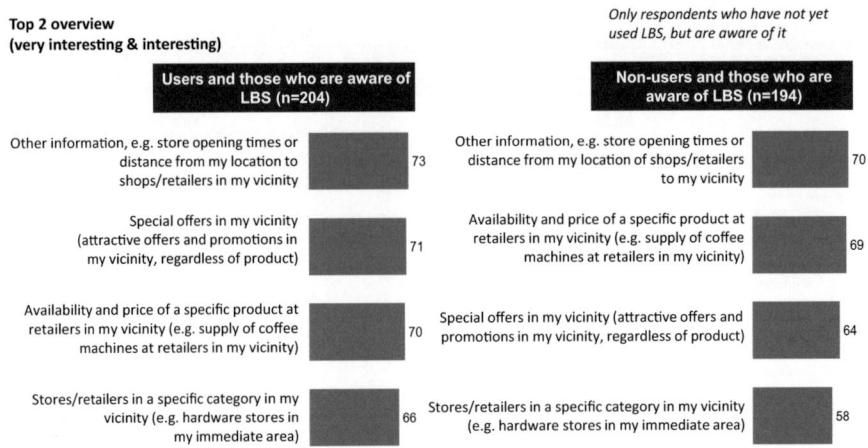

Question: "If you obtain information about shopping using location-based services, how interesting is the following information to you?"
Question: "You can use location-based services for shopping in order to obtain information on various matters. In this regard, how interesting do you find the following information?"

Fig. 5.21 Evaluation of interest in aspects of LBS usage (Source: Heinemann and kaufDA 2013)

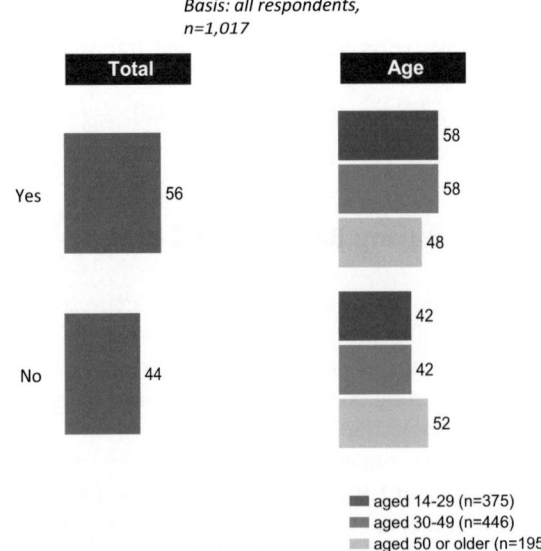

Question: "Regardless of whether you have already used location-based services, would you also order/buy the products searched and found here directly on your smartphone or tablet PC if it were possible?"

Fig. 5.22 Purchase on mobile devices following successful use of LBS (Source: Heinemann and kaufDA 2013)

5.5 "Mo": Mobile Usage of LBS

Mobile aspects related to searching for product information on smartphones will first be discussed, before examining the prerequisites for greater use of such services. The requirements for information searches on mobile devices and the specific usage of smartphones and digital displays during the shopping process are then addressed. The chapter concludes with preferences for private or provided devices.

5.5.1 Product Information Searches via Smartphones

Most respondents say they have already searched for product information using a smartphone (63 %) or tablet PC (82 %). It should be noted that younger respondents search for product information by smartphone or tablet PC more frequently than older respondents.

Both the tablet PC (39 %) and smartphone (34 %) are used several times a week to search for products.

The increase in information searches on a tablet PC in multi-person households may indicate that a tablet PC, unlike a smartphone, is used by several persons. The tablet PC could be a kind of social object in a household, which can be viewed by several people at the same time due to its larger display.

The use of smartphones to search for product information is depicted in Fig. 5.23.

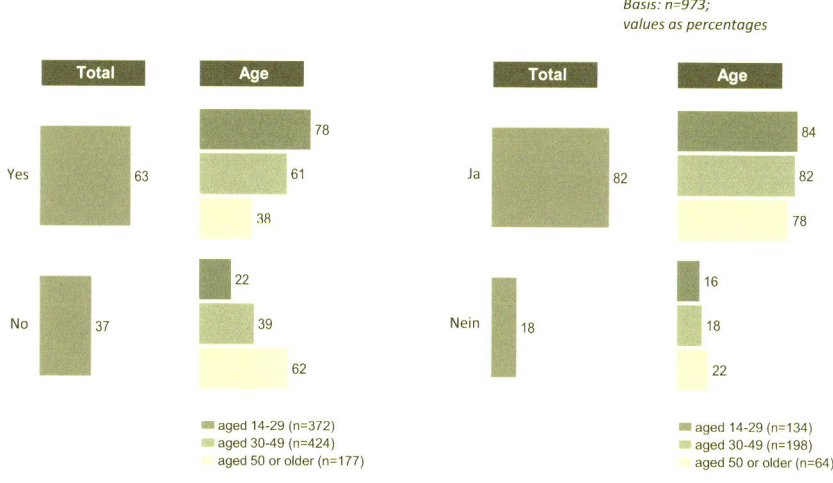

Fig. 5.23 Use of smartphone to search for product information (Source: Heinemann and kaufDA 2013)

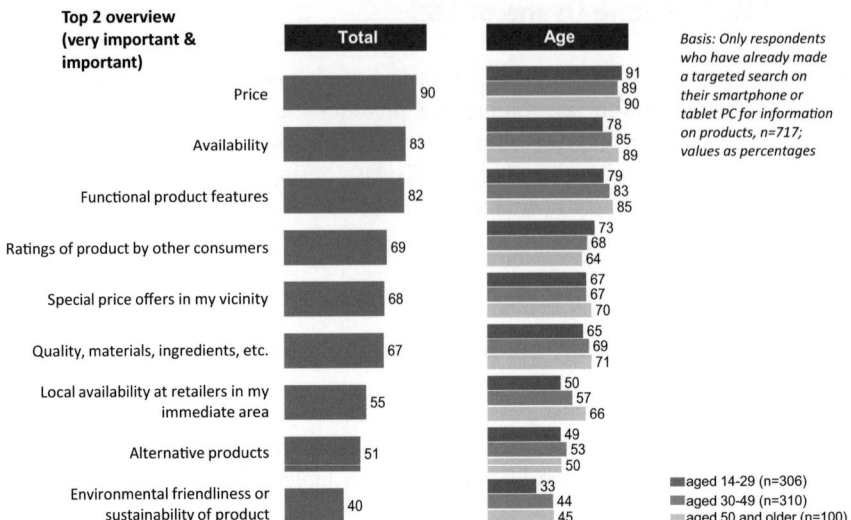

Fig. 5.24 Importance of factors when searching for product information on mobile devices (Source: Heinemann and kaufDA 2013)

In respect of the question about particularly important aspects of product searches on mobile devices, three aspects were rated very highly by respondents: price (90 %), availability (83 %) and functional product features (82 %). Reviews, price offers and product quality are just behind with almost equal ratings (69 %, 68 %, and 69 %), followed by local availability at 55 %, alternative products at 51 % and sustainability of the product at 40 %.

The high figure for availability, 83 %, could indicate that consumers want to avoid negative experiences in this regard, which are also associated with a large amount of effort in terms of time. This does not just mean accessibility of information, but also presentation of information. There is clearly a need to catch up, especially in the area of usability and optimization of the presentation of information on different displays.

Important aspects when searching for product information on smartphones are depicted in Fig. 5.24.

Relevant product categories, for which information is searched at least once a week on mobile devices, are electronic goods in first place (35 %), followed by fashion items (31 %) and books (20 %). Food, banks and drugstores are roughly equal at around 18 %, followed by sports shops, drinks and furniture at 12 %.

Product categories that are searched for during information searches on smartphones are depicted in Fig. 5.25.

Within the scope of product searches, searching for Christmas presents was surveyed as a special factor. The results are not surprising, but are roughly

5.5 "Mo": Mobile Usage of LBS

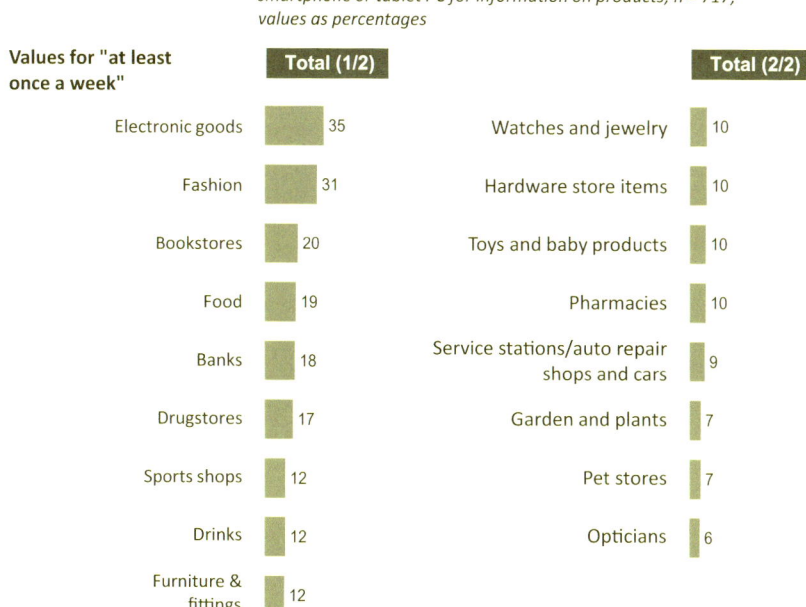

Fig. 5.25 Product categories searched for during information searches on smartphones (Source: Heinemann and kaufDA 2013)

equivalent to the ranking of current online shares in the relevant sectors. The majority (58 %) of respondents say they intend to obtain information about Christmas products via a smartphone or tablet PC this year. Amazon emerges as the most preferred source of product information (46 %), followed by eBay with 21 %. The two companies confirm that large product platforms have clearly been advanced as product information platforms or product search engines.

Information searches for Christmas presents via smartphones are depicted in Fig. 5.26.

5.5.2 Prerequisites for Greater Use of Mobile Devices

In response to the direct question about obstacles to more frequent searches for product information on mobile devices, respondents primarily mention security concerns (35 %), followed by transmission speeds (31 %) and mobile communication prices (26 %). Low distribution of WLAN (25 %) and poor network coverage (24 %) follow in fourth and fifth places.

Once again, survey results point to the fact that potential exists, but technical restrictions, such as WLAN access, transmission speeds and security concerns,

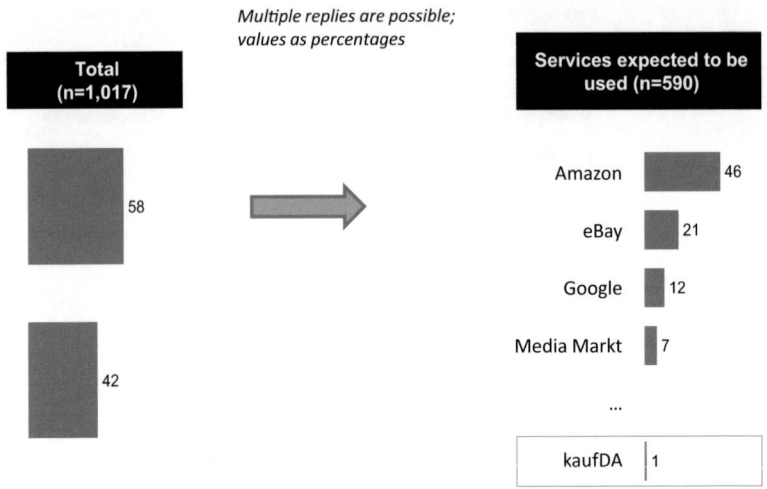

Question: "Will you be using your smartphone or tablet PC to get information about Christmas presents this year?"
Question: "Which services or for which retailers are you expecting to get information on your smartphone or tablet PC about Christmas presents this year?"

Fig. 5.26 Mobile information search for Christmas presents (Source: Heinemann and kaufDA 2013)

represent barriers to greater use of LBS. In response to the question about obstacles to conducting more frequent searches for product information using mobile devices, respondents mentioned faster transmission speeds in first place (40 %), and around one third mentioned cheaper mobile communication prices, greater distribution of hotspots and higher security in applications for smartphones or tablet PCs.

In response to the question of what users would do to obtain information about products and suppliers more frequently in the future via a smartphone or tablet PC, respondents mentioned faster transmission speeds in first place (40 %). Around one third mentioned cheaper mobile communication prices, greater distribution of hotspots and higher security in applications for smartphones or tablet PCs.

Obstacles to greater use of mobile devices are depicted in Fig. 5.27.

Survey results with regard to the question about prerequisites for greater use of mobile devices at the POS primarily specify technical barriers, such as lack of WLAN outside the home/apartment/apartment building (55 %), slow transmission speeds (42 %) and high mobile communication costs (38 %). One third of respondents mention lower costs for the devices themselves and more reliable network coverage for mobile Internet as prerequisites.

As far as brick-and-mortar retailers are concerned, this could indicate that offering free WLAN at the POS and, at least for some consumers, the provision of devices could facilitate the penetration of LBS.

The prerequisites for greater use of mobile devices are depicted in Fig. 5.28.

5.5 "Mo": Mobile Usage of LBS

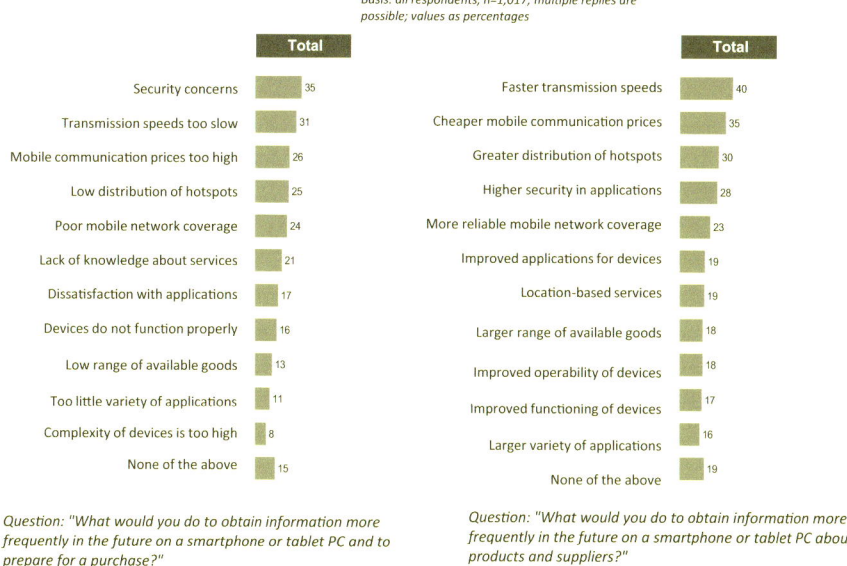

Fig. 5.27 Obstacles to more frequent product information searches on mobile devices (Source: Heinemann and kaufDA 2013)

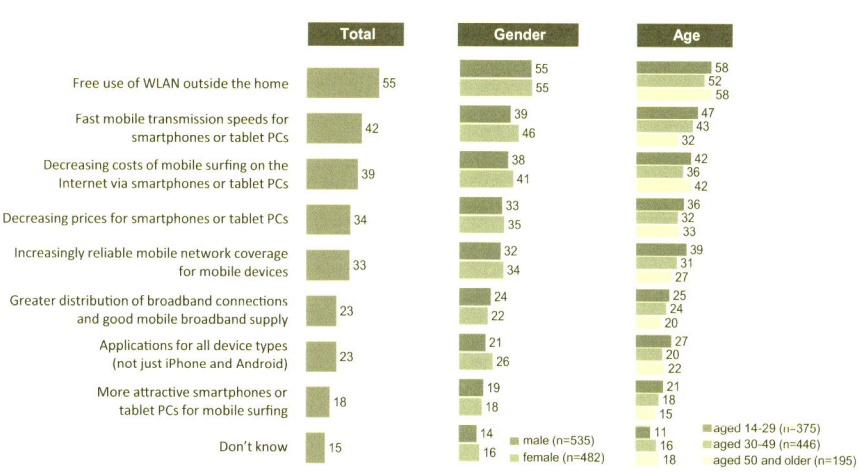

Fig. 5.28 Prerequisites for greater use of mobile devices when shopping (Source: Heinemann and kaufDA 2013)

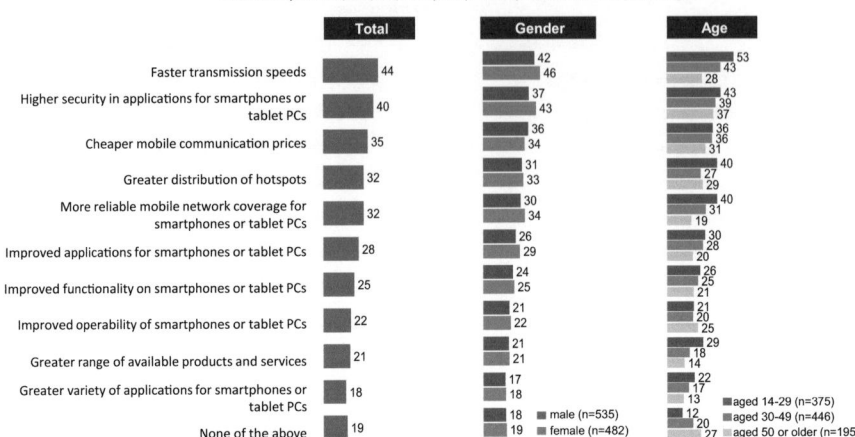

Fig. 5.29 Requirements for more frequent information searches on mobile devices (Source: Heinemann and kaufDA 2013)

5.5.3 Requirements for Information Searches on Mobile Devices

As requirements for more frequent use of product searches on mobile devices, respondents indicated "transmission speeds" in first place (44 %), followed by "higher security" (40 %) and "mobile communication prices" (35 %). "Distribution of WLAN" and "more reliable network coverage" are in fourth place (32 %).

Survey results indicate that potential also exists with regard to acceptance of and readiness for LBS. Technical limitations, such as WLAN access, transmission speeds and security concerns, represent barriers to greater usage.

The requirements for information searches on mobile devices are depicted in Fig. 5.29.

5.5.4 Use of Smartphones/Digital Displays When Shopping

Potential generally exists for support from digital displays. Around 85 % of respondents can envisage being supported by a digital display when shopping. The share of respondents who prefer to use their own device and those who prefer to use the retailer's device fluctuates slightly between around 40 % for the external device and 50 % for their own device. Contrary to the assumption that more young people utilize portable digital devices, respondents over 50 also showed a willingness to receive support from a digital display while shopping, with a figure of 80 %.

Fig. 5.30 Use of digital displays in shopping (Source: Heinemann and kaufDA 2013)

As usage/storage location for a digital shopping assistant, 47 % prefer their own device, whereas 38 % expect a benefit from using the device provided by the retailer.

These survey results indicate that consumers are very willing to be supported by a digital assistant when shopping. The share of those who reject digital shopping is around 15 %. The share among over 50s, at around 24 %, is higher than among younger respondents.

The use of smartphones and digital displays in shopping is depicted in Fig. 5.30.

5.5.5 Preferences for Private or Provided Devices

Most respondents mention trust and usage habits as reasons for using their own device (around 50 %). Essentially the 8 % of the replies specifying "constant availability of own device", 7 % replying with "for speed and practicality" and another 14 % indicating "independence" should be aggregated, producing a total of 79 %. Eleven percent of respondents are concerned about misuse of data and feel more secure with their own device. An additional 5 % mention hygiene as the reason for not using external devices.

Among respondents who advocated using an external device, the main reasons are not having to use/wear out or bring along their own device (20 %). Nineteen percent mention not having to install too much software on their own device. However, such contrary replies could indicate that there are different types of users. As far as brick-and-mortar retailers are concerned, knowledge of their specific target group is also indispensable in the digital age. Security (14 %), the external device's immediate readiness for use (13 %), less effort (10 %) and the

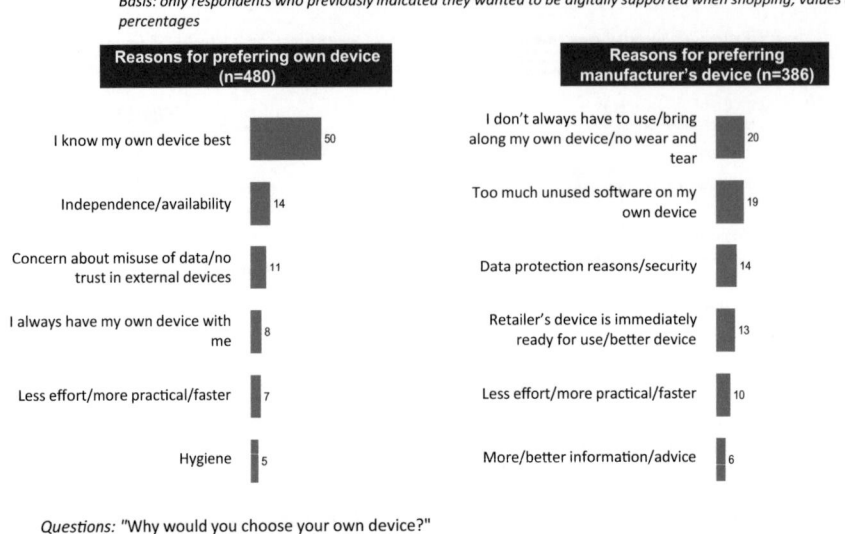

Fig. 5.31 Preferences for personal or provided devices (Source: Heinemann and kaufDA 2013)

expectation of better advice (6 %) were specified as additional reasons for using external devices.

These reasons are depicted in Fig. 5.31.

5.6 Relevance of Results to Brick-and-Mortar Retailing

5.6.1 Differentiation of Customers and Users

In the cross tabulation between "attraction of LBS" and "use of devices", it is clear that people who basically find LBS attractive are more willing to use devices, regardless of whether this is an external device or their own. "Familiarity and ownership" and "independence and availability of own device" are cited as reasons for using their own device.

It should be noted that people who find LBS unattractive are more frequently concerned about misuse of data and believe that LBS are connected with advertising. Nor do they want to divulge too much information about themselves. Among the reasons for using an external device, the results indicate that customers who find LBS unattractive justify this with "too much unused software on their own device".

When examining the relationship between "attraction of LBS" and "use of social networks", the results indicate two groups with contrary attitudes: those who find LBS attractive are also more willing to share offers in a brick-and-mortar store with their own network. A second group finds LBS unattractive and is less interested in linking local offers with their social network.

5.6 Relevance of Results to Brick-and-Mortar Retailing 183

With regard to LBS usage and social networks, the results therefore yield two clusters of respondents with opposing attitudes. In this regard there is a trend to differentiate between social networkers and network naysayers among LBS users.

Survey results identify further evidence of possible clusters: roughly an equal number of respondents prefer to use their own device or a device provided by the retailer. In response to the question about the reasons for or against using an external device, however, the reply indicates other reasons, namely "not always having to bring along their own device".

The group of respondents who use their own device because it is familiar and they maintain contact with their social network on the device clearly also have concerns about too much unused software on their own devices, but are less concerned about misuse of data. This group's attitude towards their own device suggests that it is more unusual for them to leave their own device at home. This is indicative of a second group of respondents, who do not always bring their device along, maintain contact with their social network using the device to a lesser extent, and have concerns about divulging their own data and misuse of data.

5.6.2 Conclusions and Twenty Tips on Use of LBS

The results from the kaufDA study outlined above allow us to draw conclusions about LBS usage in the form of the following 20 tips:

1. Positioning or local relevance of consumers is advised, because they show interest in local product offers and retailers.
2. LBS-specific information about especially attractive offers can change habitual buying behavior and also divert shoppers from going to "their" regular stores.
3. Customers welcome digital shopping support, which reveals LBS potential.
4. LBS potential also exists for cross-selling and spontaneous purchases.
5. From the user's perspective, there is a definite readiness for social shopping, e.g. links to social networks while shopping in a brick-and-mortar store. However, there is evidence that this has, so far, only been of interest to heavy users, or that social shopping is not consciously used.
6. A combination of online search and offline purchase is very widespread and indicative of further LBS potential as a feeder role for brick-and-mortar retailing.
7. Product searches via smartphone and tablet PC are prevalent, but used more by younger than older people.
8. The smartphone in particular could take on a role which increases conversion for brick-and-mortar stores if it were also available at the POS, e.g. provided in-store.
9. Availability of appropriate information is key during mobile product searches.
10. Optimized presentation of information on all devices is also extremely important.

11. Potential clearly exists for all product types and in particular for food-related LBS.
12. In contrast to the smartphone, which tends to be used individually, the tablet PC clearly functions as a social object. Several people often use and view one tablet at the same time.
13. LBS are highly attractive to consumers, but an absence of prerequisites prevents their usage.
14. "LBS" is still a relatively unknown term, which means there is potential in publicizing LBS.
15. From the customer's perspective, it should also become increasingly possible to utilize LBS on the move in the future.
16. From the customer's perspective, interesting LBS information includes availability of products in-store, price information, offers in the vicinity, and store opening times.
17. In social terms, product ratings from other customers and other information on product features are of interest to customers.
18. Barriers to LBS include technical limitations, such as lack of WLAN, slow transmission speeds and high mobile communication costs.
19. Among those who are skeptical about LBS, security concerns (misuse of data, lack of trust) are the primary reason for non-usage.
20. LBS can be enhanced with regard to the variety of offers and level of awareness and recognition.

In summary, it should be noted that LBS have large and previously unused potential for brick-and-mortar retailing.

5.7 Comprehensive Recommendations for Brick-and-Mortar Retailing

This study on the future and potential of location-based services (LBS) for brick-and-mortar retailing indicates a readiness for LBS on the part of customers. Results show that LBS are regarded as attractive and can already challenge habitual behavior. LBS are still in the initial phase, but display great potential.

Almost half of respondents (46 %) own a smartphone and/or tablet PC. Seventy-one percent of respondents own a traditional PC or laptop. Smartphone owners very often use their device while in the store. In a buying situation at the POS, 54 % obtain information about the product using a smartphone. Social willingness to share offers in a brick-and-mortar store with their own network on site is most common among respondents who also find LBS attractive (55.8 %). Such functions are used much less commonly by the over 50 age group. Hardly any difference can be made between genders on this issue.

The term "location-based services" is still not very prevalent in the general population: only 10 % of respondents know exactly what the name means and 72 % have never heard of it. However, the usage situation looks completely different:

among smartphone or tablet PC users, 79 % already use a location-based app which utilizes their current location (e.g. weather apps and map services). And half of them (51.3 %) already use apps to display information on price and product offers from specific retailers in the vicinity. Among communication channels, the ranking of consumer preference shows that search engines (78 %) and large shopping platforms (73 %) are used most, but apps and location-based services together are already in third place (54 %). This provides an opportunity for LBS, if successful, to move consumers' search behavior from usage predominantly on the couch (74.5 %) onto the street, and make it more widely known. Above all, searches are made on the net for fashion products (31 %) and electronic goods (35 %). Food (19 %) is almost as high up as books (20 %) on the list of most-searched for products on the Internet, and thereby underscores the potential offered by LBS.

As reasons for not using LBS, consumers criticize technical limitations (55.3 %), which retailing has not yet managed to remedy. This primarily includes a lack of WLAN (55.3 %). Moreover, consumers complain about poor network coverage (33 %) and high mobile communication prices (33.7 %).

The results of this study show that customers have certain expectations of LBS. Consumers primarily expect information on store opening times (73 %) or locations of retailers in their vicinity, current offers (71 %), and availability and price queries for products (70 %). For brick-and-mortar retailers planning to use LBS, this is an important tip in terms of creating acceptance and meeting consumers' requirements.

Overall, the results allow for the following concluding recommended actions for brick-and-mortar retailing:

1. Brick-and-mortar retailers should provide accessible and free WLAN, as well as digital displays for digital shopping support at the POS.
2. Retailers can minimize security concerns about LBS and concerns about misuse of data through relevant business communication and confidence-building, and thereby simultaneously increase the level of awareness and recognition of LBS offers.
3. Services and information provided via LBS must precisely consider the specific requirements of the relevant target group in order to offer genuine additional benefit and not be discredited as "just" advertising, because advertising is viewed as less credible information in the minds of consumers and clearly prevents them from using LBS.
4. Consumers' current expectation of LBS are based on reliable information with regard to store opening times, retailers' locations, current offers and availability and price queries for products. For brick-and-mortar retailers, this means that such information already represents basic requirements for LBS, which a consumer expects "as a hygiene factor".

Accordingly, LBS services, which can generate enthusiasm among consumers, should be carefully considered and reliably implemented.

Bibliography

Absatzwirtschaft. (2012). Internetnutzer erwarten Social-Media-Integration auf Websites, Studie zum Sharing-Verhalten. Available online at: http://www.absatzwirt-schaft.de/content/online-arketing/news/internetnutzer-erwarten-social-mediainte-gration-auf-websites;78372. Accessed 24 Oct 2012.

Accenture (Ed.). (2010). *Non-food multichannel-Handel 2015 – Vom Krieg der Kanäle zur Multichannel-Synergie*. Dusseldorf: Accenture and GfK.

Accenture (Ed.). (2010b). Mobile Web Watch Studie 2010 – Durchbruch auf Raten –mobiles Internet im deutschsprachigen Raum. Available online at: http://www.accenture.com/NR/rdonlyres/1DDC7A71-5693-446F-2EBF57F5DDA1210-/0/Accenture_Mobile_Web_Watch_2010.pdf. Accessed 27 Dec 2010.

Adzine. (2012). Kosten für Social Media Integration senken, [Online] Verfügbar unter: http://www.adzine.de/site/artikel/6690/social-media-marketing/2012/03/kosten-fuer-social-media-integration-senken-vom-06-03-2012. Zugriff am 04 July 2012.

AGOF. (2013). Dem mobilen User auf der Spur – Zahlen, Daten, Fakten (On the trail of the mobile user – Figures, data, facts). Presentation by Stefan Brax at the Mobile Summit 2013, Berlin on 28 May 2013.

Ahlert, D., Becker, J., Knackstedt, R., & Wunderlich, M. (Eds.). (2002). *Customer relationship management im Handel; Strategien – Konzepte – Erfahrungen*. Berlin: Springer.

Ahlert, D., & Hesse, J. (2002). Relationship management im Beziehungsnetz zwischen Hersteller, Händler und Verbraucher. In D. Ahlert, J. Becker, R. Knackstedt, & M. Wunderlich (Eds.), *Customer relationship management im Handel; Strategien – Konzepte – Erfahrungen* (pp. 3–22). Berlin: Springer.

Ahlert, D., Hesse, J., Jullens, J., & Smend, P. (2003). *Multikanalstrategien, Konzepte, Methoden und Erfahrungen*. Wiesbaden: Gabler-Verlag.

Ahlert, D., Große-Bölting, K., & Heinemann, G. (2009). Handelsmanagement in der Textilwirtschaft, Einzelhandel und Wertschöpfungspartnerschaften, Frankfurt/Main.

Alby, T. (2008). *Das mobile web*. Munich: Hanser.

Apple. (2011). Übertragungsgeschwindigkeiten von LTE (Transmission speeds for LTE). Available online at: http://www.apple.com/de/iphone/specs.html. Accessed 19 Dec 2010.

ARD-ZDF. (2012). ARD/ZDF Online Study 2012. Available online at: http://www.ard-zdf-onlinestudie.de. Accessed 03 Jan 2013.

Aquino, C., & Radwanick, S. (2012). 2012 Mobile future in focus. Available online at: http://www.comscore.com/Insights/Presentations_and_Whitepapers/2012/2012_Mobile_Future_in_Focus. Accessed 08 Jan 2013.

Baumgarth, C., & Kastner, O.-L. (2012). Pop-Up-Stores im Modebereich: Erfolgsfaktoren einer vergänglichen Form der Kundeninspiration. In Working Papers No. 69 of Berlin School of Economics and Law.

Beckmann, J., & Schulz, F. (2008). Online music communities und Kooperationsstrategien bei Steinberg Media Technologies GmbH/Yamaha Corp. Japan. In C. Steinmann (Ed.),

Community marketing – Wie Unternehmen in sozialen Netzwerken Werte schaffen. Stuttgart: Schäffer-Poeschel.
Bernauer, D. (2008). *Mobile Internet – Grundlagen, Erfolgsfaktoren und Praxisbeispiele.* Saarbrücken: VDM-Verlag Müller.
BITKOM & Goldmedia (Ed.). (2008). Goldmedia Mobile Life Report 2012 – Mobile life in the 21st century – Status quo and outlook, Berlin. PDF download at: http://www.goldmedia.com/publikationen/bestellung-mobile-life-2012.html. Accessed 17 Jan 2009.
BITKOM. (2007). Der elektronische Handel boomt, press release dated 25 Jan 2007.
BITKOM. (2009). Federal Association for Information Technology, Telecommunications and New Media, 2009. *Press release 23.07.2009 – 10 Millionen Deutsche spielen online.* Available online at: http://www.bitkom.org/de/markt_statistik/64026_60440.aspx. Accessed 01 June 2011.
BITKOM. (2010). Federal Association for Information Technology, Telecommunications and New Media, 2010. *Press release 28.07.2010 – Bald mehr als 5 Milliarden Mobilfunkanschlüsse.* Available online at: http://www.bitkom.org/de/markt_statistik/64046_64681.aspx. Accessed 01 July 2011.
BITKOM. (2013). New sales record for smartphones. Available online at: http://www.bitkom.org/de/markt_statistik/64086_75052.aspx. Accessed 24 Aug 2013.
Böge, B. (2012). Social Commerce. Definition und thematischer Überblick sowie Analyse der besonderen Rolle des sozialen Netzwerkes Facebook (Social Commerce. Definition and Thematic Overview, and Analysis of the Special Role of the Facebook Social Network) (presentation 2012/FH [University of Applied Sciences] Wedel).
Boersma, T. (2010). Warum Web-Exzellenz Schlüsselthema für erfolgreiche Händler ist – Wie das Internet den Handel revolutioniert. In: G. Heinemann, & A. Haug (Hrsg.), *Web-Exzellenz im E-commerce – Innovation und transformation im Handel* (S. 21–42). Wiesbaden: Gabler Verlag.
Boersma, T. (2011). Amazon Umsatz Deutschland und Gesamt 2007–2010. In Zwischendurch@Thorsten Boersma dated 31 Jan 2011.
Brohan, M. (2012). Nordstrom doubles up on the web. In: internetretailer.com, available online at: http://www.internetretailer.com/2012/02/20/nordtrom-doubles-web. Accessed 21 Dec 2012.
Bolz, N. (2008). Linking value – der Mehrwert des 21. Jahrhunderts. In H. Kaul & C. Steinmann (Eds.), *Community marketing – Wie Unternehmen in sozialen Netzwerken Werte schaffen* (pp. 251–260). Stuttgart: Schäffer-Poeschel.
Bruce, A. (2011). Multi-channeling der Zukunft – Multi-Channel-Erfolgsfaktoren im wachsenden Markt aus Sicht von Google. In G. Heinemann, M. Schleusener, & S. Zaharia (Eds.), *Modernes multi-channeling im fashion-Handel.* Frankfurt: Deutscher Fachverlag.
Buggisch, C. (2013). Social Media Nutzerzahlen in Deutschland – Update 2013. In: buggisch.wordpress.com, available online at: http://buggisch.wordpress.com/2013/01/02/social-media-nutzerzahlen-in-deutschland-update-2013/. Accessed 5 Jan 2013.
Burberry. (2013). Store experiences regent street. Available online at: http://de.burberry.com/store/experiences/regent-street/#/flagship/1. Accessed on 22 Aug 2013.
Butlers. (2013). Impressionen aus unserer Berliner Möbelfiliale (Impressions from our Berlin furniture store). Available online at: http://www.butlers.de/Videoberatung/videoberatung_lp,default,p.html. Accessed 22 Aug 2013.
BV Capital/eVenture. (2011, April). *Overview: eCommerce & online trends.* San Francisco.
BVDW. (2011). *Social commerce. Vom Hype zum Geschäftsmodell.* Düsseldorf.
BVDW (Ed.). (2012). OVK online report 2012/01. Available at: http://www.ovk.de/fileadmin/downloads/ovk/ovk-report/OVK_Report2012_1_Web.pdf. Accessed 26 Dec 2012.
BVH. (2013). "Interaktiver Handel in Deutschland"– Die Entwicklung des Multichannel Online- und Versandhandels B2C im Jahr 2012 ("Interactive Commerce in Germany" – Development of Multichannel Online and Distance Selling B2C in 2012", document for BVH annual press conference 2013), Berlin.

Bibliography

Catalyst Marketers. (2010). Dell does Twitter – do you? Available online at: http://www.catalystmarketers.com/dell-does-twitter-do-you/. Accessed 20 Aug 2013.

Chaney, P. (2012a). Shoppers count on social commerce but not mobile and tablet devices this holiday season [infographic], 16 Nov 2012. Available online at: http://networkedblogs.com/EOxsY. Accessed 20 Aug 2013.

Chaney, P. (2012b). Social commerce by definition, a cupcake or a bouncing ball? 21 Dec 2012. Available online at: http://networkedblogs.com/Gel0E. Accessed 20 Aug 2013.

Chaney, P. (2012c). Facebook launched social gifts, Amazon and Cafepress follow suit. Availabe online at: http://networkedblogs.com/G5GHn. Accessed 20 Aug 2013.

Chaney, P. (2012d). Pizza Hut offers fragrance to Facebook fans. Available online at: http://networkedblogs.com/FG5tZ. Accessed 20 Aug 2013.

Chami, N. (2012). Möglichkeiten des Mobile-Commerce für den stationären Fashion-Handel an ausgewählten Beispielen. Bachelor thesis, Niederrhein University of Applied Sciences.

Clement, R., & Schreiber, D. (2010). *Internet-Ökonomie*. Heidelberg: Physica-Verlag.

Conversity. (2010). How people influence each other. Available online at: http://www.conversity.be/blog/how-people-influence-each-other/. Accessed 20 Aug 2013.

Crossretail. (2013). Digital in-Store: Wie finde ich das richtige Konzept? Available online at: http://crossretail.de/digital-in-store-wie-finde-ich-das-richtige-konzept/. Accessed 21 Aug 2013.

DDV Dialog. (2013). "Mobile-Commerce – Nur eine Minderheit kauft unterwegs, Langsamer Abschied von den Legenden". In Feb 2013 issue, p. 22.

Der Handel. (2013). Butlers eröffnet Möbelgeschäft in Berlin, article dated 16 July 2013. Available online at: http://www.derhandel.de/news/unternehmen/pages/Wohnaccessoires-Butlers-eroeffnet-Moebelgeschaeft-in-Berlin-9875.html. Accessed 22 Aug 2013.

Deutsche-Startups.de. (2010). Smartphones ersetzen einfache Internet-Handys. Available online at: http://www.deutsche-startups.de/?p=33515. Accessed 27 Dec 2010.

dgroup (Ed.). (2012a). Im test: Click & collect von Karstadt. In: institut.diligenz.de. Available online at: http://institut.diligenz.de/2012/12/im-test-clickcollect-von-karstadt/. Accessed on 21 Dec 2012.

dgroup (Ed.). (2012b). Multichannel: Perspektiven für den Stationärhandel. Best Practice: Globetrotter. Available at: http://institut.diligenz.de/wp-content/uploads/2012/12/diligenZ_Group_ePaper_Multichannel_Dez20121.pdf

dgroup. (2013). Anzahl der smartphone Nutzer in Deutschland, internal document.

Die Welt. (2011a). Netzbetreiber beschleunigen mobiles Web, 16 Feb 2011, p. 12.

Die Welt. (2011b). Langsames Deutschland – Die Cebit macht eines deutlich: Das Internet muss viel schneller werden, 1 Mar, p. 3.

Die Welt. (2011c). Kein Spielkram, 27 Ap 2011, p. 14.

Die Welt. (2011d). Suchmaschinen für Superschnäppchen, 9 May 2011, p. 17.

Die Welt. (2011e). Teurer Schnäppchendienst, 4 June 2011, p. 12.

Die Welt. (2011f). Das Buch stirbt auf Raten, 12 Aug, p. 12.

Die Welt. (2011g). Google kauft Motorolas Handy-Sparte, 16 Aug, p. 11.

Die Welt. (2011h). Der nächste Monopolist, 27 Aug, p. 13.

Die Welt. (2012). Angriff auf Apples kleinen Klon, dated 31 Oct, p. 12.

Diller, H. (2008). *Preispolitik* (4th ed.). Stuttgart: Kohlhammer Verlag.

Digitalnext.de. (2010). Einkaufen in 3-D-online-shopping. Available online at: http://www.digitalnext.de/einkaufen-in-3d-online-shopping-wird-zum-virtuellen-erlebnis/. Accessed 28 Dec 2010.

DMC. (2013). Von der Zukunft des Handels und dem Handel der Zukunft, Dialog Digital Handeln mit dmc.cc, Stuttgart.

Duryee, T. (2012). E-commerce is head over heels for pinterest, and for good reason. Available online at: http://allthingsd.com/20120615/e-commerce-is-head-over-heels-for-pinterest-and-theres-a-good-reason-why/. Accessed 20 Aug 2012.

eBay. (2012a). Die Zukunft des Handels (The future of commerce), documentation of "Die Zukunft des Handels" ("The future of commerce") project, Berlin.
eBay. (2012b). eBay Kaufraum fact sheet (eBay showroom fact sheet). Available online at: http://presse.ebay.de/sites/ebay.de/files/factsheet_kaufraum.pdf. Accessed 22 Aug 2013.
eBay UK. (2011). eBay christmas boutique. Available online at: http://boutique.ebay.co.uk/. Accessed 22 Aug 2013.
ECC (Ed.). (2010). Empirische Daten und Prognosen zum m-commerce: Smartphones-Nutzer verhalten sich anders als Handynutzer. Available online at: http://www.ecc-handel.de/empirische_daten_und_prognosen_zum_m-commerce.php#98036701. Accessed 01 Nov 2010.
ECC. (2011). Erfahrung mit dem Bezahlen im Internet positiv, press release dated 30 March 2011.
Eckstein, A. (2013). Mobile Endgeräte als Einkaufsassistenten am POS – Die Digitalisierung des stationären Handels (Mobile devices as shopping assistants at the POS – The digitalization of Brick-and-Mortar retailing), Presentation by Aline Eckstein at the Mobile Summit 2013 in Berlin on 28 May 2013.
Eckstein, M., & Theiss, B. (2010). Eine Frage des Systems. Connect Smartphone special edition, 01/2011, p. 8 et seqq.
Eckstein, M., Kaliudis, A., & Peuckert, M. (2010). Publikumsmagneten. Connect, 12/2010, p. 36 et seqq.
EHI & KMPG (Ed.). (2012). Consumer markets. Trends im Handel 2020. Available online at: http://www.kpmg.de/docs/20120418-Trends-im-Handel-2020.pdf. Accessed 23 Dec 2012.
Eisenbrand, R. (2012). Radcarpet zeigt Entfernung zur Filiale in mobilem Banner an. In: onetoone.de [Online] Verfügbar unter http://www.onetoone.de/Radcarpet-zeigt-Entfernung-zur-Filiale-in-mobilem-Banner-an-22001.html. Zugriff am 23 Dec 2012.
Enderle, G., & Voll, L. (2011). *Turning pitfalls into Snares – Crafting a successful multi-channel strategy* (pp. 22–25). Rotterdam: OC&C Strategic Insights.
etailment.de. (2012a). Die sieben Säulen des Social-Commerce. Available online at: http://etailment.de/thema/social-commerce/die-sieben-saeulen-des-social-commerce-269/. Accessed 20 Aug 2013.
etailment.de. (2012b). Social login: Was Online-Händler von sozialen Medien lernen können. Available online at: http://etailment.de/2012/social-commerce-haendler-medien-lernen/. Accessed 20 Aug 2013.
etailment.de. (2012c). Wie Etsy den Facebook-commerce auf die website holt. Available online at: http://etailment.de/thema/tools/wie-etsy-den-facebook-commerce-auf-die-website-holt-507. Accessed 20 Aug 2013.
etailment.de. (2012d). Neue Modelle im social shopping pushen den Umsatz. Available online at: http://etailment.de/thema/tools/neue-modelle-im-social-shopping-pushen-den-umsatz-693. Accessed 20 Aug 2013.
etailment.de. (2012e). Pinterest: 6 einfache Ideen für den e-commerce. Available online at: http://etailment.de/2012/pinterest-6-einfache-ideen-fuer-den-e-commerce/. Accessed 20 Aug 2013.
Etailment. (2013). Ladengeschäfte mit Online-Logistik. Available online at: http://etailment.de/2013/ladengeschaefte-mit-online-logistik-ex-amazon-mitarbeiterin-moechte-fashion-shopping-revolutionieren/. Accessed 22 Aug 2013.
eWeb Research Center. (2012). *eWeb Research Center der Hochschule Niederrhein: Amazon und Ebay ziehen der Konkurrenz davon*. Press release of Niederrhein University of Applied Sciences dated 29 Oct 2012.
eWeb Research Center. (2013). *Web-Experte: Online-Handel in 2012 weiter auf Kosten des stationären Einzelhandels gewachsen*. Press release of Niederrhein University of Applied Sciences dated 8 Jan 2013.
Examone. (2013). Mobile internet users. Available online at: http://blog.examone.com/why-innovation-matters-to-your-applicants-a-consumer-driven-process/. Accessed 24 Aug 2013.
Fab.com. (2013). Fab showroom. Available online at: http://dby.fab.com/de/showroom.html. Accessed 22 Aug 2013.
Facebook. (2013). About social plug-ins. Available online at: https://www.facebook.com/help/443483272359009/. Accessed 20 Aug 2013.

Bibliography

Fanpagelist. (2012). http://www.fanpagelist.com. Zugriff am 01 Aug 2012.

Fashion for Home. (2013). Multichannel-Strategie mit drei neuen Showrooms in Deutschland. Available online at: http://media.fashion4home.net/press/docs/pressemitteilungen/20130502_FASHION_FOR_HOME_F.pdf. Accessed 22 Aug 2013.

Focus. (2010). Handyvergleich (comparison of cell phones). Available online at: http://www.focus.de/digital/handy/handyvergleich/tid-18828/apple-iphone-4-ausstattung-schaerfstesdisplay_aid_523701.html. Accessed 19 Dec 2010.

Focus.de. (2013a). "Die Deutschen sind keine Modemuffel", interview with top boss Claus-Dietrich Lahrs dated 14 January 2013. Available online at: http://www.focus.de/finanzen/boerse/aktien/tid-29075/wirtschaft-die-deutschen-sind-keine-modemuffel_aid_896840.html. Accessed 22 Aug 2013.

Focus.de. (2013b). Mobile Nutzung der Suchmaschinen in Deutschland. Available online at: http://www.focus.de/digital/internet/netzoekonomie-blog/mobile-suche-80-prozent-zuwachs-fuer-google_aid_986715.html. Accessed 22 Aug 2013.

FAZ-net. (2012). Mass customization – Massenware nach Maß. http://www.faz.net/aktuell/wirtschaft/unternehmen/mass-customization-massenware-nach-mass-11900853.html. Accessed 24 Oct 2012.

Firsching J. (2012). "Permalink to Geo-Tags auf dem Vormarsch Immer mehr Content enthält Ortsinformationen" Geo-Tags auf dem Vormarsch – Immer mehr Content enthält Ortsinformationen. In: futurebiz.com [Online] Verfügbar unter http://www.futurebiz.de/artikel/geo-tags-auf-dem-vormarsch-immer-mehr-content-enthalt-ortsinformationen/. Zugriff am 17 Dec 2012.

Firsching, J. (2013a). 190 Mio. monatlich aktive Google+ Nutzer weltweit. Available online at: http://www.futurebiz.de/artikel/190-monatlich-aktiver-google-nutzer-weltweit/. Accessed 20 Aug 2013.

Firsching, J. (2013b). Steigende Facebook Mobile Nutzung bringt Marken durch das Sommerloch. Available online at: http://www.futurebiz.de/artikel/steigende-facebook-mobile-nutzung-bringt-marken-durch-das-sommerloch/. Accessed on 22 Aug 2013.

Frankfurter Allgemeine Zeitung. (2008). Ebay für Zocker, no. 156 dated 7 July 2008, p. 19.

Frankfurter Allgemeine Zeitung. (2010). Offenheit ist meine religion, no. 209 dated 9 Sept 2010, p. 31.

Frankfurter Allgemeine Zeitung. (2011a). 2011 wird das Jahr des tablet-computers, no. 2 dated 4 Jan 2011, p. 15.

Frankfurter Allgemeine Zeitung. (2011b). "Ich freue mich auf das nächste Jahrzehnt bei Google" ("I'm looking forward to the next decade at Google"), interview with Eric Schmidt, no. 21 dated 26 Jan 2011, p. 16.

Frankfurter Allgemeine Zeitung. (2011c). Rabatte ohne Ende, no. 26 dated 1 Feb 2011, p. 17.

Frankfurter Allgemeine Zeitung. (2011d). Internet-Fernsehen kontra Fernsehkabel, no. 53 dated 4 Mar 2011, p. 19.

Frankfurter Allgemeine Zeitung. (2011e). Google+ bringt Facebook und Twitter in die defensive, no. 156 dated 8 July 2011, p. 11.

Frankfurter Allgemeine Zeitung. (2011f). Eine ganze Industrie findet keine Antwort auf Apple, no. 177 dated 2 Aug 2011, p. 17.

Frankfurter Allgemeine Zeitung. (2011g). Google räumt seinen Suchalgorithmus auf, no. 189 dated 16 Aug 2011, p. 17.

Frankfurter Allgemeine Zeitung. (2013a). Zwei Gewinner auf Kosten vieler Verlierer, no. 6 dated 8 Jan 2013, p. 16.

Frankfurter Allgemeine Zeitung. (2013b). "Apple kann Preise nicht ignorieren", no. 9 dated 11 Jan 2013, p. 17.

French Connection. (2013). Sketch to store. Available online at http://www.you-tube.com/user/frenchconnection. Accessed 20 Aug 2013.

Gartner. (2011). Global market shares of operating systems. Available online at: http://www.gartner.com/it/page.jsp?id=1622614. Accessed 28 Aug 2011.

Gerling, M. (2012). Goldrausch 2.0: Online-Handel und Mobile-Commerce überschätzt? In ehi. org. Available online at: http://www.ehi.org/presse/lifeehi/detailanzeige/article/goldrausch-20. html. Accessed 09 Jan 2013.

Gerlicher, A., & Rupp, S. (2004). *Symbian OS – Einführung in die Anwendungsentwicklung*. Heidelberg: Dpunkt Verlag.

Google. (2012). The New Multiscreen World: Understanding cross-platform consumer behavior, Aug 2012.

Google & Ipsos OTX MediaCT. (2012). Unser mobiler Planet: Deutschland (Our mobile planet: Germany). In: services.google.com. Available online at: http://services.google.com/fh/files/blogs/our_mobile_planet_germany_de.pdf. Accessed 2 Jan 2013.

Go-Smart study. (2012). *Always-In-Touch, Studie zur Smartphone-Nutzung 2012* (Always-intouch, study on smartphone usage 2012). Google, Otto Group, TNS-Infratest, Trendbüro.

Grabs, A., & Bannour, K.-P. (2011). *Follow me! Erfolgreiches social media marketing mit Facebook, Twitter & Co* (1st ed.). Bonn: Galileo Press.

Grahamrose. (2011). Booz & Company estimate of social commerce market size (2010–2015; in US$ Billions). Available online at: http://grahampenrose.files.wordpress.com/2011/02/social-commerce-market-in-billions.png. Accessed 20 Aug 2013.

Grebarsch, S., & Zalando. (2012). Adwords unterwegs (AdWords on the move), presentation at the Mobile Summit 2012, Management Forum, 26 June 2012, Düsseldorf.

Gruner + Jahr (Ed.). (2008). *G+J telecommunications sector profile*. Hamburg.

Haak, A., Finger, L., & Smolinski, R. (2013). Im Labyrinth der screens – Produktstrategien in einem multi-device-e-commerce. In G. Heinemann, K. Haug, M. Gehrcken, & dgroup (Eds.), *Digitalisierung des Handels mit ePace – Innovative e-commerce-Geschäftsmodelle und digitale Zeitvorteile* (pp. 27–49). Wiesbaden: Springer Gabler.

Haarhaus, H. (2013). *Opportunities for social commerce in fashion retailing with special consideration of SoLoMo – Final work of the master course of study to get the academic degree "Master of Science"*. Mönchengladbach.

Haderlein, A. (2012). Social commerce: Verkaufen im community-Zeitalter (Social commerce: Selling in the community age), sales-design. Available online at: http://de.slideshare.net/Haderlein/social-commerce-verkaufen-im-communityzeitalter. Accessed 20 Aug 2013.

Haug, K. (2013). Digitale Potenziale für den stationären Handel durch Empfehlungsprozesse, lokale Relevanz und mobile Geräte (SoLoMo). In G. Heinemann, K. Haug, M. Gehrckens, & dgroup (Eds.), *Digitalisierung des Handels mit ePace – Innovative e-commerce-Geschäftsmodelle und digitale Zeitvorteile* (pp. 27–49). Wiesbaden: Springer Gabler.

Haug, K., & Küper, J. (2010). Das potenzial vom Kundenbeteiligung im Web-2.0-Online-Shop – Produktbewertungen als Kernfaktor des "consumer-generated marketing". In G. Heinemann & A. Haug (Eds.), *Web-Exzellenz im E-commerce – Innovation und transformation im Handel* (Web excellence in e-commerce – Innovation and transformation in retail) (pp. 115–134). Wiesbaden: Gabler-Verlag.

Heinemann, G. (1989). *Betriebstypenprofilierung und Erlebnishandel*. Wiesbaden: Gabler-Verlag.

Heinemann, G. (2008). *Multi-channel-Handel – Erfolgsfaktoren und best practices* (2 Auflage). Wiesbaden: Gabler Verlag.

Heinemann, G. (2011a). *Cross-channel-management – Integrationserfordernisse im multi-channel-Handel* (3rd ed.). Wiesbaden: Gabler-Verlag.

Heinemann, G. (2011b). Der Kunde steht online im Laden, in FAZ no. 182 dated 8 Aug 2011, p. 10.

Heinemann, G. (2012a). *Der neue online-Handel, Erfolgsfaktoren und best practices* (4th ed.). Wiesbaden: Springer-Gabler.

Heinemann, G. (2012b). *Der neue mobile-commerce, Erfolgsfaktoren und best practices*. Wiesbaden: Springer-Gabler.

Heinemann, G. (2013a). *No-line-Handel – höchste Evolutionsstufe im multi-channeling*. Wiesbaden: Springer-Gabler.

Heinemann, G. (2013b). *Der neue online-Handel – Geschäftsmodell und Kanalexzellenz im e-commerce* (5th ed.). Wiesbaden: Springer-Gabler.

Heinemann, G. (2013c). Social-media als Spiegelbild des neuen Kaufverhaltens. In M. Bruhn (Ed.), *Dienstleistungsmanagement* (pp. 91–108). Wiesbaden: Gabler.

Heinemann, G., & Schwarzl, C. (2010). New online retailing – Innovation and transformation, Wiesbaden.

Heinemann, G., & kaufDA. (2013). *Study on the subject of "Zukunft und Potenziale von Location-based Services für den stationären Handel"*. Mönchengladbach.

Heinemann, G., Haug, K., Gehrckens, M., & dgroup (Eds.). (2013). *Digitalisierung des Handels mit ePace – Innovative e-commerce-Geschäftsmodelle und digitale Zeitvorteile*. Wiesbaden: Springer Gabler.

Heitmeyer, C., & Naveenthirarajah, S. (2010). Online Customer Segmentation in Shopping-Clubs – Auf dem Weg zur ultimative Kundenorientierung bei Brands4Friends. In G. Heinemann & A. Haug (Eds.), *Web-Exzellenz im E-Commerce – Innovation und Transformation im Handel* (Web excellence in e-commerce – Innovation and transformation in retail) (pp. 71–92). Wiesbaden: Gabler-Verlag.

Hengl, T. (2012). Zalando ist Deutscher Meister auf Pinterest. Available online at: http://www.lead-digital.de/start/semseo/zalando_ist_deutscher_meister_auf_pinterest. Accessed 20 Aug 2013.

Hermes, V. (2010). So profitieren Sie vom Coupon-Boom. In absatzwirtschaft 6/2010, pp. 86–89.

Heymann-Reder, D. (2011). *Social media marketing: Erfolgreiche Strategien für Sie und Ihr Unternehmen* (p. 20). Munich: Addison-Wesley.

HMWVL – Hessian Ministry of Economics, Transport and Regional Development. (2007). Internet-marketing nicht nur für kleine und mittlere Unternehmen, Wiesbaden.

Hofmann, A. (2012). Radcarpet startet mit Location-based-Advertising. In gruenderszene.de. Available online at: http://www.gruenderszene.de/news/radcarpet-location-based-advertising. Accessed 23 Dec 2012.

Hointer. (2013). Explaining Hointer's concept, a video clip. Available online at: http://www.hointer.com/ and http://www.hointer.com/blog.php. Accessed 22 Aug 2013.

Horizont. (2012a). "Internet zum Mitnehmen". In HORIZONT 42/2012 dated 18 Oct 2012, p. 19.

Horizont. (2012b). Soziale Media-Nutzung und -Erwartungen. In HORIZONT 44/2012 dated 1 Nov 2012, p. 23

IBM. (2012). Mobile retail commerce rises while social shopping drops in second quarter. Available online at: http://www-03.ibm.com/press/us/en/pressrelease/38349.wss. Accessed 20 Aug 2013.

Ich-sag-mal. (2011). E-christmas und helfende Kunden – Fallbeispiel LG Electronics, blog. Available online at: http://gunnarsohn.wordpress.com/tag/einzelhandel/. Accessed 01 Mar 2011.

IDC Retail Insights. (2010). Maximizing value from the omnichannel consumer. Available at: http://risnews.edgl.com/getmedia/f3f80ac4-a5ef-44a4-a8e7-261e56ce8299/RIS10_IDC_GG.pdf. Accessed 14 Apr 2011.

IMR. (2011). IMR World B2C Global e-Commerce Overview 2011. Available online at: http://www.imrg.org. Accessed 30 June 2012.

Immler, C., & Kaiser, D. (2010). *Das inoffizielle Windows Phone Buch* (1st ed.). Poing: Franzis Verlag.

Informatik und Gesellschaft der Universität Köln (Ed.). (2011). Entwicklung sozialer Netzwerke. Available online at: http://www.informatik.uni-oldenburg.de/~iug10/sn/html/impressum.html. Accessed 25 May 2013.

Inside FFM (Ed.). (2010). Case study: Jimmy Choo Foursquare Campaign. Available online at: http://insidefmm.com/2010/05/catchachoo-jimmy-choo-foursquare-campaign/. Accessed 23 May 2013.

Internet Retailing (Ed.). (2012a). Three-channel shoppers spend more than twice as much with Sainsbury's. In internetretailing.net. Available online at: http://internetretailing.net/2012/11/

three-channel-shoppers-spend-more-than-twice-as-much-with-sainsburys/. Accessed 21 Feb 2012.
Internet Retailing (Ed.). (2012b). Argos to 'redefine multichannel shopping' in transformation plan. In internetretailing.net. Available online at: http://internetretailing.net/2012/10/argos-to-redefine-multichannel-shopping-in-transformation-plan/. Accessed 21 Dec 2012.
Internet World Business. (2011a). Wer zuerst kommt, issue 6 dated 22 Aug 2011, p. 36.
Internet World Business. (2011b). Optimaler Zahlart-Mix, issue 9 dated 2 May 2011, pp. 26–29.
Internet World Business. (2011c). Auf die Touchpoints achten, issue 10 dated 16 May 2011, pp. 16–17.
Internet World Business. (2011d). Mobile payment ist gefragt, issue 11 dated 1 June 2011, p. 28.
Internet World Business. (2011e). Ändert dieser Button alles? Issue 12 dated 14 June 2011, p. 3.
Internet World Business. (2011f). "2020 kein Bargeld mehr", issue 13 dated 22 Aug 2011, p. 12.
Internet World Business. (2011g). Die Zukunft des Bezahlens, issue 15 dated 22 Aug 2011, p. 36.
Internetworld. (2012). Beta-Test zu same-day-delivery mit stationären Händlern. In internetworld.de. Available online at: http://www.internetworld.de/Nachrichten/E-Commerce/Dienstleistungen/eBay-forciert-Local-Shopping-Beta-Test-zu-Same-Day-Delivery-mit-stationaeren-Haendlern-68310.html. Accessed 23 Dec 2012.
internetworld.de. (2012). Geschäfte unter Freunden. Available online at: http://www.internetworld.de/Heftarchiv/2012/Ausgabe-25-2012/Geschaefte-unter-Freunden. Accessed 09 Jan 2013.
Internet World Stats. (2013). Internet usage statistics – The internet big picture – World internet users and population stats. Available online at: http://internet-worldstats.com/stats.htm. Accessed 15 Feb 2013.
Intertone. (2010). The age of on. Available online at: http://www.interone.de/iphone-studie/study.php. Accessed 20 Aug 2013.
iTunes Store. (2010a). H&M (updated on 17.12.2010). Available online at: http://itunes.apple.com/de/app/h-m/id380487409?mt=8. Accessed 29 Dec 2010.
iTunes Store. (2010b). ZARA (updated on 21.12.2010). Available online at: http://itunes.apple.com/de/app/zara/id341323282?mt=8. Accessed 29 Dec 2010.
Jahn, M., & Müller, S. (2011). Key European retail data 2010 review and 2011 forecast, dated 30 June 2011. Available online at http://www.directionsmag.com/articles/key-european-retail-data-2010-review-and-2011-forecast/186736. Accessed 23 Aug 2013.
Johnson, L. (2012). Blue moon spearheads location, context via mobile ads. In mobilemarketer.com. Available online at: http://www.mobilemarketer.com/cms/news/advertising/13202.html. Accessed 24 Dec 2012.
Josten, W. M. (2013). *BUTLERS – mit Online-Shops national und international auf Expansionskurs* (BUTLERS – On a national and international expansion course with online shops). Presentation at the 5th Commercial Real Estate Summit on 26 Feb 2013, Wiesbaden.
Kaliudis, A. (2010). Palm Pre Plus – Im Dauertest. Connect, 11/2010, p. 66 et seqq.
Kantsperger, R., & Meyer, A. (2006). Qualitatives Benchmarking von Customer Interaction-Centern im Handel. In: *Thexis: Fachzeitschrift für Marketing* (4/2006, pp. 26–30). Wiesbaden: Gabler.
Kasper, C., Diekmann, T., & Hagenhoff, S. (2007). Context-adaptive mobile systems. In D. Taniar (Ed.), *Encyclopedia of mobile computing and commerce*. Hershey: Information Science Reference.
KaufDA. (2013). *Study on the subject of "Zukunft und Potenziale von location-based services für den stationären Handel"*. Mönchengladbach.
kaufDA. (2014). Study on the subject "Zukunft und Potenziale von Location-based Services für den stationären Handel – Zeitreihenanalyse im Vergleich zu 2013", Mönchengladbach.
Kerkau, F. (2012). *Smartphone – unsere Fernbedienung des Lebens* (Smartphone – Our remote control for life). Presentation at the Mobile Summit 2012, Management Forum, 26 June 2012, Düsseldorf.

Bibliography

Kessler, S. (2011). eBay takes local shopping mobile. In mashable.com. Available online at: http://mashable.com/2011/06/16/ebay-milo-app/. Accessed 3 Dec 2012.

Kirch, N. (2012). Instagram hat 100 Millionen registrierte Nutzer – aktive Nutzer wachsen exorbitant. In: socialmediastatistik.de [Online] Verfügbar unter: http://www.socialmediastatistik.de/instagram-hat-100-millionen-registrierte-nutzer-aktive-nutzer-wachsen-exorbitant/. Zugriff am 5 Jan 2013.

Klopfleisch, M. (2009). *Mobile e-commerce: Business in motion*. Master's thesis, Jena University of Applied Sciences, Jena.

Kolbrück, O. (2012). E-commerce: Das Design-Kaufhaus Fab.com punktet mit sozialen features und einem Fokus auf mobile Kunden. In Horizont 41/2012 dated 11 Oct 2012, p. 17.

Kollmann, T. (2007). *Online-marketing – Grundlagen der Absatzpolitik in der net economy*. Stuttgart: Kohlhammer.

Kollmann, T. (2009). *E-business – Grundlagen elektronischer Geschäftsprozesse in der net economy* (3rd ed.). Wiesbaden: Gabler.

Konrad, J. (2013). *Gamification im mobile-commerce – Erscheinungsformen, Beispiele, Relevanz und Zukunftsperspektiven für Fashion Anbieter* (Gamification in mobile commerce – Manifestations, examples, relevance and future prospects for fashion providers), seminar paper. Mönchengladbach: Niederrhein University of Applied Sciences.

Kowalewsky, R. (2010). Neue Mobilfunkrevolution kommt. In RP dated 13 Apr 2010, p. A7.

Kriewald, M. (2007). Situationsabhängiges mobiles Customer Relationship Management, Analysen – Wettbewerbsvorteile – Beispiele, Hamburg.

Küllenberg, B., & Quente, C. (2006). *Kreative Markenkommunikation mit Handy & Co*. Landsberg am Lech: mi-Fachverlag.

L2 (Ed.). (2012). L2 Digital IQ Index – Specialty retail. In l2thinktank.com. Available online at http://www.l2thinktank.com/research/specialty-retail-2012. Accessed 21 Dec 2012.

Labor Intensive Design. (2012). Levi's Friends Store. Available online at: http://cargocollective.com/laborintensivedesign/Levi-s-Friends-Store. Accessed 20 Aug 2013.

Lehmann, N. (2013). Gib' der Marke ein Zuhause. In Handelsjournal (retail journal), 2010, page: 12 et seqq. Available online at: http://www.markenlexikon.com/texte/hj_lehmann_flagshipstores_01_2010.pdf. Accessed 10 June 2013.

Lehner, F. (2002). Einführung und motivation. In R. Teichmann & F. Lehner (Eds.), *Mobile commerce – Strategien, Geschäftsmodelle, Fallstudien*. Berlin\Heidelberg: Springer.

Link, J., & Seidl, F. (2008). Der Situationsansatz als Erfolgsfaktor des Mobile Marketing. In H. H. Bauer et al. (Eds.), *Erfolgsfaktoren des Mobile Marketing – Strategien, Konzepte und Instrumente*. Berlin – Heidelberg: Springer.

Link, J., & Weiser, C. (2006). *Marketing-controlling. Systeme für mehr Markt- und Unternehmenserfolg* (p. 214). Munich: Vahlen.

Logara, T. (2008). *M-Business kompakt* (2nd ed.). Norderstedt: Books-on-Demand.

Lückemeier, T. (2012). Spotlight Online Medien Management – Social commerce mit Torsten Lückemeier. Available online at: http://www.youtube.com/playlist?list=PL48A0986662ADDC18. Accessed 20 Aug 2013.

Lufthansa Exclusive. (2009). Killer gesucht, issue 03, pp. 17–21.

manager magazin new media (Hrsg.). (2010). Die bemerkenswerte zweite Gründer-Chance [Online] Verfügbar unter http://www.manager-magazin.de/unternehmen/artikel/0,2828,707576,00.html. Zugriff am 08 Dec 2010.

Marine Software (Ed.). (2012). The state of mobile search advertising in the US. How the emergence of smartphones and tablets changes paid search. In marinsoftware.com. Available online at: http://www.marinsoftware.com/downloads/mobile_search_us2012_marin.pdf. Accessed 27 Dec 2012.

Marketing-blog.biz. (2012). Guten tag. Guten tag, social shopping. Available online at: http://www.marketing-blog.biz/archives/5417-Social-Shopping.html. Accessed 20 Aug 2013.

Marsden, P. (2011a). Wired Feb. 2011: Cover story on social commerce. Available online at: http://socialcommercetoday.com/speed-summary-wired-feb-2011-cover-story-on-social-com merce/. Accessed 20 Aug 2013.

Marsden, P. (2011b). Social commerce & the smart SoLoMo customer. Available online at: http://digitalinnovationtoday.com/social-commerce-the-smart-solomo-consumer-infographics/. Accessed 20 Aug 2013.

Marsden, P. (2012a). When social media comes to e-commerce. Available online at: http://smartservice-blog.com/2011/12/13/interview-mit-social-commerce-experten-paul-marsden-part1-when-social-media-comes-to-ecommerce/. Accessed 3 Nov 2012.

Marsden, P. (2012b). How to turn social media into social sales. Available online at: http://de.slideshare.net/bostonmike/social-commerce-secrets-for-turning-social-media-into-social-sales. Accessed 02 Nov 2012.

Marsden, P. (2012c). Are you Solavei or Giffgaff? Two social commerce business models. Available online at: http://networkedblogs.com/EcprJ. Accessed 02 Nov 2012.

Marsden, P. (2012d). Shoppable videos go mainstream with YouTube: Juicy couture shows the way. Available online at: http://networkedblogs.com/Fbsv5. Accessed 20 Aug 2013.

Mashable. (2013). Signature Neiman Marcus. Available online at: http://mashable.com/2012/07/06/signature-neiman-marcus/. Accessed 31 Jan 2013.

Mayer, H.-M. (2012). Social commerce bei der internetstores AG. Available online at: http://www.youtube.com/watch?v=en4JFFzcCRM. Accessed 20 Aug 2013.

Mindwyse. (2011). *Company 2.0 social media im Unternehmen* (Company 2.0 social media in the company). Presentation document Kathrin Haug; Dt. Versandhandelskongress 2011 (German Mail Order Congress 2011), 6 Oct 2011.

Mobile Internet. (2011). Special edition of Internet World Business, Aug 2011.

Möhlenbruch, D., Dölling, S., & Ritschel, R. (2008). Web 2.0-Anwendungen im Kundenbindungsmanagement des M-commerce. In H. H. Bauer et al. (Eds.), *Erfolgsfaktoren des Mobile Marketing – Strategien, Konzepte und Instrumente*. Berlin/Heidelberg: Springer.

Mosemann, H., & Kose, M. (2009). *Android – Anwendungen für das Handy-Betriebssystem erfolgreich programmieren*. Munich: Carl Hanser Verlag.

Mücke Sturm Company. (2011). Social Gaming – Ein Trend wird zur Goldgrube (Social Gaming – A trend becomes a goldmine). Presentation by Achim Himmelreich at the 2011 Online Commerce Conference, Bonn on 18/19 Jan 2011.

Mühlenbeck, F., & Skibicki, K. (2007). *Verkaufsweg social commerce – Blogs, Podcasts, communities – Wie man mit Web 2.0 marketing Geld verdient*. Cologne: Books on Demand GmbH.

Negele, M. (2011). *Betriebssysteme im mobile-shopping – Bestandsaufnahme, Systemvergleich und Zukunftsprognosen für ausgewählte Anwendungsbeispiele* (Operating systems in mobile shopping – Survey, system comparison and future predictions for selected application examples). Bachelor thesis, Niederrhein University of Applied Sciences, Mönchengladbach.

Nielsen Global Online Survey. (2011). To what extend do you trust the following forms of advertising. http://www.nielsen.com/us/en/newswire/2012/consumer-trust-in-online-social-and-mobile-advertising-grows.html. Accessed 17 May 2014.

Nivea (Ed.). (2013). Nivea Haus. Available online at: http://www.nivea.de/ext11/de-DE/nivea-erleben/haus. Accessed 22 Aug 2013.

OC&C Strategy Consultants (Ed.). (2011). Kanal total – Kundenbasierte Strategien im multichannel-handel. Available at: http://www.atmedia.at/red/dateien/17846_Kanal_total_2011.pdf. Accessed 20 Dec 2012.

OC&C Strategy Consultants (Ed.). (2012). Stationäre Eiszeit. Wie Online-Anbieter die Handelslandschaft verändern. OC&C Proposition Index 2012. Available at: http://www.atmedia.at/red/dateien/46959_OCC-Proposition-Index_2012.pdf. Accessed 20 Dec 2012.

ohne tüte. (2012). Bist Du noch multi- oder schon Omni-channel? Available online at: http://ohnetuete.wordpress.com/dated 22.4.2012. Accessed 12 Aug 2012.

Otto Group, & Google Inc. (Eds.). (2012). Go Smart – 2012: Always-in-touch, Studie zur smartphone-Nutzung 2012 (Always-in-touch, study on smartphone usage 2012). Available online at: http://www.ottogroup.com/fileadmin/pdf/go_smart.pdf. Accessed 28 Oct 2010.

OVK. (2012). OVK online-report 2012/01 – Overview of figures and trends.
PBS Business. (2013). Die Kunden wollen es so, top issue, interview with Professor Dr. Gerrit Heinemann. In Business Partner PBS 01/2013, pp. 2–4.
Peters, P. (2011). *Reputationsmanagement im social web-Risiken und Chancen von social media für Unternehmen, Reputation und Kommunikation* (p. 113). Nordstedt: Social Media Verlag.
Pichlmeier, T. (2010). *Die Bedeutung des M-commerce als eigenständige multi-channel-strategie des stationären Einzelhandels*. Bachelor thesis, GRIN Publishing, Ingolstadt.
Pointsmith. (2013). Top-3 retailers defeating showrooming. Available online at: http://www.pointsmith.com/blog/top-3-retailers-defeating-showrooming/. Accessed 22 Aug 2013.
Pousttchi, K., Turowski, K., & Wiedemann, D. G. (2008). Mobile viral marketing. In H. H. Bauer et al. (Eds.), *Erfolgsfaktoren des Mobile Marketing – Strategien, Konzepte und Instrumente*. Berlin/Heidelberg: Springer.
psfk. (2013). Neiman Marcus app gives staff preferences. Available online at: http://www.psfk.com/2012/07/neiman-marcus-app-gives-staff-preferences.html. Accessed 31 Jan 2013.
Qype (Ed.). (2012). Über Qype (About Qype) at: qype.com. Available online at: http://www.qype.com/business_pitch/what_we_do. Accessed 20 Dec 2012.
Reilly, B. (2012). Lowe's mobile app is worth writing home about. In econsultancy.com. Available online at: http://econsultancy.com/de/blog/10666-lowe-s-mobile-app-is-worth-writing-home-about. Accessed 2 Jan 2013.
Research in Motion Limited. (2010). The company behind the Blackberry solution. Available online at: http://www.rim.com/company/. Accessed 01 Dec 2010.
RP Rheinische Post. (2009). Cebit: Das internet wird mobil, 3 Mar 2009, p. B2.
RP Rheinische Post. (2011a). Die Technik-Trends aus Las Vegas, 7 Jan 2011, p. B3.
RP Rheinische Post. (2011b). EU: Surfen per Handy wird billiger, 20 May 2011, p. B3.
Richter, T. (2009). Perspektiven für den mobilen Vertriebskanal. In Backhaus et al. (Ed.), *Multi-channel-management – Effizienzfalle oder Motor in rezessive Zeiten*. Documentation set no. 204 of the Academic Society for Marketing and Business Leadership, Leipzig.
Rio Mobile. (2010). Empirical study on the subject of "Business-Motor mobiles Internet – Wie das mobile internet unser Leben verändert und bereichert. Online at: http://www.riomobile.de/presse/download/100331_rio-mobile-Studie_Businessmotor- Internet.pdf. Accessed 16 July 2011.
Rusli, E. (2010). PopSugar launches retail therapy. Available online at: http://techcrunch.com/2010/07/20/popsugar-launches-retail-therapy-a-farmville-for-shopaholics-video/. Accessed 25 May 2013.
Salt, S. (2012). *Social location marketing – Erreichen Sie Ihre Kunden mit Lokalisierungsdiensten*. Munich: Addison Wesley.
Samsung Electronics. (2010a). What is bada. Available online at: http://www.bada.com/whatisbada/. Accessed 02 Dec 2010.
Samsung Electronics. (2010b). Samsung Wave, first bada smartphone hits the market (updated 01 June 2010). Available online at: http://www.bada.com/samsung-wave-first-bada-smartphone-hits-the-market/. Accessed 02 Dec 2010.
Scheer, A.-W., et al. (2002). Das mobile Unternehmen. In G. Silberer, J. Wohlfahrt, & T. Wilhelm (Eds.), *Mobile Commerce – Grundlagen, Geschäftsmodelle, Erfolgsfaktoren*. Wiesbaden: Gabler.
Schleusener, M. (2011). Pricing im multi-channel-Handel – Herausforderungen und Chancen für Multi-Channel-Händler. In G. Heinemann, M. Schleusener, & S. Zaharia (Eds.), *Modernes multi-channeling im fashion-Handel* (pp. 165–181). Frankfurt: Deutscher Fachverlag.
Schleusener, M. (2012). Pricing im multi-channel-Handel – Herausforderungen und Chancen für multi-channel-Händler. In G. Heinemann, M. Schleusener, & S. Zaharia (Eds.), *Modernes multi-channeling im fashion-Handel* (pp. 165–181). Frankfurt: Deutscher Fachverlag.
Schneider, D. (2001). *Marketing 2.0 – Absatzstrategien für turbulente Zeiten*. Wiesbaden: Gabler.

Schneller, D. (2008). Die Meinung der Anderen. In Statista.com on 17 Oct 2008. Available online at: http://de.statista.com/statistik/daten/studie/2051/umfrage/produktrecherche-im-internet-in-deutschland-in-2008/. Accessed 14 Oct 2009.

Shoepassion. (2013). Unser umfassendes Pressekit (Our press kit). Available online at: http://www.shoepassion.de/presse. Accessed 22 Aug 2013.

Scholz, H. (Ed.). (2010). Was ist ein mobiles Endgerät? Available online at: http://www.mobile-zeitgeist.com/2010/03/09/was-ist-ein-mobiles-endgeraet/. Accessed 27 Dec 2010.

Schott, R. (2012). Foursquare marketing: Tools for brands looking to tap in to check-ins. In searchenginewatch.com. Available online at: http://searchenginewatch.com/article/2170860/Foursquare-Marketing-Tools-for-Brands-Looking-to-Tap-in-to-Check-ins. Accessed 6 Jan 2013.

Schrödter, J. (2003). *Kundenbindung im Internet*. Cologne: Eul.

Schürmann, J. (2012). Die mobile revolution – Kernfaktoren fürein erfolgreiches mobile-business (The mobile revolution – Core factors in a successful mobile business). Presentation at the Mobile Summit, Düsseldorf on 26 July 2012.

Schwarz, T. (2007). *Leitfaden Online-Marketing, 28 innovative Praxisbeispiele*. Waghäusel: Marketing-Börse.

Schwarz, T. (2008). *Praxistipps dialog marketing – vom mailing bis zum online-marketing*. Waghäusel: Marketing-Börse.

Seidenberg, C. (2013). *Online goes offline – Online pure player erobern den stationären Handel: Fallbeispiele, Formen, Relevanz und Perspektiven* (Online goes offline – Online pure players take over brick-and-mortar retailing: Case studies, forms, relevance and prospects), seminar paper. Mönchengladbach: Niederrhein University of Applied Sciences.

SEO-united. (2011). Ausgaben für social media. Available online at: http://www.seo-united.de/blog/internet/ausgaben-fuer-social-media.htm dated 04.04.2011. Accessed 04 July 2012.

Shopanbieter. (2013). Local heroes: BUTLERS innovativer showroom startet, article dated 18 July 2013. Available online at: http://www.shopanbieter.de/news/archives/7277-local-heroes-butlers-innovativer-showroom-startet.html. Accessed 22 Aug 2013.

Siebers, B. (2011). Vertrauensbildende Maßnahmen steigern den Umsatz. In Shopanbieter.de-Blog. Available online at: http://www.shopanbieter.de/news/archives/4542-vertrauensbildende-massnahmen-steigern-den-umsatz/. Accessed 28 Oct 2010.

Silberer, G., & Schulz, S. (2008). mCRM – Möglichkeiten und Grenzen eines modernen Kundenbeziehungsmanagements. In H. H. Bauer et al. (Ed.), *Erfolgsfaktoren des Mobile Marketing – Strategien, Konzepte und Instrumente*. Berlin/Heidelberg: Springer.

Silver, H., Tan, E., & Mitchell, C. (2012). Online consumer pulse pinterest vs. Facebook: Which social sharing site wins at shopping engagement? Available online at: http://www.bizrateinsights.com/blog/2012/10/15/online-consumer-pulse-pinterest-vs-facebook-which-social-sharing-site-wins-at-shopping-engagement/. Accessed 20 Aug 2013.

Simon, H., & Fassnacht, M. (2009). *Preismanagement Strategie, Analyse, Entscheidung, Umsetzung* (3rd ed.). Wiesbaden: Gabler Verlag.

Sitzfeldt. (2013). Probe sitzen im Berliner Showroom! Available online at: http://www.sitzfeldt.com/sofa-berlin. Accessed 20 June 2013.

Socialbakers. (2012). Heart of social media statistics, Facebook pages statistics. Available online at: http://www.socialbakers.com/facebook-pages/. Accessed 18 July 2011.

Social Media. (2011). Internet World Business Guide 2011, Internet World Business.

Spehr, M., & Jörn, F. (2010). "Long term evolution" im Mobilfunk – Geduldsprobe für den mobilen Internetmenschen. In FAZ No. 63 dated 16 Mar 2010, p. T1.

Spiegel. (2011). Netzwelt. Available online at: http://www.spiegel.de/netzwelt/web/0,1518,771351,00.html. Accessed 31 Dec 2011.

Spielberg, H. (2001). Das Geschäftsmodell von @Road. In A.-T. Nicolai & T. Petersmann (Eds.), *Strategien im M-commerce* ("Strategies in M-commerce"). Stuttgart: Schäffer-Poeschl.

Springer-Gabler. (2013). *Gabler Wirtschaftslexikon*. Wiesbaden.

Bibliography

Springer-Professionals. (2013). Ohne Mobile geht nichts mehr, dated 22 Aug 2013. Available online at: http://www.springerprofessional.de/ohne-mobile-geht-nichts-mehr/4633776.html. Accessed 23 Aug 2013.

Statista. (2013). Jeder 5. nutzt Facebook ausschließlich mobil, dated 25 July 2013. Available online at: http://de.statista.com/themen/138/facebook/infografik/1077/facebooks-mobile-nutzer/. Accessed 20 Aug 2013.

Stambor, Z. (2012). Pinterest cozies up to businesses. Available online at: http://www.internetretailer.com/2012/11/15/pinterest-cozies-businesses?cid=FB-Article-2012. Accessed 20 Aug 2013.

Steimel, B. (2011). Interview with social commerce expert Paul Marsden, Part 1: When social media comes to e-commerce. Available online at: http://smarter-service.com/2011/12/13/interview-mit-social-commerce-experten-paul-marsden-part1-when-social-media-comes-to-ecommerce/. Accessed 20 Aug 2013.

Steimel, B. (2012). Abschied von AIDA. Available online at: http://smartservice-blog.com/2012/10/04/abschied_von_aida/. Accessed 03 Nov 2012.

Steimel, B., Gentsch, P., & Dimitrova, T. (2012). Praxisleitfaden. Social commerce – "Show me the money!" An empirical study for Mind Business Consultants.

Stock, L. (2012). Chris Morton von Lyst prognostiziert einen stark personalisierten eCommerce (Chris Morton of Lyst predicts highly-personalized e-commerce). Available online at: http://d-lab.com/?s=chris+morton. Accessed 20 Aug 2013.

Strategic Marketing Advisors. (2011). To what extent do you trust the following forms of advertising, Nielsen Global Trust. Available online at: http://www.strategic-marketingadvisors.com/images/reviews.jpg. Accessed 20 Aug 2013.

Stracke, T. (2005). Profilieren statt ignorieren: Internet-Nutzer zwingen Hersteller zum Umdenken. In Direct Marketing 11/2005, pp. 24–27. Available at: http://www.pangora.com/versions/de/assets/mentasys_in_der_Direktmarketing-0511.pdf. Accessed 14 Oct 2009.

Subramani, M. R., & Rajagopalan, B. (2003). Knowledge-sharing and influence in social networks via viral marketing. *Communications of the ACM, 46*(12), 300–307.

Sugar Publishing (Ed.). (2010). Sugar Inc. und ShopStyle starten Social Fashion-Game "RetailTherapy". Available online at: http://press.shopstyle.de/Sugar-Inc-und-ShopStyle-starten-Social-Fashion-Game-Retail-Therapy-mit-begleitendem-weltweiten-Designer-Handtaschen-Wettbewer-10097004. Accessed 25 May 2013.

Syzygy. (2013). Digital at point of sale. Reinventing retail for the connected customer. Available online at: http://syzygy.de/. Accessed 22 Aug 2013.

Telekom (Ed.). (2013). Telekom and Groupon form strategic partnership to accelerate local commerce offerings across Europe. In telekom.com. Available online at: http://www.telekom.com/media/company/99368. Accessed 04 Jan 2013.

Thaeler, J. (2012). Guess launched pinterest contest based on color. Available online at: http://pinnablebusiness.com/guess-launched-pinterest-contest-based-on-color/. Accessed 20 Aug 2013.

Thollot, B. (2014). 4 bonnes raisons de vendre sur Facebook, unter: http://www.ecommercewall.com/2011/07/ecommerce/4-bonnes-raisons-de-vendre-sur-facebook/. Accessed 17 May 2014.

Thelen, K. (2009). Eignung des Mobile-Shopping für Bekleidung (Suitability of mobile shopping for clothing). Seminar paper at Niederrhein University of Applied Sciences, Department of Textile and Clothing Technology, Mönchengladbach.

Tiramizoo. (2013). Company presentation. At: tiramizoo.com. Available online at: https://www.tiramizoo.com/docs/tiramizoo_teaser_deutsch.pdf. Accessed 21 Jan 2013.

Tollmien, S. (2011). The outernet – Meet your future client. Presentation by Achim Himmelreich at the 2011 Online Retail Conference, Bonn on 18/19 Jan 2011.

Top-handy-apps.de. (2009). Vor- und Nachteile des smartphones. Available online at: http://www.top-handy-apps.de/2009/09/27/smartphone-vor-und-nachteile-des-touchscreen/. Accessed 18 Dec 2010.

Turowski, K., & Pousttchi, K. (2004). *Mobile Commerce – Grundlagen und Techniken*. Berlin/Heidelberg: Springer.

Twitter. (2013). Dell outlet. Available online at: http://twitter.com/delloutlet. Accessed 20 Aug 2013.

Unterberg, B. (2008). Consumer generated advertising; Konsumenten als Markenpartner in der Werbung. In H. Kaul & C. Steinmann (Eds.), *Community marketing – Wie Unternehmen in sozialen Netzwerken Werte schaffen* (pp. 203–216). Stuttgart: Schäffer-Poeschel.

von Kunhardt, F. (2012). Aus SoLoMo-Fans werden Kunden (SoLoMo fans turn into customers). Presentation at the Mobile Summit 2012, Management Forum, 27 June 2012, Düsseldorf.

von Kunhardt, F. (2013). Beschleunigte conversion – Sellaround Widgets als modernes Verkaufsinstrument im Zeitalter des SoLoMo. In G. Heinemann, K. Haug, M. Gehrckens, & dgroup (Eds.), *Digitalisierung des Handels mit ePace – Innovative e-commerce-Geschäftsmodelle und digitale Zeitvorteile* (pp. 315–329). Wiesbaden: Springer Gabler.

Waldeis. (2013). Selling on Facebook. Available online at: http://www.wald-eis.de/wp-content/uploads/2011/05/F-Commerce-Infographic.png. Accessed 20 Aug 2013.

Walsh, M. (2012). Mobile Traffic Tops Desktop for Groupon, LivingSocial. In mediapost.com. Available online at: http://www.mediapost.com/publications/article/181460/mobile-traffic-tops-desktop-for-groupon-livingsoc.html#axzz2H0BflZsu. Accessed 04 Jan 2013.

WAMS – Welt am Sonntag. (2013). Daddeln auf allen Kanälen, no. 33 dated 18 Aug 2013, p. 50.

Weave. (2012). Social commerce. In issue 05.12.: Trends – Social commerce, pp. 223–225

webhelps. (2011). internetwerbung-immer-wichtiger. Available online at: http://www.webhelps.de/blog/2011/02/28/internetwerbung-immer-wichtiger/. Accessed 13 Aug 2012.

Wegener, M. (2004). Erfolg durch kundenorientiertes multichannel-management. In H.-C. Riekhoff (Ed.), *Retail business in Deutschland, Perspektiven, Strategien, Erfolgsmuster* (pp. 197–218). Wiesbaden: Gabler.

Weinberg, T. (2010). *Social media marketing, Strategien für Twitter, Facebook & Co* (Social media marketing: Strategies for Twitter, Facebook & Co). Cologne: O'Reilly.

Weiss, M. (2010). Retail therapy: Popsugar bringt Facebook-Game für Modefans. Available online at: http://www.excitingcommerce.de/2010/07/popsugars-retail-therapy-verbindet-facebook-game-mit-shopping.html

Welt am Sonntag. (2011). Abschied von der Festplatte, no. 26 dated 26 June 2011, p. 12 and p. 63.

Welt am Sonntag. (2013a). Daddeln auf allen Kanälen, no. 33 dated 18 Aug 2013, p. 50

Welt am Sonntag. (2013b). Brillenträger haben das Internet immer vor Augen, no. 5 dated 3 Feb 2013, p. 50.

Werner, A. (2012). Guest contribution: Pinterest in Deutschland – Für welche Unternehmen lohnt es sich, schon jetzt loszulegen? Available online at: http://www.futurebiz.de/artikel/pinterest-in-deutschland/. Accessed 20 Aug 2013.

WhatIs.com. (2010). Social graph. Available online at: http://whatIs.techtarget.com/definition/social-graph. Accessed 22 Feb 2013.

Wiecker, M. (2002). Endgeräte für mobile Anwendungen. In W. Gora & S. Röttber-Gerigk (Eds.), *Handbuch mobile-commerce – Technische Grundlagen, Marktchancen und Einsatzmöglichkeiten*. Berlin/Heidelberg: Springer.

Wiedmann, K.-P., Reeh, M.-O., & Schumacher, H. (2008). Near field communication im mobile marketing (Near field communication in mobile marketing). In H. H. Bauer et al. (Ed.), *Erfolgsfaktoren des mobile marketing – Strategien, Konzepte und Instrumente*. Berlin/Heidelberg: Springer.

Wieschowski, S. (2008). Um Mitternacht gibt es Schnäppchen. In Welt am Sonntag no. 27 dated 6 July 2008, p. 47.

Wikipedia. (2008). Blog, tag and wiki. Available online at: http://en.wikipedia.org/wiki. Accessed 12 Oct 2008.

Wikipedia. (2010). Applications. Available online at: http://en.wikipedia.org/Applikationen. Accessed 09 Dec 2010.

Wikipedia. (2012a). E-commerce. Available online at: http://en.wikipedia.org/wiki/E-commerce. Accessed 09 Dec 2012.
Wikipedia. (2012b). Social shopping. Available online at: http://en.wikipedia.org/wiki/Social_shopping. Accessed 09 Dec 2012.
Wikipedia. (2012c). Wikipedia: Flagshipstore (Flagship store). Available online at: http://de.wikipedia.org/wiki/Flagshipstore. Accessed 15 June 2013.
Wikipedia. (2013). Social. Available online at: http://en.wikipedia.org/wiki/Social. Accessed 20 Aug 2013.
Wilhelm, S. (2012). Verkauf spielt bei Facebook keine große Rolle. In Der Handel 10/2012 dated 04 Oct 2012, p. 50
Wirtz, B. W. (2008). *Multi-channel-marketing, Grundlagen – Instrumente – Prozesse*. Wiesbaden: Gabler Verlag.
Wolter, A. (2012). Desktop war gestern – Mobile ist die Gegenwart! – Auch für die Zukunft? (Desktop was yesterday – Mobile is now! – And for the future?). Presentation at the Mobile Summit 2012 on 26.6.12 in Düsseldorf.
Zalando. (2012). Zalando Pop-up Store. Available online at: https://blog.zalando.de/team/2012/03/zalando-pop-up-store/. Accessed 22 Aug 2013.
Zander, C. (2011). *Möglichkeiten des cross-channel-management unter besonderer Berücksichtigung der Integration des m-shopping* (Opportunities for cross-channel management with particular consideration for the integration of m-shopping), seminar paper. Mönchengladbach: Niederrhein University of Applied Sciences.
ZDNet. (2013). Android erreicht fast 75 Prozent Marktanteil. Available online at: http://www.zdnet.de/88154889/gartner-android-erreicht-fast-75-prozent. Accessed 22 Aug 2013.
Zobel, J. (2001). *Mobile business and m-commerce – Die Märkte der Zukunft erobern*. Munich: Carl Hanser Verlag.

Index

A
Aggregation platforms, 58–60
Applications/apps, 106–107, 130–131
AR app retail, 69–71
Attraction, 169–174

B
Bargaining, 86–88
Bonus cards, 90–91
Brick-and-mortar formats, 9–12
Bundling platforms, 58–60
Business concepts, 127–129
Business models, 35–37, 123–131
Buying behavior, 163–164
Buying process, 37–41

C
Channel hopping, 44, 45
Commercialization, 30–33
Consumer-generated advertising, 41–43
Context-sensitive services, 84–86
Couponing, 86–88
Cross-technology platforms, 129–130
Customer involvement, 41–43

D
Digital in-store applications, 63–77
Digital in-store fittings, 73–74
Direct *vs.* indirect social-commerce, 30, 31
Dynamic pricing, 88–95

E
E-payment, 88–95

F
Facebook commerce, 33–35
Flagship brick-and-mortar stores, 73–74
Forms, 26
Functions, 159–160
Future prospects, 16–17, 107–111
Future prospects for mobile commerce, 101–111

G
Gamification, 65–67

H
History, 15–16

I
Information-seeking behavior, 162–163
In-store apps, 76–77
In-store navigation, 69–71

L
Local, 7
   real-time offers, 62–63
   referral marketing, 60–62
   search optimization, 55–58
Localization functions, 84–86
Location-based services, 55–99, 155–185

M
Manifestations, 27–37
mCRM, 138–141
Mobile, 7

Mobile (cont.)
  commerce, 101–154
  commerce added value, 111
  devices, 114–117
  e-payment, 91–93
  marketing, 77–81, 131–148
  operating systems, 117–120
  universe, 1–3
  usage, 175–182
Mobile-relevant trends, 120–123
Multi-channel environment, 93–95

N
Near field communication (NFC), 141–144
New, 159
NFC. *See* Near field communication (NFC)

O
Omni-channel use, 43–46

P
Phases, 15–16
Pop-up stores, 71–73
Prerequisites, 177–180
Purchase, 159

Q
QR scan retail, 68–69

R
Relevance, 18–20
Role of SoLoMo, 52–54

S
Sellaround widget, 34–35
Share of mobile commerce, 2, 3
Showrooming, 68–69, 74–76
Significance, 16
Situational adequacy, 77–81

Situation-oriented CRM, 81–84
Smart natives, 47–49
Smartphones, 5–6, 180–181
  owner, 157–161
  usage, 46–49
Social, 7
  commerce, 13–54
  commerce market size, 22, 23
  graph, 14
  media, 13–17, 30–33
  media channels, 165
  networks, 3–5, 17
  referral marketing, 60–62
Socialization, 27–30
SoLoMo, 13–99, 101–154
  communication, 51
  convergence, 51–52
  efficiency, 50–51
  usability, 50
Special characteristics, 18–20
Stages of development, 23–25

T
Tablet shopping, 107–111
Telematics, 129–130

U
Usage, 157–161, 169–174
Usage locations, 164–165
Use, 180–181
Users of social networks worldwide, 4

V
Value chain, 126
Viral marketing, 144–148
Virtual community forms, 15
Virtual coupons, 90–91

W
Websites, 130–131

About the Authors

Christian Gaiser is CEO of Bonial International Group with local brands in nine countries and offices in Chicago, Berlin, Paris, Barcelona, Sao Paulo, Moscow and Munich, providing location-based "research online an purchase offline" services to retailers, manufacturers and consumers. In 2008, Christian Gaiser and his team founded kaufDA, "the star among location-based services in Germany", according to Werben & Verkaufen, the leading German magazine for communication and marketing. In early 2011 Axel Springer SE, one of Europe's largest media companies, became kaufDA's majority investor. From Germany, Mr. Gaiser went on to launch the kaufDA concept as Bonial in France, Lokata in Russia, Ofertia in Spain, Guiato in Brazil and Retale in the United States. Since the birth of kaufDA in 2008, Christian and his team have successfully partnered with 600 retailers and 12 million consumers. Prior to Bonial, Mr. Gaiser worked in various positions at Goldman Sachs, McKinsey and SAP. He is a graduate of the WHU Otto Beisheim School of Management, Vallendar and HEC, Montrèal.

Gerrit Heinemann is Director of the eWeb Research Center and Professor of Retail and Trade at Niederrhein University for Applied Sciences in Mönchengladbach, Germany. Prior to this role, he occupied several top management positions in the retail sector inluding Douglas Holding, Kaufhof/ Metro and as a management consultant with Droege & Comp. Where he specialized in retailing for international clients. Professor Heinemann is a frequent lecturer at international conferences and author of numerous articles in professional press and academic publications. He works as a senior advisor for retail companies and is author of several best-selling books on multi-channel and online-retailing (e.g. 'New Online Retailing: Innovation and Transformation' (2010), 'Web-Excellence in E-Commerce – Innovation and Transformation'(2010), 'Cross-Channel Management' (2011) and 'No-line Retailing' (2013). As member of the board of some leading online retailing companies – such as buch.de internetstores AG – he is also involved in all the actual key issues effecting the e-commerce sector.

MIX
Papier aus verantwortungsvollen Quellen
Paper from responsible sources
FSC® C105338

If you have any concerns about our products,
you can contact us on
ProductSafety@springernature.com

In case Publisher is established outside the EU,
the EU authorized representative is:
**Springer Nature Customer Service Center GmbH
Europaplatz 3, 69115 Heidelberg, Germany**

Printed by Libri Plureos GmbH
in Hamburg, Germany